ALIEN LIAISON

ALIEN LIAISON

THE ULTIMATE SECRET

TIMOTHY GOOD

With a commentary by Admiral of the Fleet,
The Lord Hill-Norton GCB,
Chief of Defence Staff 1971-73

CENTURY

LONDON   SYDNEY   AUCKLAND   JOHANNESBURG

Published in 1991 by Century
Random Century Ltd
20 Vauxhall Bridge Road, London SW1V 2SA

Random Century Australia (Pty) Ltd
20 Alfred Street, Milsons Point, Sydney, NSW 2061, Australia

Random Century New Zealand Ltd
9-11 Rothwell Avenue, Albany, Auckland 10, New Zealand

Random Century South Africa (Pty) Ltd
PO Box 337, Bergvlei 2012, South Africa

Reprinted 1991 (six times)

Typeset in Linotronic Baskerville by
SX Composing Ltd, Rayleigh, Essex

Printed and bound in U.K. by
Butler and Tanner Ltd, Frome, Somerset

A catalogue record for this book is available from the British Library.

ISBN 0-7126-2194-6

Contents

To Admiral of the Fleet,
The Lord Hill-Norton GCB

Commentary

Admiral of the Fleet
The Lord Hill-Norton GCB,
Chief of Defence Staff 1971-3

I have known Tim Good for about ten years, during which I have formed the opinion that he is both honest and reliable. I am quite sure that he is not a 'nut-case', and equally sure that his long and diligent investigations have been efficiently conducted, and the results carefully and accurately reported. All this makes the astounding revelations in this book impossible, certainly for me, to dismiss, unless or until they are equally publicly disproved.

The plain fact is that either what he reports here is true, or it isn't. If his accounts of recovered UFOs, and their alien occupants, being in the hands of United States Government agencies (and perhaps those of the Soviet Union too) are not true, then it seems that many important and distinguished former public servants have perhaps lied, or have been grossly mis-reported. In the latter event one must expect and hope that they will take the appropriate legal action to set the record straight.

In the same way, the apparently hard evidence of all sorts of other UFO information given by dozens of people, many of them prominent persons in Australia, Belgium, Brazil, Puerto Rico, the United States and the Soviet Union, is either true or they are lying, hallucinating or (again) have been grossly misrepresented. Since they are all named by Tim Good in this book they must now either put up or shut up.

[Signed]
Hill-Norton

Acknowledgments

I would like to record my thanks to the following individuals and organizations who – either directly or indirectly – have contributed information and material contained in this book:

Jeffrey Acosta, Tom Adams, Dr John Altshuler, Gerald Anderson, Walter Andrus and the Mutual UFO Network, Associated Press/Topham Picture Library, Ron Banuk, Ron Bartels, Timothy Green Beckley, Paul Bennewitz, Howard Blum, Robert Bowker, Curt Brubaker, Larry Bryant, Dr and Mrs Howard Burgess, Ellen Carney and the *Idaho State Journal*, the Central Intelligence Agency, Citizens Against UFO Secrecy (CAUS), Colonel William Coleman, Gordon Cooper, Vicki Cooper and *UFO* magazine, Riley Crabb and the Borderland Sciences Research Foundation, Gordon Creighton and *Flying Saucer Review*, Marie-Thérèse de Brosses and *Paris Match*, Colonel Wilfried De Brouwer, the Defense Intelligence Agency, Richard Doty, the Federal Bureau of Investigation, Stanton Friedman, the Fund for UFO Research, Peter Gersten, James Goodall, Barry Goldwater, Billy Goodman and KVEG Radio (Las Vegas), Stan Gordon, John Grace and the Nevada Aerial Research Group, Lee Graham, Gerard Grede, Barry Greenwood, William Hamilton III, Robert Hastings, Everett Hineman, Alan Holt, Mike Hunt, Raymond Ingraham, Robert Kirchgessner and Kenneth Feld Productions, John Lade, Bill Lear, Elsa Lee and Quest International, Nikolai Lebedev, Beverly McKittrick, General Igor Maltsev, Dr Jesse Marcel, Michael Michaud and Headline Book Publishing, Al and Elizabeth Merritt, Norman Miller, the Ministry of Defence, Dr Henry Monteith, Charles Moody, the North American Aerospace Defense Command, the National Aeronautics & Space Administration, the National Security Agency, Bob Needham, Richard Nixon, Hans Petersen, Bob Pratt, the Public Record Office, Ronald Reagan (Hon KBE), Bill Scott and *Aviation Week & Space Technology*, Elias Seixas, Rear Admiral Sumner Shapiro, Paul Shartle, Wilson Sosa, Leonard Stringfield, Robert Suffern, Christa Tilton, Robert Todd, Harry Tokarz and the Canadian UFO Research Network, the US Air Force Office of Special Investigations, the US Army, the US Department of the Interior, the US Department of Naval Intelligence, Gabriel Valdez, Jacques Vallee, William Veenhuizen, Dorothee Walter, Philip Waterhouse, and others too numerous to mention here but who are credited elsewhere.

I am especially indebted to my friend Bob Oechsler, who gave me so much of his time and invaluable information (at considerable personal risk); Admiral Bobby Ray Inman, for making the acquisition of some of that information possible; Bob Lazar, for what could be the story of the millennium; Gene Huff, for his kindness in helping me with additional information on the Lazar material; John Lear, who gave me a lot of his time, introduced me to Bob Lazar and provided me with photographs and material relating to Groom Lake/Area 51 ('Dreamland'); George Knapp of KLAS-TV (Las Vegas), for giving me much valuable information and for the use of copious material from his excellent programmes on the subject, as well as from his private interviews with Bob Lazar; Linda Howe, for allowing me to extract so much information from her book on the animal mutilations, *An Alien Harvest*; Bob Emenegger, for helpful information, as well as for use of the Holloman AFB story in his book, *UFOs Past, Present & Future*; Bill Moore and Jaime Shandera, for the use of lengthy extracts from their interviews with 'Falcon' and 'Condor' (to whom I would also like to extend my thanks) and for information from their publication, *The MJ-12 Documents*; Michael Seligman and Lexington Broadcast Service, for extracts from the pioneering TV documentary, *UFO Cover-Up? Live*; Drs John Derr, Peter Van Arsdale and Berthold Schwarz, without whom the 'Colorado Breakthrough' chapter could not have been written; William Steinman and Wendelle Stevens, for the use of important cases relating to 'Dreamland', extracted from their book, *UFO Crash at Aztec*; Daniel Fry, for his hospitality and time, as well as for extracts from his book, *To Men of Earth*; Nicholas Redfern, for giving me many documents he obtained from the FBI on the cattle mutilations, and other documents from the Public Record Office; Robert Dorr, for helpful information on the US Government's flying disc project; Dr Leopoldo Díaz, for his co-operation, and Michael Packer of WOAI Radio (San Antonio), for extracts from his interview with Dr Díaz; Travis Walton, for his time and for extracts from his book, *The Walton Experience*; Jorge Martín, for his research into the Puerto Rico/US Navy aircraft incidents, and for arranging for me to meet the witnesses; Beverley Bean, her mother and sisters, for so kindly sharing information about Melvin Brown's involvement in the Roswell incident; Ralph Noyes, for generously allowing me the use of his word-processor when mine packed up; and Admiral of the Fleet, the Lord Hill-Norton GCB, for his outspoken Commentary.

Finally, I am indebted to those who contributed but cannot be named.

Introduction

So vast is the complexity of this multifaceted subject that it resists a single, all-encompassing hypothesis to account for the many inherent paradoxes that confront us. In *Alien Liaison*, I have chosen to concentrate on those facets of the UFO enigma which I hope will shed new light on the overall picture.

As far back as 1952, the then Director of Central Intelligence, Walter Bedell Smith, recognized the need for a multidisciplinary approach to the subject. 'It is my view that this situation has possible implications for our national security which transcend the interests of a single service,' he wrote in a memorandum to the Executive Secretary of the National Security Council. 'A broader, co-ordinated effort should be initiated to develop a firm scientific understanding of the several phenomena which apparently are involved in these reports . . .'

Thousands of documents on UFOs have now been released under provisions of the Freedom of Information Act (FOIA) in the United States, by agencies such as the Atomic Energy Commission, CIA, Defense Intelligence Agency, Department of State, FBI, National Security Agency, and the Air Force, Army and Naval intelligence branches. The fact that research into UFOs by these and other agencies was long denied (with a few exceptions), and that thousands more documents remain classified and therefore exempt from disclosure, is proof – if proof were needed – of just how seriously these matters are taken.

While my last book, *Above Top Secret*, proves beyond any doubt that a massive cover-up has been in effect since the late 1940s, *Alien Liaison* takes us one stage further by partially exposing what has been hitherto withheld, i.e. that some UFOs are indeed extraterrestrial in origin, that alien bodies have been recovered, a few craft have been test-flown, and that contact has been established – even at an official, if restricted, level.

Since these claims are certain to be misrepresented, let me emphasize that only a relatively few people in governments and the intelligence community are aware of this situation. The most sensitive information about UFOs is handled at a 'need-to-know' level, restricted to those with very high security clearances – in some cases, as we shall learn, as high as thirty-eight levels above Top Secret.

Given that there is truth behind these allegations, I readily concede that even the knowledgeable élite remain baffled by the bewildering diversity of reports with which we are regularly confronted, and I am certain that considerable confusion exists in high circles as to the nature of the more bizarre encounters. I have not shied away from these reports, such as the animal mutilations (Chapter 2) and the extraordinary but illuminating experiences which befell several witnesses on a ranch in Colorado (Chapter 3). Much of this information is controversial and disturbing.

Alien Liaison does not go into an in-depth analysis of either abduction or contact stories, except in those few cases I have cited that reflect my own bias in support of certain relevant hypotheses. The stories I have selected stretch the boundaries of belief, and although scepticism is warranted, it should never be forgotten that many extraordinary technological and other human developments which we now take for granted were initially regarded with disbelief or ridicule. How many of us would have believed, for example, that the Berlin Wall would be dismantled in 1989? When marvellous events are said to have happened, the natural tendency is to disbelieve, partly because we do not want to appear gullible, but also because we are simply confounded when presented with unfamiliar concepts. I am certain therefore that the concept of extraterrestrial visitation will become increasingly acceptable in due course.

As described in Chapters 6 and 10, the US Government has made several attempts at indoctrinating the public about some of the realities involved in the UFO phenomenon. Although what has been revealed is undoubtedly diluted with disinformation intended to confuse and deceive, it is important to stress that official disinformation on the UFO subject would be pointless if there was nothing to cover up. In addition, both covert and overt disinformation usually incorporates a certain amount of genuine information that sometimes provides signposts to the truth, as we shall learn in the concluding chapters.

Since I was personally invited to participate indirectly in the latest US Government attempt at public indoctrination, I can confirm that there is a sincere desire on the part of those in authority to release certain unequivocal material, but that there continues to be a reluctance to do so, owing to economic, political, religious and sociological considerations.

It is to be hoped that the revelations made available to me for publication in *Alien Liaison* will facilitate the official release of some of this material in the not-too-distant future.

January 1991

· 1 ·

Aerial Confrontation

It was a clear night in the early summer of 1947. The young pilot was growing tired as he cruised in his Lockheed P-38 Lightning at 9,000 to 10,000 feet, en route from Grand Rapids, Michigan, to Los Angeles, where he was due to participate in the Bendix Trophy Race the following day.

Shortly after passing over the Colorado River near Blythe, California, he was alerted by something so startling that it has left an indelible impression to this day.

'Suddenly I looked off to my left side and I saw a round fuselage, with round windows in it,' Bill Lear told me. 'And of course at that time the only commercial airliner that was flying that had round windows was a DC-4. And instantly, judging from my position in relation to that body, I judged that I was about 50 feet from running into the trailing edge of the wing of that airplane. So, no matter how hopeless it seems, you always try to avoid something.

'I was gaining on it, so I immediately racked the P-38 over into a 90-degree bank to the right and pulled as hard as I could, almost with my eyes closed, expecting to crash into the wing of that airplane. And to my astonishment, nothing happened!

'I breathed a sigh of relief, and when I figured I was about 90 degrees off the westerly heading, which would have put me north, I rolled out. And as I rolled out, I looked to my left, and it was still there! And this is out over the desert – I'd already passed all the lights behind me – and there it still was, with the little round windows, looking for all the world like DC-4 windows. But the light behind the windows was not white; it was a bit yellowish.

'And here I was, in exactly the same position as I had been before, and I thought, this is totally impossible. But the brain won't accept that. When you're about to die, and when you're about to crash into the trailing edge of the wing of another airplane, you don't stop to think how the hell did it get there, you just get out of there! There's no time to think. So I simply executed the same manoeuvre, rolled to the right again in a 90-degree bank, pulled as hard as I could again, thinking to myself, "My God, what is happening? That DC-4 *can't* follow me!" But nonetheless, there it was.

'And when I rolled out the second time, heading east, it was gone. But there was no question, if it *had* been an aircraft, I would – on the first occasion – have ploughed into the trailing edge of the wing. The second time, there was no way it could have been an aircraft. In 1947 I had not read anything about any flying saucers or the cigar-shaped things. I was so relieved that I hadn't run into any airplane. Nothing could have stayed pace with me like that thing did. I couldn't explain it, and I was so tired that I simply made a 180 [-degree turn] and continued on to the west and landed in California.'

Bill Lear is a son of the late William P. Lear, designer of the Lear Jet, and together with his brother John – also a pilot – he has done a considerable amount of research into UFOs, as I soon learned when we discussed the subject in his London home in 1990. One aspect of the 1947 sighting bothered me, however.

'Bill, the sceptic would say that you were just overfatigued and were hallucinating,' I remarked, after listening to his account.

'When you're flying along and you see something that you recognize, you suddenly come very much awake,' he replied. 'I mean, the adrenalin starts pumping. And I was awake, standing right on my tiptoes in the airplane, practically, because *that* really gets your heart started! To see something casually, OK, I'll buy hallucination – possible hallucination – because of fatigue. Or you misinterpret lights on the ground for something that might be flying next to you. But when you turn into the black sky at 10 or 11 o'clock at night, and there are only stars above you, and there are these round windows, that fuselage that you can make out the shape of, and those round windows with very pale yellow lights behind them, and you don't know what the hell it is, except the only thing you recognize is if it's got a fuselage it must have wings, and you're about to plough into the trailing edge of the wing – you move, and get the hell out of there!

'OK, the first time, you panic and break right, and if there's nothing, OK, you just saw some lights on the ground and you were tired and perhaps had a mild hallucination. Second time – black sky – still there – no way!'[1]

Sightings by pilots cannot easily be dismissed. According to Dr Richard Haines, who has devoted much of his professional career as an aerospace scientist to investigating the mysteries of human vision and perception, there have now been well over 3,000 sightings of UFOs by military and civilian pilots.[2]

Near Misses with Helicopters

Thanks to Elsa Lee of Quest International, who first uncovered the basic details of the case, I interviewed a helicopter pilot who had an alarming near miss with an unidentified flying object in England in 1988. Because the name of the witness is internationally known, he has requested anonymity, and I have deleted certain names and places from the following report.

The incident occurred on 21 February 1988 at 18.50 hours, in the vicinity of Chipping Warden, Northamptonshire, as the pilot, accompanied by his wife, was flying a Bell JetRanger en route from Bakewell, Derbyshire, to his home in a southern county.

'. . . passed 5 miles west abeam Daventry VOR at 2,200, 1033,' his report begins. 'First noticed extremely bright red flashing light from the south-west. Initially thought to be an aircraft but light looked too bright and wasn't moving relative to the background illuminations. Then thought to be a beacon marking the top of the mast, though seemed to be far too bright and high.

'I continued on 170 track and after an estimated 3 minutes, during which time [my wife] had been continuously watching the light, we suddenly appeared to be on a collision course with the flying object carrying this light. I immediately commenced descent, maintaining 120 knots air speed, but the object appeared to be homing in on us and also descending.

'Throughout this the object had been at approximately 2 o'clock. The object continued to appear to home in on us until I had descended to 1,300, closing at an estimated speed of 300 to 400 knots, when it suddenly commenced a turn to the right, ending up on a track parallel to my own and perhaps 800 yards to the west.

'At this point I estimate my position to have been 5 miles north-east of Banbury [Oxfordshire]. Once the object moved approximately half a mile ahead it appeared to stop and then reverse direction on a reciprocal to my own at an estimated 1,800 feet, again approximately 800 yards to the west.

'The object had a very bright red light and two dimmer white lights each side of it and was very large; estimated size 300 feet long. The speed of its reciprocal and final seen course was estimated 500 knots relative to my own. I then climbed to 1,800 feet and continued en route . . .'

The witness immediately reported the near miss to London Information. Subsequent inquiries about conflicting traffic to London Information, Luton, Cranfield, Birmingham, Coventry, Brize Norton, Upper Heyford, and Hurn (Bournemouth), established that none 'had any traffic that was even remotely likely to have been in the area at the time'. (Following receipt of a UFO report, air traffic controllers are required to contact London Air Traffic Control Centre immediately, and to submit a written report to the Ministry of Defence.[3])

Visibility had been excellent at the time – 30 miles – the pilot told me. He was unable to determine precisely the shape of the object, but indicated that it could have been rectangular. The red light flashed in a regular sequence, while the white lights remained constant, yet he is absolutely convinced that the object he saw bore no other resemblance to any conventional aircraft. The red light was far too bright for a normal anti-collision light, and he added that he could think of no plane that could change direction or stop so quickly.[4]

Another incident involving a helicopter's near miss with a UFO took place in the vicinity of Nalchik Airport, Georgia, USSR, on 7 March 1990, when the crew of a MiL-2, commanded by V. Silka, was ordered to investigate a low-flying unidentified object that had been tracked on radar since 10.40 a.m. The helicopter was at 800 metres when visual contact was made with the object, which was flying at a lower altitude. Described by the crew as spherical in shape and about 3 metres in diameter, the UFO then ascended to the same height as the helicopter and began to move away, but the helicopter soon caught up. Suddenly, the UFO turned and approached the helicopter at high speed. The pilot made a 90-degree turn to avoid a collision, and the UFO made the same manoeuvre. An immediate descent by the helicopter was not reciprocated by the UFO, however, which stopped and then returned to its original position before disappearing.

The air traffic controller reported that both the helicopter and UFO could clearly be seen on radar until the moment the helicopter began to make its approach from a distance of 6 kilometres, at which point both 'targets' disappeared from the screen for about twenty seconds. The incident, lasting twenty-three minutes, was also tracked by an air defence radar station.[5]

Ultimate Confrontation

Although cases involving the disappearance of aircraft during confrontations with UFOs (such as that of the young Australian pilot Frederick Valentich in 1978[6]) are rare, there have now been a sufficient number to warrant serious concern. And in two incidents that occurred in Puerto Rico in 1988, both thoroughly investigated by Jorge Martín, witnesses came forward who claim to have actually observed these dramatic events as they happened.

On the evening of 16 November 1988, Yesenia Velázquez observed a huge ball of yellow light in the municipality of San Germán. She summoned her family, and they all then witnessed an extraordinary sight.

'Suddenly, two jet fighters appeared from the south, chasing the object,' recalled Yesenia's father, Santiago. 'The UFO stopped in mid-air . . . and the jets began flying over it, under it, and all around it. Then suddenly, they seemed to enter the object from underneath it, and disappeared! We couldn't see them any more, and the sound of their engines couldn't be heard any more. Then two smaller balls of light came out of the UFO and shot away at great speed. After that, the [main object] also disappeared at high speed.'

Then, on 28 December 1988, many witnesses in the Cabo Rojo area observed a huge, triangular object similar to that reported by over 2,600 Belgian witnesses in 1989–90. 'It was enormous,' reported Wilson Sosa, 'blinking with many coloured lights. I ran and got my binoculars and could then clearly see that it was triangle-shaped and slightly curved at its rear side.

'It made a turn back and then came over lower, appearing much larger. It was then that we noticed two jet fighters [F-14 Tomcats] right behind it . . . one tried to intercept it and passed right in front of it, at which point the UFO veered to the left and made a turn back, reducing its speed. The jets tried to intercept it three times, and that's when the UFO slowed down and almost stopped in mid-air . . .

'The second jet remained at the right side of the UFO and the other one positioned itself at the left rear side. Then – I don't know exactly what happened – if the jet entered the UFO by the rear, by its upper side, or what. That was when we all yelled, because we were afraid there would be a collision and maybe an explosion. The jet in the back just disappeared on top or inside of the UFO, because I was observing everything through my binoculars and it didn't come out from the rear, the upper side or the other sides.

'The second jet remained very close to the right side of the UFO. It looked very small alongside that huge thing. As the UFO flew a little to the west, the jet disappeared, as well as its engine sound . . .'

After 'trapping' the jets, the UFO lowered its position and came close to the ground over the Samán Lake. 'It stood still in mid-air for a moment,' Sosa continued, 'then "straightened" its corners and gave off a big flash of light from the central ball of yellow light. It then divided itself in the middle into two separate and distinct triangular sections . . . That's when they both shot away at great speed. You could see red sparks falling from it when it divided itself.'

Although the Federal Aviation Administration denied that this incident had occurred, Jorge Martín subsequently obtained confirmation from a US Navy source, who said that there were radar tapes showing what had happened, which were immediately classified and sent to Washington, DC.

'We were able to see what happened on the radar systems of the ships that were stationed nearby,' the Navy source revealed. 'We saw when the smaller targets on the radar, which represented the jets, merged with a bigger one. After that, the big target seemed to split, and shot off at great speed. A lid has been placed on the whole incident. Many things like this have been happening, but we are not allowed to comment on anything.'[7]

In August 1990 I went out to Puerto Rico and visited the areas where the incidents had taken place. Jorge Martín introduced me to the principal witnesses, all of whom impressed me with their sincerity.

Do these events signify hostility, or could something even more sensational be involved? While I was in Puerto Rico, I heard rumours to the effect that the US Government could be engaged in some type of liaison with the aliens. An outlandish suggestion, of course, but there is no doubt that some very odd happenings are reported to have occurred in this area, as we shall learn in Chapter 10.

Official Soviet Recognition

In an official statement made in April 1990, General Igor Maltsev, Chief of the General Staff of the USSR's Air Defence Forces, admitted that over 100 observations of UFOs had been reported to him on 21 March that year.

'According to the evidence of eyewitnesses,' he stated, 'the UFO is a disc with a diameter from 100 to 200 metres. Two pulsating lights were positioned on its sides. When the object flew in a horizontal plane, the line of the lights was parallel to the horizon. During vertical movement it rotated and was perpendicular to the ground. Moreover, the object rotated around its axis and performed an "S-turn" flight, both in the horizontal and vertical planes.

'Next, the UFO hovered above the ground and then flew with a speed exceeding that of the modern-day jet fighter by two or three times. All of the observers noticed that the flight speed was directly related to the flashing of the side lights: the more often they flashed, the higher the speed . . .'

The object was observed as a 'blip' from a radar target on the screens of aircraft gun-sights as well as on several ground-based radar units, Maltsev added. The Soviet newspaper in which this information appeared commented that General Maltsev's testimony was important confirmation for claims that UFOs are piloted craft, contradicting theories that they are merely atmospheric phenomena.

Maltsev provided a report from a Soviet Air Force pilot of the incident, which took place in the vicinity of Pereslavl Zalesskiy, about 80 miles north-east of Moscow:

'I, Lieutenant Colonel A. A. Semenchenko, received the command to go on an alert exercise. At 21.38 hours, I received the command for take-off. In the air, in the region of Pereslavl, I received my task of detecting and identifying a target at an altitude of 2,000 metres.

'I visually detected the target, designated by two flashing white lights, at 22.05 hours. I was following a true course of 220 degrees and it was ahead and to the right, at an angle of 10 degrees. The target altered its altitude by amounts ranging up to 1,000 metres and changed its direction of flight. With the permission of the command centre, I locked my sights on to the radiation after checking to be sure the weaponry was switched off.

'The target did not respond to the "identify – friend or foe" request. In addition to the target, three or four regularly scheduled airliners could be observed on the screen. As ordered by the command post, I carried out a banked turn. While completing the turn, I observed a luminous phenomenon, reminiscent of the aurora borealis but with a weak intensity, to the north and north-west.

'I approached the target to within about 500 to 600 metres. I passed above the target, trying to define its character. I observed only two bright flashing white lights. I briefly saw the silhouette of the target against the background of the illuminated city. It was difficult to determine its nature and classification due to the limited lighting. At the order of the command centre, I ended my mission and returned to the airfield.'

Another official report confirms that the UFO was tracked at a radar centre near Pereslavl Zalesskiy:

... At 21.55 hours the object disappeared at an azimuth of 240 and a range of 40 kilometres ... At 21.59 hours there was an observation of an airplane at an azimuth of 250 degrees, a range of 30–50 kilometres, and a course of 330 degrees. The object is turning and, at great speed, is approaching the airplane. After an approach to a distance of about 20 kilometres, the object disappears from the field of observation and appears again to the rear and above the plane. The object is moving in an arc at azimuth 270.

At 22.01 hours, the object is hovering in place at an azimuth of 190-200 degrees and a range up to 100 kilometres. At 22.03 hours, a fighter aircraft appeared . . . at an azimuth of 240 degrees. While the fighter was approaching the object, the latter disappeared. At 22.05 hours, the object appeared at an azimuth of 190-220 degrees, hovered, and after one to two minutes, disappeared.

'The object looked like a flying saucer with two very bright lights along the edges,' reported another observer, Captain V. Birin. 'Its diameter was approximately 100–200 metres (judging by the shining lights). A less intense light, which looked like a porthole, could be seen between the two bright lights . . . The trajectory depended on the flashing of the bright side lights: the more often they flashed, the faster the speed of the UFO and vice versa. While hovering, the object extinguished its lights almost completely. At 22.30 hours the object headed off in the direction of Moscow.'

'The movement of the UFO was not accompanied by sound of any kind and was distinguished by its startling manoeuvrability,' commented General Maltsev. 'It seemed that the UFO was completely devoid of inertia. In other words, they had somehow "come to terms" with gravity. At the present time, terrestrial machines hardly have any such capability.'[8]

A number of additional Soviet Air Force UFO incidents have been brought to my attention by Nikolai Lebedev, a leading Soviet researcher. On 8 October 1990, for example, two huge unidentified targets were tracked on radar over the vicinity of Grozniy, near Tbilisi, Georgia, according to S. Prokoshin, commander of the local air unit, and an interceptor jet was sent to investigate.

'At 11.27 hours I was given the co-ordinates of the target and the task of finding it,' reported the pilot, Major P. Riabishev. 'According to information from the command unit, the object was at an altitude of 4.5 kilometres. The weather was cloudless and visibility fine, but the search proved to be in vain. I informed the command unit then made a turn and headed back to base. Suddenly, something forced me to turn round. Behind me and to the right, I saw two cigar-shaped objects, of considerable dimensions. The length of the first was about 2 kilometres, the length of the second about 400 metres. They were positioned one beside the other and were clearly visible. The small object was streaked with silver, reflecting the sun, while the larger one looked dull.

'I noticed that the UFOs were moving sideways at great speed. I made a turn and began to approach them, but suddenly both targets disappeared instantly from my field of vision, although traces of the targets remained on the radar screen.'[9]

Glasnost has led to a relatively open attitude towards the subject of UFOs in the USSR. In January 1989, for example, I was invited to express my own views openly in an interview on Leningrad TV, whereas on previous visits such an opportunity would not have been available. I was also astonished when, in the space section of the Exhibition of Economic Achievements in Moscow, I came across a UFO stand featuring a display of photographs, books and magazines – including Britain's *FSR*, one of the world's leading journals on the subject.[10]

In response to a question on UFOs from a group of workers in the Urals in early 1990, President Mikhail Gorbachev stated that *'the phenomenon of UFOs does exist, and it must be treated seriously . . .'*[11]

Times have certainly changed, but I must point out that the Committee for State Security (KGB) still maintains firm control over the dissemination of information on the subject, principally through its Third Chief Directorate, which deals with military counter-intelligence.

Hide-and-Seek in Belgium

In addition to the USSR, the Belgian Defence Ministry has now openly admitted that unexplained aerial objects have intruded into its airspace. Since November 1989, over 2,600 witnesses, including military personnel, pilots, police, air traffic controllers, engineers and scientists, have reported sightings in Belgium. The UFOs are usually described as huge, triangular- or rectangular-shaped devices.

On the night of 30/31 March 1990, ten days after the Soviet incidents, several police patrols and other witnesses reported a UFO, which was confirmed by radar units at Glons and Semmerzake. Two Belgian Air Force F-16 fighters were sent to intercept, guided by police on the ground.

The pilots succeeded in 'locking on' to the target with their radar. At first, the object had been moving very slowly – as low as 40 k.p.h. – but suddenly it accelerated at an incredible speed; from an altitude of 2,000 metres to below 200 metres in the space of a second!

On three occasions that night, the F-16s locked on to the target, and each time the object took evasive action, playing hide-and-seek with the planes by diving to below 200 metres – out of radar range – then leisurely climbing back into radar range.

'There was a logic in the movements of the UFO,' declared the Belgian Air Force Chief of Operations, Colonel Wilfried De Brouwer, who ruled out meteorological or electromagnetic phenomena as the

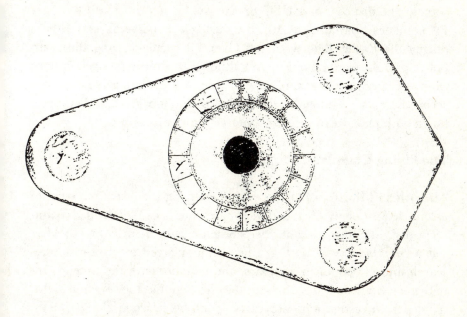

Fig. 1.1
One of the aerial devices seen over Belgium by several thousand witnesses, including pilots and police, between 1989–90. This object was seen over Mazy on 11 December 1989. *(Gerard Grede)*

source of the radar echoes.

The incidents, lasting for seventy-five minutes, were observed by many witnesses on the ground, including twenty policemen. Thanks to the Belgian Defence Minister, Guy Coëme, tapes from the F-16 'black boxes' have now been made available, clearly indicating the target (which was close to the planes) as it was automatically tracked by computer.[12]

Although the Air Force refused to allow the pilots to give interviews, in order to avoid unwelcome publicity, Colonel De Brouwer nevertheless fully endorses their reports. 'They're young guys, and they think it was something special,' he remarked. 'They're convinced that it was something.'[13]

In an unprecedented degree of official co-operation, the Belgian Air Force placed a number of aircraft, including a Hawker Siddeley 748 twin-turboprop equipped with infrared and other sophisticated sensors, at the disposal of a UFO group, the Société Belge d'Étude des Phénomènes Spatiaux (SOBEPS), during a massive skywatch held during the Easter 1990 weekend. Over 1,000 citizens, together with police patrols, were involved, and although a number of observations from the ground were made, each time the aircraft arrived on the scene the mystery intruder descended to rooftop level, which, combined with poor weather, made interception impossible.[14]

The Flying Complaints Flight

The British Ministry of Defence will be among the last, I am sure, to acknowledge openly the fact that our airspace is being intruded by unidentified, intelligently controlled aerial devices. As disclosed in *Above Top Secret*, the Royal Air Force has been engaged in clandestine research into UFOs for many years, and together with the Defence Intelligence Staff and the Directorate of Scientific and Technical Intelligence, investigations are carried out by a secret 'lodger' unit, sequestered under the Flying Complaints Flight, based at RAF Rudloe Manor in Wiltshire, headquarters of the Provost and Security Services (P&SS). A new independent source has subsequently come forward with corroborative details as well as additional relevant information.

My new informant, a former special investigator for the Provost and Security Services, has learned that certain UFO sightings are initially investigated by the Provost and Security Police Special Investigators attached to the Flying Complaints Flight at Rudloe Manor. I have been given to understand that the unit is staffed by senior non-commissioned officers and officers trained in all aspects of special investigations and counter-intelligence.

Reports are forwarded to the Director of Security and Provost Marshal (RAF) at the Metropole Building in Northumberland Avenue, London, then to the appropriate department within the Ministry of Defence – most probably DI55 of the Defence Intelligence Staff, as the MoD has admitted to me. Interestingly, it was in the Northumberland Avenue building that Gordon Creighton was working as an intelligence officer in a certain department when he had several opportunities to discuss the subject with CIA and US Air Force personnel who were liaising with their British counterparts in the Air Ministry on top secret investigations into the phenomenon. Creighton learned that the Deputy Directorate of Intelligence (Technical) employed full-time researchers during this period (the 1950s), a fact consistently denied by the MoD. And in 1957, *Reynolds News* revealed the existence of Room 801, on the ninth floor, where all reports were collected and analyzed. Room 801, it was claimed, was top secret, its interior never seen by unauthorized persons.[15]

A former non-commissioned officer who also worked as a senior investigator with the Provost and Security Services confirmed to my source that the Flying Complaints Flight dealt with UFO reports and that these were forwarded to the Provost Marshal's office, then to the appropriate department in the Ministry of Defence.

Prior to moving to Rudloe Manor, the Flying Complaints Flight operated from an office in Government Buildings, Bromyard Avenue, in Acton, London, I was informed. A former counter-intelligence investigator (whose name is known to me) revealed to my informant that although he was security-cleared to the highest category, he was denied access to this office during the period he worked there, from 1963 to 1965.

'I had access to every Top Secret file there was, except Low Flying, because I understand they dealt with UFOs,' the investigator disclosed, adding that the unit was small, situated in a well-locked office at the end of a corridor. 'We could get in anywhere, but not in that department. I remember they used to have an Air Ministry guard in the passage – you couldn't get past them. We could see the Provost Marshal's top secret files but yet I couldn't get into the place dealing with UFOs . . .'

Rudloe Manor does not serve as a 24-hour 'tracking station', as I had been told by an earlier source, but RAF Police investigators there do operate a 24-hour service for UFO reports, as well as at a number of other P&SS units around the country.

'From my personal experience as a serving member of the RAF Provost and Security Services,' my source concluded, 'also from the information obtained from my two informants, I am sure beyond any reasonable shadow of doubt that all initial investigations into UFOs are carried out by investigators of the P&SS who are serving in a small secret unit with the Flying Complaints Flight based at HQ, P&SS, Rudloe Manor.

'I believe the activities of this unit to be so secret that fellow investigators serving in the Special Investigations and Counter-Intelligence sections of the RAF are not fully aware of the activities of the FCF . . .'

My informant went on to elaborate on the possible operational procedures involved in the handling of UFO reports:

1. UFO incident reported and channelled through FCF.
2. File opened and investigation activated.
3. Notification sent to Provost Marshal's office, Northumberland Avenue, followed by regular reports.
4. Provost Marshal's office forwards memos and copies to DI(55) who in turn issues memos/instructions etc. back to the Provost Marshal's office, who in turn instructs FCF. There would be no general direct contact between DI(55)B and FCF, but on occasions, in very important cases, FCF and DI(55)B staff could well work together. The Security Service (MI5) *could* also become involved in certain cases.
5. DI(55)B would in any event report to the Security Service (MI5) HQ, Curzon Street, London, who would in turn liaise

with the Prime Minister, depending on the nature of the investigation.

6. Throughout any UFO investigation it is most likely that private UFO research groups, as well as witnesses, would be subjected to an official monitoring operation.

None of this proves, of course, that Her Majesty's Government liaises with aliens, nor indeed does it prove that the phenomenon is even extraterrestrial in origin. What it does show, however, is that the Government takes the whole issue a great deal more seriously than we have been led to believe, and in company with the US Intelligence Community classifies its findings at an above Top Secret level.

Security Threat

In *Above Top Secret* I suggested the probability that the UK Government liaises with a number of US agencies on UFO research, including the National Security Agency and Defense Intelligence Agency; the former, via the Government Communications Headquarters (GCHQ), and the latter via the Defense Intelligence Agency Liaison branch at the Ministry of Defence (DIALL). Evidence for the involvement of the DIALL has now been provided for me by researcher Nicholas Redfern, who in 1990 received some material from the DIA via the DIALL at the MoD's Main Building in Whitehall, as is clearly marked on the envelope.

Nicholas Redfern has also provided me with a number of recently released RAF reports dating back to the 1950s, many of which had been forwarded to the Deputy Directorate of Intelligence (Technical). A 1953 memo from Headquarters, Southern Sector, for example, states:

It has been decided that sightings of aerial phenomena by Royal Air Force personnel are in future to be reported in writing by Officers Commanding Units immediately and directed to Air Ministry (DDI (Tech.)) with copies to Group and Command Headquarters ... It is essential that the information should be examined at the Air Ministry and that its release should be controlled officially ... Personnel are to be warned that they are not to communicate to anyone other than official persons any information about phenomena they have observed, unless officially authorized to do so.[16]

During his inquiries into the RAF Topcliffe incident of September 1952,[17] Redfern was advised by the Public Record Office that although it was possible that some records of the Ministry of Defence's Scientific Intelligence Branch may become available for inspection in 1991, 'because of the nature of these files many will be under extended closure and so closed for fifty, seventy-five or one hundred years.'[18]

In my previous book I cited a number of incidents involving civilian witnesses who had been approached by Government investigators and asked not to communicate their reports to the media. A Ministry of Defence spokesman disclaimed MoD responsibility for these visits when I discussed the matter with him, yet I continue to receive information from both military and civilian sources indicating that such requests have indeed been made.

Shortly after 5.30 a.m. on 2 December 1982, Elizabeth Merritt was driving to work in Bury St Edmunds from her home in Honington, Suffolk, when she was surprised by an unusual sight.

'I had just passed Troston, and as I approached the junction where The Bull public house is, there were three bright white beams of light coming straight down,' she related to me. 'There was no shape behind the lights: they seemed to be in a triangle, but not particularly symmetrical. I couldn't believe it, so I stopped my car, turned off my radio and opened the car door. I couldn't hear anything. I thought I must be imagining it, so I carried on driving, put the radio back on, and took the right junction. After that, it's a straight road. And this contraption followed me up the road – I could see the bright lights moving along in the rear mirror.

'My heart was absolutely thumping by that time. It was so real. I'll admit I wasn't very brave – I was really shaking. But I'm a very cool-headed person in emergencies. Then this thing veered off to the right – and the lights were gone. And I thought it must be just my imagination: it's not a spaceship, it's nothing peculiar. So I drove on to the office in Bury St Edmunds. I was a bit unnerved, but I said nothing to anybody.'

The following morning Mrs Merritt left home at exactly the same time and took the same route, stopping her car in the same locations as the previous morning, but no lights that might have accounted for the sighting could be seen. 'I just wanted to make sure that I hadn't imagined it,' she told me.

Returning home at lunch-time, Mrs Merritt asked her husband, who worked at nearby RAF Honington, to check at the base if there had been any helicopter movements during the time in question, then went on to recount the sighting to him. 'So he rang up air traffic control. They wanted to know why he was asking, and he explained that I thought I had seen helicopter movements. And they didn't say yes or no.'

Shortly afterwards, an intelligence officer from the base telephoned to ask Mrs Merritt for precise details of her sighting. 'I know what I saw, and I know I didn't imagine it,' she told him, 'and this is why I asked my husband to confirm that there were no helicopter movements, because they're the only aircraft that would have such bright lights shining down to the ground like that.'

The flight lieutenant made no comment, but phoned back later the same day. 'He asked me to go over the story again,' Mrs Merritt said. 'Well, I have a very good photographic memory, and I went over it line for line. And he said, "Now, I don't want you to go to the media about this". I said, "Well, I'm not interested in the media, but can you confirm that I didn't imagine it?" I never got a yes or no.'

The following Monday morning, 6 December, as Al Merritt was working at RAF Honington, an interesting message was relayed over the Tannoy system. 'It was to the effect that if anyone had seen anything unusual in the sky, they were to see the intelligence officer and were not to communicate with anyone else about it,' Mr Merritt told me, adding that in his opinion the announcement was directly related to his wife's sighting and subsequent interview.[19]

In a 1989 letter to Member of Parliament Andrew Mitchell regarding an inquiry on the subject by Nottingham constituent Bob Needham, Michael Nuebert, Parliamentary Under-Secretary of State for Defence for the Armed Forces, responded (in part) as follows:

... the Ministry of Defence's sole interest in these matters is to establish whether or not reported sightings of UFOs present a threat to the security and defence of the United Kingdom, using a judgement based on military expertise and an analysis of the available information. Unless we judge that they do present a threat, *and this is not normally the case*, no further attempt is made to investigate or identify the phenomenon.

Moreover, I am sure you will appreciate that we do not have the resources to undertake in-depth studies and that we could not justify the use of Defence Funds on scientific investigations unless a clear threat to the security of the UK had been identified . . .

The MoD does not possess any positive evidence to suggest that 'alien' spacecraft have landed or crashed on the planet nor are we aware of any form of communication with extraterrestrials . . .[20] [My italics]

The fact that threats to UK security are 'not normally the case' implies that such threats have indeed occurred. And as to the lack of Defence funds to undertake in-depth investigations, I have learned otherwise. Via an academic source who was involved in secret research for the Ministry of Defence, I was informed that in 1978, for example (a year of intensive UFO activity), no less than £11 million had been appropriated.

The same source confirmed that secret research by the RAF had determined the extraterrestrial origin of UFOs, and furthermore suggested that the origin of humankind was in some way connected with the visitors. Unfortunately, I am unable to substantiate these claims except in apocryphal terms. Hundreds of people throughout the world – and I have personally interviewed many – claim to have had actual communication with extraterrestrial beings, and the theme of genetic links with humanity is a recurrent one.

I have yet to find any convincing evidence that alien spacecraft have crashed in the United Kingdom, although in 1958 Dr Olavo Fontes was informed by naval intelligence sources in Brazil that one such incident had taken place. No details were given.[21] But there is ample evidence that crashes and retrievals have occurred in other countries, particularly in the United States, as will be discussed in later chapters.

A 'Deal'?

John Lear is the only pilot to hold every airman certificate issued by the Federal Aviation Administration, and has not only flown over 160 types of aircraft in over fifty countries, but has also flown many missions worldwide for the CIA. He first became interested in UFOs in early 1987, after talking with US Air Force personnel who had witnessed the landing of a UFO outside the USAF/RAF bases at Woodbridge/Bentwaters, England, in December 1980.[22]

Based on his research, drawn from a number of independent sources and blended with published material, Lear believes that during 1969–71, a secret US Government group made a 'deal' with an alien species, called 'Extraterrestrial Biological Entities', or 'EBEs', as they are referred to in the controversial 'Majestic-12' briefing document allegedly prepared for President-elect Eisenhower in 1952 (see Chapter 6).

The 'deal' supposedly stipulated that in exchange for technology which the aliens would provide us with, the Government agreed to 'ignore' the abduction of humans and suppress information regarding the mutilation of animals. The abductions were alleged to be for the purpose of monitoring the development of our civilization, while the mutilations – involving the extraction of enzymes or hormonal secretions – were said to be essential to the aliens' survival.

There is more to this unbelievable scenario, including the allegation that the abductions turned out to have a more sinister purpose: the insertion of probes in the abductees, post-hypnotic suggestions to carry out certain specific activities, and genetic experiments, including the impregnation of human females and early termination of pregnancies to secure crossbreed infants;[23] theories proposed, for example, by Budd Hopkins in his important books on the abduction phenomenon.[24]

John Lear's statements have naturally provoked a great deal of outrage, effectively alienating him from the mainstream of 'serious' UFO research. He has admitted to me that some of his sources have proved to be unreliable and that he has occasionally made rather extreme statements. Yet he maintains that the scenario is basically true. And in one respect, at least, he could be right.

The idea that aliens could be involved in animal mutilations goes back several decades, and is now inextricably woven into the fabric of UFO lore. But is there any truth to this bizarre and disturbing theory?

Notes

1 Interview with the author, 16 February 1990.
2 Letter from Dr Richard Haines to the author, 4 October 1990.
3 *Manual of Air Traffic Services*, Part I, Amendment 31, 5 July 1984.
4 Interview with the author, 6 May 1988.
5 *Izvestia*, 26 March/2 April 1990.
6 Good, Timothy: *Above Top Secret: The Worldwide UFO Cover-Up*, Sidgwick & Jackson, London, 1987, pp. 170–7.
7 Martín, Jorge: 'US Jets Abducted by UFOs in Puerto Rico', *The UFO Report 1991*, edited by Timothy Good, Sidgwick & Jackson, London, 1990, pp. 192–204.
8 *Workers Tribune*, Moscow, 19 April 1990.
9 Ibid., 20 October 1990.
10 *Flying Saucer Review* is published by FSR Publications Ltd, P.O. Box 162, High Wycombe, Buckinghamshire HP13 5DZ.
11 *Soviet Youth*, 4 May 1990.
12 De Brosses, Marie-Thérèse: 'A UFO on the F-16's Radar', *Paris Match*, 5 July 1990 (translated by Gordon Creighton).
13 Walker, Tom: 'Could Be It's Full of Martians Hoping To Get In On 1992', *Wall Street Journal*, Brussels, 5 October 1990.
14 Kellaway, Lucy: 'Flying triangle has Belgians going round in circles', *Financial Times*, 18 April 1990. See also 'The Belgian Wave of Sightings 1989–90' by Pieter Hendrickx, published in *The UFO Report 1991*.
15 Good, Timothy: op. cit., pp. 48–9.
16 Memo from Flight Lieutenant C. P. B. Russell, for Senior Air Staff Officer, Headquarters No. 11 Group, 16 December 1953.
17 Good, Timothy: op. cit., pp. 29–31, 446.
18 Letter to Nicholas Redfern from the Public Record Office, Kew, 21 September 1990.
19 Interview with the author, 4 October 1990.
20 Letter to Andrew Mitchell MP from Michael Neubert, Parliamentary Under-Secretary of State for Defence for the Armed Forces, Ministry of Defence, 19 April 1989.
21 Letter from Dr Olavo Fontes to Coral Lorenzen, 27 February 1958.
22 Good, Timothy: op. cit. pp. 78–95.
23 Statement by John Lear, 29 December 1987, revised 25 March 1988.
24 Hopkins, Budd: *Missing Time: A Documented Study of UFO Abductions*, Richard Marek, New York, 1981; *Intruders: The Incredible Visitations at Copley Woods*, Random House, New York, 1987.

· 2 ·

A Question of Need?

On 9 September 1967, a three-year-old colt named Lady was found dead near Alamosa, in the San Luis Valley area of southern Colorado. The entire head of the animal was stripped clean of all flesh and muscle, and the brain, organs and spine were missing. No signs of blood or tyre tracks near the animal could be found.

Fifteen circular 'exhaust' marks were discovered in the vicinity, and a 3-foot circle of six or eight holes in the ground, each about 4 inches across and 3 to 4 inches deep, was found near a damaged bush 40 feet away from the animal's body. A Forest Service Ranger checked with a Geiger counter and found evidence of radiation around the 'exhaust' marks, but the radiation count decreased the closer he approached the horse's carcass.[1]

Dr John Altshuler, currently Assistant Clinical Professor of Medicine (Haematology) and Pathology at the University of Colorado Health Sciences Center in Denver, investigated the case ten days later and was profoundly shocked by what he found:

When I got close to the horse I could see that it was also cut from the neck down to the base of the chest in a vertical, clean incision. At the edge of the cut, there was a darkened colour as if the flesh had been opened and cauterized with a surgical cauterizing blade. The outer edges of the cut skin were firm, almost as if they had been cauterized with a modern-day laser. But there was no surgical laser technology like that in 1967 . . .

I cut tissue samples from the hard, darker edge. Later, I viewed the tissue under a microscope. At the cell level, there was discolouration and destruction consistent with changes caused by burning.

Most amazing was the lack of blood. I have done hundreds of autopsies. You can't cut into a body without getting some blood. But there was no blood on the skin or on the ground. No blood anywhere. That impressed me the most.

Then inside the horse's chest, I remember the lack of organs. Whoever did the cutting took the horse's heart, lungs and thyroid. The mediasternum was completely empty – and dry. How do you get the heart out without blood?

As he further describes in Linda Howe's authoritative book on the animal mutilations, *An Alien Harvest*, Dr Altshuler was also witness to a sighting of UFOs in the Great Sand Dunes National Monument park, shortly before becoming involved in the mutilation investigation. He had heard about sightings in the vicinity and one night went into the park by himself.

'About 2–3 a.m., I saw three very bright, white lights moving together slowly below the Sangre de Cristo mountain tops,' Dr Altshuler reported. 'I knew there were no roads up on those rugged mountains, so the lights could not be cars . . . Those lights were below the tops of the mountain range and moved at a slow, steady pace. At one point, I thought they were coming toward me because [they] got bigger. Then suddenly, they shot upward and disappeared . . .'

So shocked was Dr Altshuler by both the sightings and the subsequent investigation of the mutilation that he refused to allow his name to be associated with either. 'I was unbelievably frightened,' he said. 'I couldn't eat. I couldn't sleep. I was so afraid I would be discovered, discredited, fired, no longer would have credibility in the medical community. My experience in 1967 was so overwhelming to me, I denied the experience to everyone, even to myself . . .'[2]

I had the pleasure of meeting Dr Altshuler during the Ozark UFO Conference in Arkansas in 1990, and was struck by the warmth of the man. He let me handle preserved samples of tissue taken from a mutilated cow and tissue that had been cut with a laser, and the difference is readily apparent.

The Alamosa case was the first to attract worldwide attention, and thousands of similar cases have been reported since that time. In about 90 per cent of cases, cattle are involved, but horses, sheep, goats and other animals (including domestic species) have been found mutilated in similar circumstances. The phenomenon is by no means restricted to the United States.[3]

In many cases, sex organs are removed from the animals, and this has fuelled speculation that satanic cults are responsible. While this may be so in some cases, it is doubtful if such cults would be able to excise the organs with such immaculate precision, leaving no signs of blood or other traces. Neither has anyone yet been caught in the act, although large rewards (as high as $45,000) have been offered for information leading to the arrest of those responsible. Predators have also been blamed for the mutilations, but, as we shall see, this theory can only apply in a minority of cases. A more plausible theory is that the mutilations are done as part of a secret US Government research project, such as germ warfare experimentation. Again, while there are definite indications of Government involvement in some cases, such as is described in the following account, evidence of *direct* Government responsibility remains tenuous.

A Military Connection

In 1988 I received some interesting information from a man whose superficial investigation of the Alamosa mutilation led to a curious sequel with the military.

Raymond Ingraham was a sophomore engineering student at the University of Colorado, Boulder, in the autumn of 1967 when he met with Mike Kellenbarger, a keen student of the UFO subject who was a member of the Aerial Phenomena Research Organization (APRO). During the Christmas break that year, Raymond, Mike and another friend decided to travel to the San Luis Valley, where further animal mutilations and UFO sightings had occurred. 'Quite frankly, it was more of an adventure than a serious research effort,' Ingraham told me.

The distance from Boulder to the San Luis Valley is about 300 miles, and on the way the group stopped in Colorado Springs to pick up some food supplies from the US Air Force Academy, where Mike's father was an officer, then proceeded on their journey.

'We arrived in the Valley very late on a Friday evening and merely pulled off the road, as we were in a camper. The evening was bitter cold, but uneventful.' The following day, the group was fortunate to meet the farmer whose family owned Lady (presumably Harry King, who had discovered the carcass).

'Althouth initially very suspicious and somewhat hesitant to even speak to us, he gradually warmed up to our visit, and spoke freely of the experience. He took us to the spot where Lady was found, and even then, so many months after the event, one could plainly see the outline of the horse, as nothing would grow there.

'It was at this time that I noticed a grey station-wagon about a quarter-mile down the road from the farmhouse. I had my camera with me and had an 80–210 mm zoom lens on it. As the farmer was talking, I raised my camera up and slowly panned toward the car. As I began to zoom in and focus on the car, it abruptly started up and raised a cloud of dust, obscuring the vehicle completely.

'The farmer stated nonchalantly that that sort of thing happened *all* the time, and had increased many-fold since he reported the horse mutilation. But he went on to state that it had happened *prior* to the mutilation as well, after he had complained to the Air Force about un-marked helicopters skimming across the valley, shooting at coyotes, and sometimes frightening livestock. He stated that B-52 bombers from an Air Force base in New Mexico would come in low at night and do mock bombing runs at the sand dunes, creating deafening noise and disruption.

'Returning to the house, the farmer told us several unbelievable tales of lights, strange vehicles, and saucers that were fairly common in the area. Quite frankly, the isolation of the farm and the strange-ness of the farmer led me to believe that he wasn't completely sane, but on the other hand, his tale of harassment by the press and the Air Force was not totally unbelievable. He seemed to be sincerely sorry that he had reported the mutilation in the first place.

'During this trip, on one other occasion while in Alamosa, we spotted a grey station-wagon parked down the street from us while we were refuelling our truck. We never were sure if they were watching us, although there was a person in the driver's seat even when it was parked.

'The trip was, other than the interview with the farmer, fairly uneventful. We saw no unexplainable phenomena, even though we spent two nights scanning the skies with binoculars and cameras. We all agreed that the San Luis Valley would be an ideal spot for UFOs to hide, as the vastness of the area is difficult to describe. We journeyed back to Boulder. Over time, we all went our separate ways. I dropped out of school in 1969, and lost track of Mike.

'I received my draft notice in January of 1970, and after shopping all the armed services, elected to enlist in the US Army, and was accepted in the Army Intelligence section, with a specialty in photo reconnaissance. I proceeded to Fort Leonard Wood, Missouri, for my basic training. In my initial screening/clearing interview, I was asked point-blank *why* I had gone to Alamosa in 1967 and *what* was I doing there.

'Needless to say, I was flabbergasted (a) that they knew I was there and (b) why on earth it concerned them. When the discussion of APRO ensued, they asked me if I had joined, to which I honestly replied "No". This apparently satisfied them. Due to a pre-existing stomach ulcer I never got into Army Intelligence, and was discharged in March 1970 . . .'[4]

Official Investigations

In the latter days of Project Blue Book, Dr J. Allen Hynek was asked by Major Quintanilla of the Blue Book office to interview a farmer who had written to Secretary of Defense Robert McNamara immediately following a UFO/cattle incident in February 1968. The farmer, who lived about 30 miles north of Kansas City, Missouri, had been awakened at 3.20 a.m. by the bawling of his cattle. Outside, he saw the cows staring up at an illuminated object that appeared to be at least 100 feet in diameter, hovering about 20 to 25 feet off the ground, making a pulsating, swishing noise.

The farmer explained that his cows scattered, and the object eventually took off rapidly. 'I have been losing a cow or two now and then, undoubtedly stolen without trace', he wrote to McNamara. 'On seeing the craft, I remember thinking, "No wonder I have found no evidence! They are being hauled off by air!"'

Dr Hynek conducted an interview by phone and was impressed by the witness, though he regretted not having conducted a personal interview. 'Blue Book did not, of course, consider it worthwhile to expend time and money for me to visit this witness,' he reported. The case was simply filed away as 'unexplained'.[5]

In April 1973, US Attorney Allen Danielson asked the FBI to launch an intensive investigation, following a spate of mutilations in Iowa. Although an agreement was reached to co-operate with the Iowa Bureau of Criminal Investigation and several county sheriffs,[6] the FBI appears to have been reluctant to investigate cases.

Another request was made to the FBI two years later. In August 1975, following 130 cases of cattle mutilations in a two-year period, confirmed by the Colorado Bureau of Investigation, Senator Floyd Haskell wrote to the FBI requesting assistance. In his letter, Haskell noted that some rural residents had reported being chased by helicopters and that ranchers were arming themselves to protect their stock and families. 'I talked with FBI Director Clarence Kelley and also with his chief assistant in Washington, and they looked into possible grounds for the FBI to enter the case,' Haskell reported. 'But since there is no evidence of interstate movements in connection with the reported mutilations, the FBI concluded that it has no jurisdiction. Although the FBI assistance would have been welcome, after talking with CBI [Colorado Bureau of Investigation] officers I am satisfied that agency is conducting a thorough investigation. I am hopeful that, with the co-operation of local law enforcement officials, the CBI will be able to learn who or what is behind the mutilations and put an end to the fears of rural Coloradans.'[7]

By 1974, ranchers in Nebraska had become so angered with the mutilations that they armed themselves with rifles and shotguns and formed vigilante groups. 'I've never seen anything like this,' Nebraska State Senator Jules Burbach commented in September 1974. 'Folks are almost hysterical.' Since so many unmarked helicopters had been seen in the areas where the mutilations had occurred, the ranchers began shooting at them. After two bullets penetrated the canopy of a utility-company helicopter checking power lines, the Nebraska National Guard ordered its pilots to cruise cross-country at higher altitudes than normal to avoid being fired on by irate ranchers and farm-hands.[8] In some areas, helicopters were grounded.

In addition to the helicopters, strange lights and UFOs continued to be seen by the ranchers. 'I have had reports of UFOs in this area, but have never seen any myself,' said Sheriff Richards of Cochran County, Colorado, in the spring of 1975. 'The people who have been reporting this all tell the same story. It is about as wide as a two-lane highway, round, and looks the colour of the sun when it is going down and has got a blue glow around it. When these people see this thing, in two or three days we hear about some cows that have been mutilated.'[9]

Later that year, Colorado Governor Richard Lamm expressed his anger during a meeting of the state's Cattlemen's Association. 'The mutilations are one of the greatest outrages in the history of the western cattle industry,' he announced. 'It is important that we solve this mystery as soon as possible. The cattle industry already is hard hit from an economic point of view. From a human point, we cannot allow these mutilations to continue.'[10]

In early 1975, the Coryell County Deputy Sheriff and Department of Public Safety (DPS) officials investigating the mutilation of a calf near Copperas Cove, Texas, discovered that, typically, the sex organs had been removed bloodlessly. Peculiar markings were found near the carcass, consisting of concentric circles pressed into the hard ground, and in an open field about 40 yards from the calf an area about 30 feet in diameter was scarred by similar markings. Clumps of dried grass had been pressed down in a circular pattern as if by some tremendous force, which had also dug up the ground and moved small rocks. Some of the clumps of grass seemed to have been 'rotated' so fast that they had been uprooted.

The DPS officials speculated that an aerial vehicle had been used in the operation. It was later learned that several residents near Copperas Cove and Killeen had observed a yellowish-orange light hovering over the farmland at around the same time as the mutilation.[11]

With the FBI's initial refusal to become involved, investigations were mostly left to local law enforcement officials. The following abridged official report (released by the FBI) by Officer Gabriel Valdez of the New Mexico State Police provides an interesting example of an official investigation into the mutilations. The incident had occurred on 13 June 1976 at a ranch owned by Manuel Gomez near Dulce, New Mexico:

> ... At the scene, writer examined carcass of a 3-yr.-old black White-Faced cow which was lying on its right side. The left ear, the tongue, the udder, and the rectum had been removed with what appeared to be a sharp precise instrument. No traces of blood were left on the skin of the cow ... Other evidence on the cow was a small puncture on the brisket. No other evidence was available as to cause of death.
>
> Investigations continued around the area and revealed that a suspected aircraft of some type had landed twice, leaving pod marks positioned in a triangular shape. The diameter of each pod part was 14″. The perimeter around the three pods was 16½′ (6′ × 5′ × 5½′). Emanating from the two landings were smaller tri-angular-shaped tripods 26″ apart and 4″ in diameter. Investigation at the scene showed that these small tripods had followed the cow for approximately 600 feet. Tracks of the cow showed where she had struggled and fallen. The small tripod tracks were all around the cow. Other evidence showed that grass around the tripods, as they followed the cow, had been scorched. Also a yellow oily sub-stance was located in two places under the small tripods. This sub-stance was submitted to the State Police Lab. The Lab was unable to detect the content of the substance ...
>
> On 06-17-76 writer contacted a Mr Howard Burgess from Albu-querque, N.M. to proceed to the scene and conduct a radiation test. This was 3 days after the incident had occurred. His findings were that around the tripod marks and in the immediate tracks, the radiation level was twice the normal background reading. Mr Bur-gess's qualifications may be checked as he is a retired scientist from Sandia Lab, Albuquerque. It is the opinion of this writer that radia-tion findings are deliberately being left at the scene to confuse in-vestigators ...

The cow had a 3-month-old calf which has not been located since the incident. This appears strange since a small calf normally stays around the mother cow even though the cow is dead . . .

Officer Valdez noted that in all the cattle mutilations that had occurred in New Mexico and surrounding states at that time, 'the object of the mutilations has been the lymph node system'. And he reported that on one of the mutilated cows, 'a high dosage of Atropine insecticide was analyzed in the blood system'. Since Atropine is a tranquillizing drug, this would imply that either government agents or private individuals were responsible in this case, yet the presence of the drug need not necessarily be related to the mutilation, and investigations into later cases failed to confirm the presence of such drugs.

During his investigations, Valdez studied several theories for the mutilations, including 'Satan worshippers' and predators. 'Both have been ruled out due to expertise and preciseness and the cost involved to conduct such a sophisticated and secretive operation,' Valdez noted in his report. 'It should also be noted that during the spring of 1974 when a tremendous amount of cattle were lost due to heavy snowfalls, the carcasses had been eaten by predators. These carcasses did not resemble those of the mutilated cows.'

In one of the New Mexico mutilated cows, a substance analyzed showed the presence of 'an ion exchange resin and Vitamin B_{12}'. Valdez concluded in his report that investigations had narrowed down to those theories which involved (1) the experimental use of Vitamin B_{12}, (2) the testing of the lymph node system, and (3) what was involved in germ warfare testing, and the possible correlation of these three factors.[12]

In another case reported by Manuel Gomez of Dulce, involving the mutilation of an eleven-month-old Hereford-Charolais bull on 24 April 1978, Officer Valdez reported some additional unusual findings:

. . . Investigation showed that this . . . bull [had been] dropped by some type of aircraft north of Mr Gomez's ranch house . . . The rectum and sex organs had been removed with a sharp and precise instrument . . . The bull sustained visible bruises around the brisket, seeming to indicate that a strap was used to lift and lower the animal to and from the aircraft . . .

Prints were found . . . north of the slain animal. These 4″ diameter round footprints led to the animal and . . . apparently returned to a hovering aircraft. The imprints appeared to be quite heavy since the ground was dry and hard . . . These imprints appeared to have scraped the ground as they moved.

The liver and heart of this animal were removed by this writer. Both the liver and heart were white and mushy. Both organs had the consistency of peanut butter. The carcass was dehydrated. The heart was taken to the Los Alamos Medical Laboratory to be analyzed and the liver was taken to 3 different laboratories . . . The liver was checked against a healthy food-market liver which showed a difference from the mutilated bull's liver. The bull's liver contained no copper, and 4 times the amount of phosphorous, zinc, and potassium. No explanation for this condition is available at the present time . . . Also the blood which came off the bull's nose when it was presumably dropped was light pink in colour . . .

The hide on the animal was brittle and . . . flesh underneath the hide was pinkish in colour. A probable explanation for the pinkish blood is a control type of radiation used to kill the animal, according to radiation experts. The red corpuscles are destroyed leaving the pale pinkish colour . . . It is believed that this type of radiation is not harmful to humans, although approximately seven people who visited the site complained of nausea and [illegible]. However, this writer has had no such symptoms after checking approximately eleven mutilations in the past four months.

The only entrance to this mutilation site is through Mr Gomez's front yard. No vehicle was seen or heard entering the pasture . . . However, a Mr Martinez, who was visiting his son-in-law Mauricio Gomez (brother of Manuel Gomez) heard a low-flying aircraft in the vicinity of where the mutilated bull was found at approximately 3 a.m. on 4-24-78 . . .

Investigation of these strange mutilations has been hampered by an inability to find laboratories which will perform tests and report accurate findings . . . It is writer's opinion that these animals have been marked for some time before they are mutilated . . . It is writer's theory that these animals are picked up by aircraft, mutilated elsewhere and returned and dropped from aircraft. This is indicated from bruised marks and broken bones on cattle.

Identical mutilations have been taking place all over the South-West . . . no eyewitnesses to these incidents have come forward . . . One has to admit that whoever is responsible for the mutilations is very well organized with boundless technology and financing and secrecy . . .[13]

Substances Tested

Howard Burgess, the retired Sandia Laboratories scientist who conducted a great deal of research into mutilations in northern New Mexico and southern Colorado, including, as confirmed in the preceding report, those that had occurred on Manuel Gomez's ranch, pointed out in 1979 that up to that time an estimated 10,000 cases had taken place in the United States. 'To the general public the term "mutilation" has come to mean a crude sex operation done by some unknown cult,' he commented. 'This is not true for the animals we are examining. In these animals the same parts of the lymphatic and digestive tract are removed from each animal in a very precise and bloodless operation. The operation is generally performed in the air and the dead animal dropped. Many times the animals appear to have received some form of radiation.'

Burgess discovered that 90 per cent of the mutilated cattle were four- to five-year-old cows and heifers of less than one year old. Theorizing that the animals had perhaps been 'marked' in some way, Burgess arranged for ultraviolet light tests to be run on a herd of live cattle belonging to Gomez's ranch on the Apache Indian Reservation near Dulce. Late on the night of 5 July 1978, 100 mixed cattle were checked, using five different types of ultraviolet lamps ranging through the spectrum, which were put in place over a narrow chute into which only one animal could pass at a time.

'To our amazement,' Burgess reported, 'three four-year-old cows and two young heifers had bright flourescent splashes on their backs or top sides, fitting the pattern of animal types being mutilated in that area at the period. No markings were found on their sides, underneath, or lower parts. We were not able to find any liquid or solid in the corral or pasture that glowed with the same colour or brilliance as the marks on the animals. The fluorescent marking was not from material picked up locally. If the animals were marked in advance, how was it done? When? By whom?'

Near midnight, Tribal Police Chief Raleigh Tafoya of the Apache Indian Police stopped by to see how the operation was going. 'Did you see the orange light moving around in the sky a while ago?' he asked. 'It was the kind that always shows up when there's a mutilation. Maybe they're watching you tonight.' Later that night two mutilations occurred a few miles away on a remote mountain slope.

About four weeks after the fluorescent hair – containing some apparently metallic, organic material – had been removed from the animal (for analysis by the Schoenfeld Clinical Laboratories in Albuquerque), the fluorescence suddenly and inexplicably 'turned off'.

Four days before the ultraviolet test, on 2 July, about twenty witnesses observed a disc hovering directly above a state highway inspector's pick-up truck, outside his home in Taos, New Mexico. The object was described as being about 25 to 30 feet in diameter, glowing a brilliant pinkish-orange and emitting a 'crackling' noise similar to that of an electrical high-tension corona discharge. As the witnesses watched, flaky material from the UFO showered down to the ground, some falling on the truck. The small light grey flakes, averaging about one-sixteenth of an inch by about three-sixteenths and as thick as heavy paper, resembled chips of dried paint. Leroy Graham, the highway inspector, collected a substantial amount of the substance in a sterile fruit jar, and Dr Burgess (after having learned of the incident six months later) arranged for an analysis to be conducted by the Schoenfeld laboratory. Dr Robert Schoenfeld found twenty-two elements that generally occur in organic material, plus trace elements of europium, lanthanum, yttrium, platinum and vanadium. In addition, substantial quantities of magnesium and potassium were found.[14]

Dr Schoenfeld told journalist Larry Statser that the substance he tested was of the same chemical composition as the substance discovered on the cow hides he had analyzed previously. He explained that the material was similar to 'slivers or chips of grey paint' with an 'extremely high' quantity of potassium and magnesium. In fact, the potassium content was about seventy times higher than the normal amount for earth samples in the Taos area. A test under a spectrometer showed the substance to be similar to Teflon in composition, although both samples proved to be basically organic, 'as opposed to a metal compound such as used on aircraft', Schoenfeld said.[15]

Perhaps coincidentally, a mutilated animal, fitting the general age pattern of those marked, was found later that year (or possibly 1979), a short distance from the point where the UFO had hovered over Leroy Graham's home in Taos. On the night before the mutilation, a similar UFO to the one reported in July was again observed in the area.[16]

In a report to the FBI Director alluding to the Taos incident, retired FBI agent Kenneth Rommel, Jr, who came out of retirement to head a $50,000 FBI investigation established in early 1979 (the Animal Mutilation Project), concluded as follows:

> . . . Some of the individuals that are most vocal to the media have inferred that these flakes are identical with a substance that was taken from cowhides in a controlled test conducted in the Dulce, New Mexico area . . . I have not been able to locate a sample of the substance reportedly collected in the Dulce test, but it has been described as a fluorescent material.
>
> I have to date been unable to confirm any connection between these two substances, and have been told by those that have seen both that they are not identical. However, I would appreciate it if through the use of a G.S. Mass spectroscopy test or any other logical test, these flakes can be identified. This in itself would go a long way to assisting me to discredit the UFO–Cow Mutilation association theory . . .[17]

The FBI Laboratory Report identified the material as a 'white enamel paint typical of an acrylic latex/emulsion-type exterior house paint' which 'appears to have originated from a wood substrate', but that the 'particular origin and/or manufacture of this paint cannot be determined'.

Commenting on the animal mutilations in general, Rommel concluded that 'most credible sources have attributed this damage to normal predator and scavenger activity'[18] (Appendix, Fig. 2.4), a conclusion he reaffirmed in his 297-page final report in June 1980. But critics, including Officer Valdez, pointed out that Rommel had failed to investigate the 'classic' cases, concentrating instead on those cattle that had obviously died more naturally, and had not bothered to talk with the ranchers and investigators who were most familiar with the problem. Valdez complained that the report 'looks very convincing because it comes from an FBI agent, but everything he put in the report was speculation.'[19]

Another critic was New Mexico Senator Harrison Schmitt, whose request to the US Attorney General had led to the FBI investigation (Appendix, Fig. 2.3). Senator Schmitt, a former astronaut with a PhD in geology from Harvard, had declared earlier: 'To date, the mutilations have been as mysterious as they've been grisly. Either we've got a UFO situation or we've got a massive, massive conspiracy which is enormously well funded.'[20]

An Alien Connection?

Inevitably, charges of a cover-up were made, particularly since ranchers and other investigators had found scant evidence of predator or scavenger activity: in most cases, in fact, predators would not go anywhere near the mutilated carcasses. And in numerous instances, sightings of unidentified flying objects, including mysterious helicopters which behaved in an unconventional manner, continued to be reported in areas where mutilations had occurred.

By 1980, researcher Tom Adams had compiled a catalogue of about 200 mutilation incidents that involved sightings of UFOs or helicopters. In late 1975, the Federal Aviation Administration began an official investigation into sightings over north-eastern New Mexico, but in response to Freedom of Information requests made some years later to various FAA offices, the FAA denied having any information about the mystery helicopters and UFOs, or any investigation thereof.

In the early autumn of 1976, following twenty-two confirmed mutilation cases in Madison County, Montana, between June and October, a hunter from Bozeman, Montana, observed an unmarked black helicopter as it disappeared below a hill in the Red Mountain area near Norris. Climbing to the top of the hill, the hunter saw a black helicopter (which appeared to be a Bell JetRanger) on the ground, its engine still running.

Seven men had disembarked from the craft and were walking up the hill towards the witness. As the hunter waved and shouted greetings, he noticed that the men all appeared to be Oriental, with slanted eyes and olive skin, and were talking among themselves in an undecipherable language. Suddenly, they headed back to the helicopter, and the hunter followed. As he came to within about 6 feet, the 'Orientals' broke into a run, jumped into the helicopter, and took off.[21]

Shy Oriental tourists, perhaps? A conventional explanation is suggested in this particular case, even if puzzling questions remain. Other cases are completely puzzling, especially those involving more 'conventional' UFOs.

In one of many incidents cited by Linda Howe in *An Alien Harvest*, rancher Pat McGuire and his cousin Mark Murphy sighted a large, orange-glowing object hovering near a ridge on McGuire's ranch in Bosler, Wyoming, in late 1976. Cows could be heard bellowing in the distance. Viewing the object from 1.8 miles away through a rifle hunting scope, the men could see red, yellow, blue and white lights rotating around the top and bottom of the object. Suddenly, the cows became silent. Frightened, the men did not investigate until the following morning, when it was discovered that a cow was missing.[22]

Linda reports that witnesses in the ranching community of Sterling, Colorado, frequently observed a large, hovering white light, with smaller lights that appeared to be entering or leaving it. The sightings continued 'almost nightly' between November 1976 and the spring of 1977.

Logan County Sheriff Harry 'Tex' Graves tried to get closer to the objects in a light aircraft, but was always unsuccessful. 'No matter how we tried, we could never get closer than 5 miles to it,' he told Linda. 'Several times we observed smaller lights come out of this big [light] and then come down toward earth. This huge brilliant light would hang in the air and then when it would move, it could move up and down, backwards, forwards, travel very rapidly, and after a while these smaller lights would join up with the larger one and then they would disappear.'[23]

Graves, who by April 1977 had exchanged information on the mutilations with law enforcement officials in twenty other states, was informed by Deputy Sheriff Keith Wolverton of Cascade County in Montana that on one occasion a UFO was observed on radar, hovering at 21,000 feet before climbing to 44,000 feet – in the space of three and a half seconds.[24] Bill Jackson, a reporter from the *Sterling Journal-Advocate*, succeeded in taking a number of photographs of the strange object with telephoto lenses (reproduced in *An Alien Harvest*), and had several close encounters with UFOs. One cloudy night, a huge object flew towards him as he was driving north on Colorado Highway 61, about 30 miles from Sterling:

> . . . I pulled to the side of the road thinking I was really going to be on a big story – maybe a 747 coming down in the prairie. I stood outside my car and watched it fly right over me. It was completely silent – not a sound . . . There were all kinds of lights – green ones, white ones, red ones, orange ones – maybe a hundred of them. I couldn't see any definite shape, but the lights seemed to run in lines, maybe like a rectangle or an oval. It was as big as a football field, at least 300 feet long, and moving slowly below the clouds.[25]

During his extensive study of the mutilation phenomenon, Dr Henry Monteith, a retired Sandia Laboratories engineering physicist, found that Indians were so terrified of the mutilations that they buried the carcasses immediately and were reluctant even to discuss the subject. 'They don't say anything about it because they know it's being done by "star people",' he is quoted as stating in a 1979 interview. 'They know why they're doing it, so therefore we should leave it alone. Those are their exact words . . . the "star people" know what they're doing and should be trusted.'[26] Monteith was convinced that the mutilations were part of an 'environmental testing programme' by aliens who were able to make themselves invisible, thus frustrating all efforts at catching them.[27]

In an interview with Linda Howe, Sheriff Lou Girodo, who was chief investigator of mutilations for the District Attorney's office in Trinidad, Colorado, also admitted that aliens could be responsible. 'It's possible that these mutilations are being done by creatures from outer space,' he declared. Girodo also volunteered his opinion that the mystery helicopters could be spacecraft 'camouflaged as helicopters'.[28]

The idea is not as absurd as it seems. Mysterious unmarked aircraft have long been associated with the UFO phenomenon, as I have shown in my previous book, and it seems to me to be entirely feasible that aliens might disguise their vehicles or even produce facsimile aircraft (sometimes of preposterously unaerodynamic design), as well as render their craft and themselves invisible, in order to keep us in a perpetual state of confusion. A clue to this deception is provided by a number of reports from New Mexico describing UFOs that imitate helicopter sounds.

During 1978, Howard Burgess reports, a Taos city policeman heard what he thought was a helicopter hovering over his police car. Stepping out of the car, he observed a large wingless cigar-shaped vehicle hovering motionless above him. It then took off and disappeared over mountains. In another incident, a witness reported seeing a large round object near Dulce which made a noise like that of an old two-cylinder tractor![29]

Yet it is equally possible that in many cases US Government helicopters have been involved in secret investigations into the mutilations, and as a counter-intelligence operation make a point of being seen in areas where mutilations have occurred, thus drawing attention away from the actual perpetrators. This theory is endorsed by one of the principal witnesses in the Colorado Ranch case, as we shall learn in the following chapter.

Little Green Men

Other theorists allege that the US Government is involved with the mutilations as part of a clandestine liaison with the aliens. I first learned about this bizarre theory from Paul Bennewitz, who in 1980 had taken some 8 mm films of UFOs near Kirtland AFB, Albuquerque, New Mexico – described in Air Force Office of Special Investigations (AFOSI) documents (see *Above Top Secret*) – and who had intercepted and monitored some unusual low frequency radio signals which he believed were communications from the aliens. Whatever the nature of the signals, they were sufficiently sensitive to necessitate counter-intelligence measures directed against Bennewitz in order to discredit him, according to William Moore, who was himself asked by the OSI to monitor the progress of the disinformation that Bennewitz was fed.

'Bennewitz was the subject of considerable interest on the part of not one but several government agencies,' Bill Moore discovered. 'I was personally aware of the Intelligence Community's concerted efforts to systematically confuse, discourage and discredit Paul by providing him with a large body of disinformation on the subject of UFOs, the malevolent aliens who allegedly pilot them, the technology they employ and the underground bases they supposedly possess and occupy . . . I watched Paul become systematically more paranoid and more emotionally unstable as he tried to assimilate what was happening to him.'[30]

Perhaps some of that disinformation is contained in one of Bennewitz's letters to me in 1985:

> . . . Research and computer communications would indicate that humanoids are made from the specific cattle parts . . . The humanoid is apparently green . . . A deal was made between the Government and the aliens. I can only surmise what it was, but based upon my evidence we helped build the base – gave them the land – in trade for the atomic ship and technology . . . We agreed to the cattle mutilations and lately are or were apparently helping in unmarked helicopters . . .

The 'green humanoids' are supposedly manufactured by the aliens, one of whose bases is said to be under the Archuleta Mesa near Dulce, New Mexico (where, interestingly, a preponderance of mutilations has occurred), and the 'atomic ship', I was told, is the alleged 'Snowbird' craft, which during a test flight in December 1980 (escorted by over twenty helicopters) was observed by Betty Cash and two other witnesses in Huffman, Texas, as described in my previous book. Whatever that craft was, it undoubtedly irradiated the witnesses and made them very ill.[31]

In 1985 Bennewitz invited me to fly with him and photograph evidence of this alleged base near Dulce, but regrettably chose to cancel the visit. In July 1989, however, I was shown some of Bennewitz's photographs by his friend, Colonel Ernest Edwards, who had been in charge of security at the Manzano Nuclear Weapons Storage Area at Kirtland AFB at the time of the 1980 sightings. Edwards confirmed the sightings to me, and pointed out where they had taken place, but neither of us was able to distinguish any unusual evidence in the photographs.

This is not to say that I reject totally the scenario presented by Bennewitz. In order to be effective, disinformation should contain some elements of truth, and the following story – if true – confirms at least one aspect of the 'green humanoids' scenario.

In April 1980, near Waco, Texas, a rancher who had been searching for a missing cow that was ready to calve encountered two 4-foot-high 'creatures' in a clearing between mesquite trees about a hundred yards away.

'They was wearin' some kind of tight-fittin' green clothes like the colour of mesquite leaves in the spring,' the rancher told Linda Howe. 'Even the feet was covered. The hands was shaped like eggs, with the pointy end down toward the ground. Between them they was carryin' a calf. Their arms swung back and forth right together. The hands was the same colour as everything else, all sort of greenish. No other colour on them.'

The rancher said the beings looked like small adults, neither fat nor skinny, but slightly muscular. No noses or hair could be distinguished. Suddenly, their heads turned in unison and the rancher was able to see the eyes, which were angled upward and pointed at the end. They were 'sloe-eyed', he reported, 'like big, dark almonds. I was afraid of them seein' me. I've read all about them abductions and I didn't want them takin' me away in some flyin' saucer! I took off down the hill pretty fast . . .'

The rancher was so disturbed by the experience that he remained silent about it for two days. Finally he confided in his wife and son, and together they returned to the site where he had seen the beings. There, on the hill, was the remains of a calf, presumably the same one carried by the two beings, with its hide pulled back over the skull and folded inside out on the ground. No blood was in evidence, and a complete calf backbone – minus ribs – was found about a foot away from the empty hide.[32]

The Harvest Continues

Many researchers reject the possibility that the animal mutilations could be caused by alien or non-human intelligences, and favour less exotic hypotheses. George Erianne, for example, a private investigator who spent seven years investigating the subject, concluded in 1982 that the US Government was conducting a secret germ warfare study that necessitated the random selection of cattle (supposedly to attract less attention). According to Erianne, helicopters were used to transport the tranquillized animals to a location where laser surgery removed the organs and the blood was drained for testing. He pointed out that the reproductive systems of beef and dairy cows closely resemble those of humans, and that other physiological similarities include extremely sensitive mucous membranes in the eye cavity, coronary system, and lungs.

Erianne claims to have received death threats when he publicized these findings, which would seem to indicate that he was on the right track.[33] Possible support for his theory is the recent manufacture of a blood product derived from cows which may well be used in the near future as a temporary substitute for human blood. The substitute, Hemopure, already successfully tested on animals, is a purified haemoglobin, the substance in blood that transports oxygen. Hemopure lacks the potential to transmit diseases such as AIDS and Hepatitis B, and can be given to people irrespective of their blood group.[34] This may have no relevance to the mutilations, though it does lead to interesting speculation. It is possible, for instance, that the blood drained from cattle, as reported in most mutilations, is used for additional testing in chemical-biological experiments owing to its similarity (in many respects) to human blood.

But many experts remain puzzled by the fact that traces of blood are seldom found at the mutilation sites or in the carcasses. Questioned about this by Linda Howe, Dr Albert McChesney, a Colorado State University pathologist, responded: 'I would say that it would be virtually impossible to withdraw not even all of the blood from an animal without leaving some tell-tale mark that blood vessels had been cut or that the animal had been killed in this manner.' Dr McChesney added that closer examination of the carcasses might have revealed the presence of blood that had gravitated to the deeper organs or the down side of the animal, but he confessed to bewilderment about the blood-draining (exsanguination) technique used.[35]

Linda Howe told me in 1990 that the animal mutilations have continued, but admits that in the majority of cases no UFOs are reported. In August 1987, however, a security guard patrolling the grounds of a large corporation in Denver, Colorado, saw a large circle of stationary lights over a pasture a few hundred feet away. He was loathe to report the incident at the time for fear of losing his job, but later came to regret this decision when the following morning he watched a farmer collect a couple of dead and mutilated cows from the pasture. 'What kind of technology are we talking about?' he asked Linda. 'I never took my eyes off those lights. There was no beam, no sound – nothing. How did they do it?'[36]

A particularly gruesome multiple mutilation occurred on or around 10 March 1989, when five pregnant cows were found dead by L. C. Wyatt on his property near Hope, Arkansas. On arrival at the scene, reporter Juanita Stripling noted that the cows seemed to have dropped dead in their tracks. 'One cow was lying on her right side,' she reported. 'There was a large, round cut-out area with the calf lying just outside the cow and still in the embryo sac . . . There was no blood on the ground or on the body of the cow or calf. There was also no dampness on the ground of water or body fluids.'

Pathologist and haematologist Dr John Altshuler, whose comments and photomicrographs of samples from these cows are published in Linda Howe's book, stated that 'one would have to conclude that the surgical procedure performed on these animals took place quickly, probably in a minute or two, and utilized high-temperature heat (e.g. laser) as a cutting source applied in a fine probe or cutting instrument.'[37]

A sales engineer claims that a laser required to make the type of cuts on these animals would be the size of an average office desk and weigh about 550 pounds. Using existing laser equipment, the engineer believes, surgery on one cow alone would take about an hour.[38]

The unlikelihood of Government mutilators is further reinforced by these findings, although it is certain that new and secret types of laser equipment have been developed by the military. Even as far back as 1983, IBM announced that it had developed an ultraviolet excimer laser which is able to cut without charring and operates at low temperatures and 'breaks selective bonds between atoms', thus producing smaller molecules that vaporize at a lower temperature. According to IBM, however, there were problems with aiming the tiny beam precisely.[39] And even if a perfected device was used to mutilate the cows at Hope, we are still left with Dr Altshuler's findings (for example, indications of *high*-temperature use), as well as a complete lack of evidence for human intrusion at the mutilation site.

Dr Chris Oates, an Idaho veterinarian who performed an autopsy on a mutilated steer in December 1989, found not only organs and blood msising but also discovered that the heart appeared to have been given a powerful electric shock. 'I opened it everywhere,' she said. 'I've thought about it a lot and I can't explain it.'[40]

I can't explain it, either. Perhaps we should remain open to the possibility that some alien intelligences require certain substances from animals, either for their own sustenance or genetic experiments – or both. After all, do we humans not abuse animals for similar reasons?

In 1984 I discussed the question of mutilations with Dr Pierre Guérin, the French astrophysicist, as we enjoyed a steak in a Paris restaurant. 'The testimonial facts are always doubtful,' he said, 'but the material facts, independent of the witnesses – as in the case of the mutilations – are of a superior degree than testimonial evidence.'

Dr Guérin shares my opinion that the mutilations are a manifestation of extraterrestrial activity, and is unequivocal in his condemnation of the official FBI 'Animal Mutilation Project' report, which he regards as proof of the deliberate intention of the American authorities to deceive public opinion on the UFO phenomenon.[41]

Notes

1 Howe, Linda Moulton: *An Alien Harvest*, Linda Moulton Howe Productions, P.O. Box 538, Huntingdon Valley, Pennsylvania 19006-0538, 1989, p. 2; Duplantier, Gene: *The Night Mutilators*, SS&S Publications, 17 Shetland Street, City of North

York, Willowdale, Ontario M2M 1X5, 1979, p. 30.
2 Howe, Linda Moulton: op. cit., pp. 2–5.
3 Duplantier, Gene: op. cit.
4 Letter to the author from Raymond C. Ingraham, 22 July 1988.
5 Hynek, Dr J. Allen: *The Hynek UFO Report*, Sphere Books, London, 1978, pp. 193–5.
6 Harpster, Charles: 'Burgeoning Losses Bring FBI into Rustler's Probe', *The Des Moines Register*, Des Moines, Iowa, 19 April 1973.
7 *Gazette Telegraph*, Colorado Springs, 24 September 1975.
8 *Newsweek*, 30 September 1974.
9 Howe, Linda Moulton: op. cit., p. 22.
10 Ibid., p. 23.
11 Blann, Tommy Roy: 'The Mysterious Link between UFOs and Animal Mutilations', *UFO Report*, Vol. 3, No. 1, April 1976, pp. 70, 72.
12 New Mexico State Police Report, 15 December 1976.
13 New Mexico State Police Report, 31 July 1978.
14 Burgess, Howard and Burgess, Lovola: 'Close Encounter at the Old Corral', *True UFOs & Outer Space Quarterly*, Summer 1979, pp. 28–33; Lorenzen, Jim: *Cattle Mutilations – The UFO Connection*, APRO Symposium, San Diego, California, 16–18 November 1979; Statser, Larry: 'Cattle Mangled by UFOs?', *Amarillo Globe News*, (?) May 1979.
15 Statser, Larry: op. cit.
16 Burgess, Howard and Burgess, Lovola: op. cit.
17 Letter to the FBI Director from Kenneth M. Rommel, Jr, Director, Animal Mutilation Project, Office of the District Attorney, First Judicial District, Espanola, New Mexico, 5 March 1980.
18 Ibid.
19 *APRO Bulletin*, Vol. 28, No. 11, 1980, Vol. 30, No. 4, 1982.
20 Barnhill, William; Pratt, Bob; Wright, David: 'FBI Joins Investigation of Animal Mutilations Linked to UFOs', *National Enquirer*, 5 June 1979.
21 Adams, Thomas R.: 'The Choppers – and the Choppers', Project Stigma, P.O. Box 1094, Paris, Texas 75460, 1980.
22 Howe, Linda Moulton: op. cit., p. 46.
23 Ibid., pp. 35–6, 43.
24 Aldridge, Dorothy: 'Do UFOs Fly in Colorado?', *Gazette Telegraph*, Colorado Springs, 24 April 1977.
25 Howe, Linda Moulton: op. cit., p. 36.
26 Barnhill, William; Pratt, Bob; Wright, David: op. cit.
27 Jackson, Bill: 'Mutilations – Predators . . . or UFOs?', *Greeley Tribune*, Greeley, Colorado, 2 November 1980.
28 Howe, Linda Moulton: op. cit., pp. 44–5
29 Burgess, Howard and Burgess, Lovola: op. cit.
30 Moore, William L.: *UFOs and the US Government* (Part 1), MUFON Symposium, Las Vegas, 1 July 1989. Available from William L. Moore Publications & Research, 4219 W. Olive, Suite 247, Burbank, California 91505.
31 Good, Timothy: *Above Top Secret: The Worldwide UFO Cover-Up*, Sidgwick & Jackson, London, 1987, pp. 296–9.

32 Howe, Linda Moulton: op. cit., pp. 83–4.

33 *Arizona Wildcat*, University of Arizona, 14 September 1982.

34 Alderson, Andrew: 'Beefing up the Blood Banks', *Sunday Express*, London, 21 January 1990.

35 *A Strange Harvest*, produced by Linda Howe, 1980. Videotapes are available from Linda Moulton Howe Productions, P.O. Box 538, Huntingdon Valley, PA 19006-0538, or Quest Publications International Ltd., 15 Pickard Court, Temple Newsam, Leeds LS15 9AY.

36 Howe, Linda Moulton: '1989 – The Harvest Continues', *The UFO Report 1991*, edited by Timothy Good, Sidgwick & Jackson, London, 1990.

37 Howe, Linda Moulton: *An Alien Harvest*, pp. 94–103.

38 *Little River News*, Ashdown, Arkansas, 20 April 1989.

39 *Science Digest*, October 1983.

40 Garber, Andrew: 'Mutilated cattle baffle Idaho ranchers, police', *The Idaho Statesman*, Boise, Idaho, 10 June 1990.

41 Good, Timothy: op. cit., pp. 136–9.

· 3 ·

Colorado Breakthrough

Although reports of alien beings associated with the animal mutilations are relatively rare, there have now been a sufficient number, in my opinion, to justify the hypothesis of alien or at least non-human involvement. The following case provides us with an excellent example, highlights some complex aspects of the multifaceted nature of UFO encounters, and provides us with important clues as to the nature of the phenomenon and its interaction with human beings – and animals.

The case was investigated for the Aerial Phenomena Research Organization by Dr Leo Sprinkle, a University of Wyoming psychologist, Dr John Derr, a seismologist, his wife Janet, and Dr Peter Van Arsdale, an anthropologist. As a prerequisite to relating their experiences, the witnesses insisted on anonymity and requested that the precise location of their ranch in Colorado should not be divulged.

The principal witnesses were 'Jim', a former US Air Force security officer and public relations officer with professional training in physical and biological sciences; 'John', who at the time held a management position in a large corporation; his wife 'Barbara' and their teenage sons; and a law officer.

Prior to the experiences, John and Barbara had pooled their financial resources together with Jim in order to purchase the ranch, which is located in the Rocky Mountains area. The property included grazing area, woods, and springs feeding a pond near the ranch house. After settling in, unusual events began to occur, including untraceable humming sounds, electrical power failures, sounds of someone or something walking around outside the house, sightings of UFOs and humanoids, 'Bigfoot' type creatures observed in the woods, 'messages' broadcast on the radio and stereo systems – and cattle mutilations.

On approximately 16 October 1975, during the night, Jim noticed that the cattle were braying loudly and went outside to see what was disturbing them. 'We have a large coon hound that was watching the property,' Jim recounted, 'and the dog was extremely afraid of something. He was on the porch and wanted in, and I grabbed a gun and went out.

'Range cattle do not usually come close to you, [but they] were packing me so tight that I could hardly get through the middle of the herd. I walked about halfway to the dam and above the dam was a large lighted object. It was orange and trapezoidal shaped. I was going to see what it was and I got about halfway there when I realized that whatever it was, I didn't need to know! That was during the cattle mutilation days and I had a small-calibre rifle and I decided to leave well alone.'

Jim later learned that a large reward for the arrest of the cattle mutilators had been offered, and one night decided to go hunting for them with a 12-gauge shotgun. But he found himself unable to move from the couch he had been sitting on. 'It was like paralysis,' he said, 'like I was drugged.'

Barbara suddenly experienced an increase in her heart rate, accompanied by a sense of panic, a change in her 'thinking pattern', and a flood of memories (in common with the sensations described by Bob Oechsler in Chapter 10). 'I remembered things that I had completely forgotten, and that frightened me,' she explained. 'And by that time I was screaming and Jim came to from whatever his problem was – he couldn't seem to talk. Shortly after that, John showed up. I started to tell him what happened but I couldn't talk about it. Every time I started to, I would stutter. Jim then started telling him what happened, and then I was able to talk about it. That was the first strange thing . . . it had never happened to me before in my life.'

The First Mutilations

Some time later (date not given) Joe, the eldest son, together with some friends, discovered a mutilated cow about 200 yards from the house. 'They came back in a panic,' Jim said. 'It was snowing heavily and we decided the first thing to do was get into town and get the law officer. The boys were pretty upset . . . because they felt that something was following them. I assumed it was a natural paranoia. We went out and I followed the route and we found huge footprints that had followed them all the way from the cow to the horse barn, and the footprints were even in the soft manure inside the horse barn. They were, I guess, 18 inches. I didn't measure them but they were quite large – what I guess you would call a "Bigfoot" footprint.'

The cow exhibited classic signs of mutilation. 'The udders were removed surgically – the sac under the udders wasn't perforated,' explained Jim. 'One eye was missing. One ear was missing. And that was it. There was no blood – all the blood had been removed. And there were no tracks in the snow around the cow . . . the rectum was also removed.'

Jim reported the incident to the law officer, who promised to investigate a few days later. He never showed up.

Two weeks later, a second mutilation was discovered, although the animal (a bull) did not belong to the ranch. Its head was twisted back and various organs and parts of the body removed as if by surgical operation. Jim drove into town and called on the law officer, who suggested meeting in a restaurant. 'I asked him why I hadn't heard from him and why he wasn't trying to solve this,' Jim said.

'He explained to me that they knew what the mutilations were and they had known for some time. They only report one in four, and in this county alone there had been over 400 reports by that time. *It was being done by extraterrestrials*, and they had spoken to the FBI about it. I told him that I couldn't believe it, that if he couldn't solve the crime, at least don't blame it on something like that. I made an enemy of the man and I frankly didn't care because we had lost two cattle.'

No Known Species

One night, at about 10 o'clock, two visiting friends and a rancher heard a strange noise emanating from the cistern south-east of the house and about 60 yards up a slope. 'All of a sudden, after listening to this noise,' Jim told the investigators, 'a huge, dark object pushed its way through the barbed wire and came straight at them down the hill. They all came running into the house . . . We subsequently went back and traced the route and sure enough, there were some foot-prints.

'I removed some hair from the fence, noticing that it [had] pushed its way through the barbed wire: it didn't jump the fence but just by force alone spread it and went through. There were long strands of hair . . .'

Jim collected the hair and took photographs of the footprints. Samples of the hair were sent to a biogeneticist in Denver, who reported that it matched 'no known species'.

'By then I was getting more and more upset about the activities,' Jim related. 'One law officer was encouraging me to keep my mouth shut about it because he didn't want a full-scale panic in the county. I told him I wasn't interested in panics – I was interested in finding out who was mutilating my cattle.'

A Creature Shot?

By this time, as tensions mounted, everyone in the house had become fearful and depressed. Jim began to sleep near the front door, with a gun beside him, staying awake for most of the night, hoping to catch the 'culprit'. 'I was beginning to suspect that somehow the real-estate man was involved; that he was trying to make us break the contract so he could resell the house.'

Alerted by a humming sound at about 2 a.m. one night, Jim looked out of the window and saw a disc-shaped object flying slowly past the front of the house and up the gully.

On other occasions, Jim saw the hairy creature running near the house. 'I was tolerating it to a certain degree. One night I didn't. I went out and one was running beside the corral and I shot it. Barbara came running out, and when Harry and Roger came back from town we went tracking to see if we could find what I had shot. It didn't seem to hurt it at all. There was a little flinch – I'm a good shot so I know I hit it. There was no blood, no traces, no signs. We pursued it on to the property next to us. Then I heard this most unusual sound, like a double sound: it was a whine with almost a beeping noise inter-mixed.'

Nothing was found, however. 'We returned to the house and I noti-fied the law officer that I had shot one. He gave me hell and told me I was lucky this time and he didn't want anybody killed.'

Further Intrusions

One night, following further disturbances, Jim lost his temper and stormed outside the house. 'I don't remember exactly what I said but most of it can't be repeated. I think I threatened that if we can't have the land, then you won't either – I'll blow the whole thing away. I meant it too: I would have destroyed it before I would have moved right then.'

Jim returned to the house and calmed down, then later went out-side again. 'While outside,' he said, 'this voice just came out of no-where and said four words, "*Dr Jim, we accept*". I think that was the first time I was really shaken rather than it just angering or dis-orienting me. That was all. [It was] just like FM stereo; it came from everywhere.

'There were many smaller incidents that were unnerving. We had several friends come out who were harassed one way or the other and terrified. I went in and talked to the law officer again. If he really felt we were in any danger, I would move the boys. He said that nobody he knew of had been hurt. They had lost horses, a lot of cattle and animals of one kind or another, and people had been terrified. The mutilations were going on at a much heavier rate during this period – this was 1976, [and] they were occurring weekly.'

Also during that period, two airline pilots came out to the ranch, asking if they could put an airstrip on the land in exchange for Jim's use of their plane. Jim consented to the plan. About three weeks later, one of the pilots and two others were killed in a crash nearby. Others who had enquired deeply into the mutilations, Jim learned, had disappeared mysteriously, including the editor of a magazine.

Jim also learned that two Air National Guard interceptors, sent up to pursue UFOs in the vicinity, had crashed. The next night, two squadrons of interceptors circled the area. 'I was with Air Defense Command,' Jim said, 'and I know that when they bring them out, they are nuclear-armed and they don't fly them around for games.' He counted twenty-six aircraft, which appeared to be surveying everything, presumably in an effort to locate parts of the crashed planes.

'All this was a little unnerving so I decided I was going to stop my enquiry,' Jim told the investigators. 'I was going to just quietly mind my own business.'

One night, at about 2 a.m., *nine* discs allegedly landed in the front yard, observed by Jim, Barbara and Harry, a friend. David, another friend, was asleep upstairs, but did not respond when called. Jim bravely walked out of the house and approached the objects. Curiously, although he and Barbara clearly saw disc-shaped devices, Harry saw 'large, dark football shapes, as if they were blocking part of the view'.

As Barbara watched this incredible scene, her face pressed close to the window, she was suddenly struck forcibly in the forehead by something, knocking her senseless to the floor for a short time. While the others attended to her, the objects disappeared.

'I thought about it subsequently and wondered why they didn't do it to me since I was the one walking toward them,' Jim commented. 'But then I began to understand that they did the most practical thing that could be done to get me back inside and get both people away from the window. And I think I really began to respect how clever they were. Then I began to suspect that maybe the Government was doing it to us. Except that there were a lot of unusual things. For instance, David had been paralyzed during the incident: he could hear us calling but couldn't get up until it was over. But then he went out walking with me and what we call ultrasonics – the extremely high-pitched sounds – were going on out there and continued through the night. David was sick for three days. The sound would sometimes give us headaches but not all of us at once – to different individuals at different times.'

The Broadcast

At about 2 a.m. one night, in the presence of guests, the lights went out in the house and a mechanical-sounding voice was heard coming from all the radio and TV speakers. 'We were sitting right in front of a console stereo,' said Jim, 'and the voice came out of it. I can almost recite the words exactly. They are burned in my memory:

"Attention. We have allowed you to remain. We have interfered with your lives very little. Do not cause us to take action which you will regret. Your friends will be instructed to remain silent concerning us."'

One of the guests, Dan, a computer and electronics specialist, was determined to find a rational explanation for the mysterious broadcast, and dismantled the stereo set. 'He went through the whole unit and said he couldn't figure it out,' Jim related. 'He checked and the stereo was off; the phonograph was on when the lights went off, but the radio receiver part was off – it was on phono. We found that the type of transmitter it would take, from even close range, to cause a signal of that intensity to go through the house would be beyond our means to ever put up.'

The Black Box

In another conversation with the law officer, Jim learned about a bizarre incident involving a strange 'box'. 'He said he was out on patrol one night and he saw, in a group of trees, this box that was blinking. He didn't want to go in alone so he raced back to town and picked up another law officer. When he got back, the trees were gone, the box was gone – everything was gone. He thought they had gone into the ground; he had seen things go into the ground before. I've never seen that happen.' But Jim did see one of the boxes.

Together with the older son, Joe, Jim, on a compulsion, drove up one night in January 1977 to the top of a hill to where a 35-foot circle had been for some time and nothing had grown. In the trees, a yellow light could be seen, apparently shining on the car.

'We got out and walked over, and there was a box on the ground,' Jim said. 'I told Joe to stay back about 10 feet. It was making a buzzing sound and there was a light, like inside it but not on it – hard to describe. It was night but there was a full moon, and as I walked to about 4 feet from it, it changed its tone entirely. It sounded like a bunch of angry bees. The sound went up so I backed away and told Joe to go back to the car and watch me as I walked up to the box. We then walked back to the car and I told Joe that whatever happens, do not leave the car. Then I walked back and the box was gone!'

Contact

Later that night, Jim noticed another light in the trees. 'I told Joe to go on to the house, and I walked down into the trees. And I think that's the closest I ever came to being afraid. I had to force my legs to take me down because I didn't know what I would see.

'I walked down to the light and there were two individuals waiting for me in the light. The light didn't come from anywhere – I can't describe it – it was just light. They obviously weren't nervous and as soon as I walked up, they spoke to me by name and told me – I can quote that exactly: "How nice of you to come." It was just as though I had been expected. Down below, possibly 50 to 60 feet from us, was a disc on the ground. It was lightly lit, just light enough to see.

'And I had no doubts that these were two men. They were approximately 5 feet 6 inches tall, I would say. They had on tight-fitting clothing, you know, like a flight suit. I noticed the clothing changing colours, from brown to silver, but I don't know how. They were very fair, had large eyes and seemed perfectly normal, completely relaxed. They had blond hair with something over the head, but I could still see their hair. The hair was obviously blond and wasn't long; it didn't make much of an impression. The thing that impressed the most was the eyes . . . Their facial features were finer. They were almost delicately effeminate [and] completely self-assured.

'I was up there maybe five minutes. They apologized for the inconveniences they had caused us, and told us that a more equitable arrangement would be worked out between us, whatever that means. I wanted to ask a lot of questions but found that I didn't – you know, like, "Where are you from?" I didn't ask any of that. There are several things they asked me not to repeat that have no significant meaning at all. I think maybe they were just checking to see if I would keep my mouth shut. I told them that if they were mutilating cattle, it was very foolish to do so and draw that much attention to themselves. They didn't give me any earth-shattering information or even admit they were mutilating the cattle. The only thing I found out for sure is that this big fuzzy thing, "Bigfoot", obeys the commands.

'They mentioned the box and that I did the right thing backing away from it – it was what I called an implied threat. They nodded, and approximately 20 to 30 feet away, "Bigfoot", as I called him, got up and walked toward the box. The box changed tone and he dropped. They said, "As you can see, they are quite lethal."

'They said that they would come back and talk again. There were no goodbyes: I just somehow felt it was time to go. They did tell me that my memory wouldn't be tampered with. I thought about all of the things I would have liked to have asked . . . I hadn't decided they came from space and I'm still not sure of that. They looked enough like people . . . that was my first thought; that somehow the Government was trying to do this. They were completely self-assured; they spoke vernacular English.

'I was pretty rocked, because I did see the disc and it was quite clear. I walked on back to the house . . . I was excited over the "more equitable arrangement": I guess I had some illusion that they were going to give me the cure for cancer or a billion dollars or something . . . I couldn't figure why they had even bothered to talk to me. It was obvious that I was supposed to come. They didn't say anything that would indicate why, except "a more equitable arrangement".'

Purpose

Jim felt sure that some kind of permanent alien installation was located on the ranch. 'Our ranch overlooks a military installation: we have a perfect view,' he explained to the investigators. 'I can only assume that they are watching us – watching our military potential.

'I'm reasonably sure that they play rough. It's not big brothers from space who are interested in us as spiritual beings or whatever. I'm absolutely convinced that they couldn't care less if we live or die. We're nuisances, although I think they may be more humanitarian than we are. I have no doubts that they are mutilating the cattle –

none at all. The cattle are being lifted into the air, they are being drained of blood, they are being mutilated, and they are being lowered. If they wanted to do just biological research on cattle, they could have disposed of the remains without them being found. It is obviously some intent to instil fear and it has been quite successful.

'I figured out early in the game that the government is sending in helicopters in large numbers from several sources, but they are doing it to cover what is really happening. I'm absolutely sure that the helicopters have nothing to do with the mutilations. And the helicopters are not of sufficient size to lift a 2,600-pound bull. Also, you could hardly carry a bull away in a helicopter in a manner so that it wouldn't be seen.'

During a discussion about the mutilations with an officer at the nearby Air Force base, Jim learned that the base had had its share of troublesome UFO incidents, and that directives existed on how to deal with them. The officer also asked Jim if he had experienced any trouble with 'Bigfoot'. (In fact, about twenty people witnessed them on various occasions at the ranch.) Apparently, the Air Force had directives on these elusive creatures, too.

A Rational Explanation?

'It is possible it could have been a totally subjective experience,' Jim rationalized, in summing up these and other extraordinary experiences at the ranch. 'Even with all of us, it could have been hallucinations. It could have been a lot of things. Maybe none of it happened. Maybe everybody there was deceived in some way. I can't picture how, but just because I can't picture it, doesn't mean it couldn't happen.'[1]

I asked Dr Leo Sprinkle, one of the investigators, for his impressions of the witnesses. 'My initial reaction was one of doubt,' he replied. 'The witnesses seemed so cautious, even evasive. However, later, I viewed them as reliable and sincere. Perhaps the initial meeting with three PhDs was intimidating ... [the wife] worried about their experiences being publicized and affecting her husband's business relations ... I conducted no formal psychological testing: however, my impressions – and those of the other investigators, John Derr and Pete Van Arsdale – support the view that the witnesses described events as accurately as they could: they truly were puzzled by the events – as were we!'[2]

The investigators all agreed that the witnesses were intelligent, articulate, and perceptive. 'The intellectual and emotional doubts (and courage) which are experienced by these witnesses are apparent in their conversations and in the way they have conducted themselves in the interviews,' they concurred at the time. 'The witnesses seem to be patriotic Americans, and yet are convinced that "US Military Operations" is not sufficient explanation to account for the strange events which they have experienced.'

This exceptional case incorporates so many facets of the UFO enigma that it lends itself to any number of interpretations. Hard-headed rationalists will undoubtedly invoke psychological explanations, such as mass hallucination. Yet there seem to me to be sufficient grounds for assuming that at least some of the incidents have a basis in objective reality, even if we are unable at present to comprehend the nature of that reality.

Notes

1 Derr, Dr John S.; Sprinkle, Dr R. Leo: 'Multiple Phenomena on a Rocky Mountain Ranch', *APRO Bulletin*, Vol. 27, Nos. 1–7, 1978–9.
2 Letter to the author from Dr Leo Sprinkle, 18 July 1990.

· 4 ·

Alien Dimensions

'My dear Friend,' the letter began, 'I have just returned from Muroc. The report is true – devastatingly true!'

The letter, from Gerald Light to his friend and colleague Meade Layne of the Borderland Sciences Research Foundation, described sensational events that he claimed to have witnessed over a two-day period in April 1954 at Muroc Air Base (Edwards AFB), Muroc Dry Lake, California.

'I made the journey,' Light continued, 'in company with Franklin Allen of the Hearst papers and Edwin Nourse of Brookings Institute (Truman's erstwhile financial adviser) and Bishop McIntyre of LA (confidential names, for the present, please).

'When we were allowed to enter the restricted section (after about six hours in which we were checked on every possible item, event, incident and aspect of our personal and public lives), I had the distinct feeling that the world had come to an end with fantastic realism. For I have never seen so many human beings in a state of complete collapse and confusion as they realized that their own world had indeed ended with such finality as to beggar description. The reality of "otherplane" aeroforms is now and forever removed from the realms of speculation and made a rather painful part of the consciousness of every responsible scientific and political group.'

The 'otherplane aeroforms' were supposedly craft flown by the 'Etherians', as the Borderland Sciences Research Foundation called the occupants of UFOs, which had landed at Edwards AFB some time prior to Gerald Light's visit, and had allegedly given startling demonstrations to various different groups of scientists and other carefully selected individuals, including President Eisenhower in February that year.

'During my first two days' visit,' Light claimed, 'I saw five separate and distinct types of aircraft being studied and handled by our air-force officials – with the assistance and permission of The Etherians! I have no words to express my reactions. It has finally happened. It is now a matter of history.

'President Eisenhower, as you may already know, was spirited over to Muroc one night during his visit to Palm Springs recently. And it is my conviction that he will ignore the terrific conflict between the various "authorities" and go directly to the people via radio and tele-vision – if the impasse continues much longer. From what I could gather, an official statement to the country is being prepared for de-livery about the middle of May.'

Needless to say, no such statement was forthcoming. But a mystery remains about Eisenhower's whereabouts on the evening of 20 February 1954. The President, who had been staying with his friend Paul Roy Helms at the Smoke Tree Ranch in Palm Springs, ostensibly for a golfing holiday, 'disappeared' for four hours, causing consider-able confusion and leading to pandemonium at the subsequent press conference. The official explanation given was that Eisenhower had merely lost a cap on his tooth while chewing on a chicken leg, and had to be taken to a local dentist for treatment. No evidence for the dental trip (such as White House memos) has ever emerged, however.[1]

Light implies that the demonstration he witnessed in April 1954 in-cluded dematerialization and materialization, a process with which he had become familiar during his research into the paranormal, and he describes the reactions of the scientists and others alleged to have been present: 'I watched the pathetic bewilderment of rather brilliant brains struggling to make some sort of rational explanation which would enable them to retain their familiar concepts,' he wrote.[2]

The letter (Appendix, Fig. 4.1) is unquestionably genuine, but the sensational disclosures contained therein are harder, if not impossible, to substantiate. Gerald Light is now dead, as are the other witnesses mentioned, none of whom ever spoke about the matter publically and refused even to acknowledge receipt of letters sent by various investigators. Nevertheless, others have come forward with testimony indicating that some remarkable events did indeed occur at the time.

During a visit to California in the summer of 1954, British writer Desmond Leslie spoke with an Air Force man who claimed to have seen a disc 100-foot in diameter land on the runway at Muroc on a certain day. Men coming back from leave were suddenly not allowed back on the base and were given orders to 'get lost'. The saucer was allegedly housed under guard in Hangar 27, and President Eisenhower was taken to see it during his Palm Springs vacation.[3]

Further details have subsequently come to light. The Earl of Clancarty, better known as Brinsley Le Poer Trench, the pioneering UFO researcher and author, has spoken with a former US test pilot (now a retired colonel) who claims to have been present at Edwards AFB during the Eisenhower visit on 20 February 1954.

'The pilot says he was one of six people at the meeting,' Lord Clancarty told a reporter. 'Five alien craft landed at the base. Two were cigar-shaped and three were saucer-shaped. The aliens looked human-like, but not exactly,' he said, adding that they had the same proportions as humans and were able to breathe our atmosphere. They did not say where they came from.

The aliens spoke English, and supposedly informed the President that they wanted to start an 'educational programme' for the people of Earth, then reportedly demonstrated their paranormal powers by making themselves invisible, causing Eisenhower considerable embarrassment.[4]

The retired colonel, who had been sworn to secrecy, refused to allow his name to be disclosed, and I have been unable to persuade Lord Clancarty to reveal it to me, which of course leaves us with just another unsubstantiated story to add to the collection of rumours about the Edwards AFB affair.

There are other similar accounts of the aliens' knack of rendering themselves and their craft invisible. My favourite is a report by the South African contactee Ann Grevler, who claimed to have encountered a human-type extraterrestrial in the Eastern Transvaal in the 1950s. Prior to a trip in a spacecraft, the alien made her car invisible with a small rod-like device, and when Grevler walked incredulously to where her car had been, she gashed her leg on the invisible number plate. Fortunately the spaceman was able to give first aid, accomplished by directing his gaze to the wound, which promptly healed. He explained that although it was possible to render objects invisible by the power of thought, it was a rather exhausting business and gadgets were normally used for the job.[5]

In a more recent incident, during a series of landings witnessed by adults and children at Voronezh, USSR, in late September and early October 1989, one of three giant, silver-suited space beings reportedly 'zapped' a boy with a beam of light from a 50-centimetre-long tube, so that the boy vanished totally from the scene, to reappear only after the alien craft and its occupants had departed.[6]

As a postscript to the Edwards AFB affair, it is worth noting that Gordon Cooper, the ex-astronaut and pilot, disclosed in an interview with Lee Spiegel that in either 1957 or 1958, while he was project manager of the Flight Test Center at Edwards, a flying disc landed at the base. Cooper said that it was 'hovering above the ground, and then it slowly came down and sat on the lake bed for a few minutes.'

A camera team in the area filmed the entire scene. 'There were varied estimates by the cameramen on what the actual size of the object was,' Cooper said, 'but they all agreed that it was at least the size of a vehicle that would carry normal-sized people in it.'

Although Cooper did not witness the sighting, he did study the film. 'It was a typical circular-shaped UFO. Not too many people saw it, because it took off at quite a sharp angle and just climbed out of sight . . . I think it was definitely a UFO. However, where it came from and who was in it is hard to determine, because it didn't stay around long enough to discuss the matter — there wasn't even time to send out a welcoming committee!'

The film was sent to Washington, DC, and nothing more was heard about it. Cooper also revealed that 'there were always strange things flying around in the air over Edwards'.[7] And on several occasions in 1951, while serving as a pilot with the Air Force in Germany, Cooper chased groups of metallic, saucer-shaped vehicles. 'I do believe UFOs exist and that the truly unexplained ones are from some other technically advanced civilization,' he wrote in a statement to the United Nations in 1978.[8]

A British Connection

In September 1962, Swiss researcher Lou Zinsstag received an interesting letter from her friend Waveney Girvan, a publisher who was editor of *Flying Saucer Review* at the time:

'. . . a colleague at the office where I work – an important editor of one of our women's papers – approached me with a sensational story. She hadn't previously realized that I was interested in the subject. Her brother, she tells me, is an extremely important expert with one of our famous aircraft firms. Five years ago, he was invited to the United States with several of his colleagues in the industry to inspect a landed saucer and to meet its pilot. He went, and the pilot was exactly as [George Adamski] has described such a person; he communicated by telepathy and he told those assembled that beings like himself had infiltrated amongst us . . .'[9]

Further details of the alleged 1957 meeting were revealed by Girvan's friend and colleague, John Lade, in a letter to Richard Hall, then secretary of the National Investigations Committee on Aerial Phenomena (NICAP) in the US:

Waveney Girvan wants me to tell you that we have had a leak of information through a man who a few years ago was called to an international meeting on your side to view a saucer, of the type resembling two saucers one above the other. The pilot (who was long-haired, ski-suited, and one of distinctly Aryan appearance) addressed the gathering of scientists and aeronautical experts telepathically, and we are told that it was an extraordinary experience to hear the audience break through the silence by laughing together sometimes, thus proving that they were receiving successfully. However, as the pilot proceeded to describe the motive power of the craft, the audience lost grip and even the most advanced scientists present could no longer follow the concepts offered to them . . .

Ross Hall, the aeronautics 'expert' (whom I have so far been unable to trace), was dismayed to learn that his sister had related the story, having signed an oath of secrecy in the USA, and on 11 July 1963, when John Lade met him at the De Havilland Aircraft Company,

Hatfield, he denied everything.

'I told him of my active interest in getting at the truth of our subject and my reason for approaching him, ending with the question if the story Waveney heard was true,' Lade wrote to Zinsstag. 'At first, he avoided my question and began to give his views on saucers which were rather primitive, but I felt he was treating them seriously and I brushed them aside to return to the question.

'He did not admit to having pulled the leg of his sister but he confessed that he regarded her as being connected with the newspapers and he might have said something to her, but he confirmed that he had never seen a saucer on the ground, nor heard a lecture, nor had his visits to America had anything to do with the subject. When he left he said he would speak to his sister and I felt he meant he would put things right.'[10]

If Ross Hall had merely teased his sister, he did a good job. Waveney Girvan had been impressed with the fact that she had been genuinely perplexed and interested in the subject, and had never spoken about the matter with anyone else as far as he knew – certainly not to the press.

If it were not for the fact that I have spoken with a number of completely honest 'closet contactees' around the world, who claim to have had similar experiences, I would have rejected such stories long ago. In 1963, for example, a close friend of mine whom I have known since 1952 and whose account is the most convincing I have come across, observed the landing of a flying disc in the north of England and subsequently made contact with two extraterrestrials. The meetings lasted over a period of about a year, usually in the presence of a few scientists who were liaising with the aliens on a highly secret project. On one occasion, my friend had the opportunity of seeing one of the craft at close quarters, but was not allowed to go inside.

Apart from a barely noticeable difference in the eyes, the aliens were very similar to humans. A great deal of information was given during the course of these meetings, as well as a few demonstrations of technical and mental abilities which transcended those of normal human beings. At no time did they reveal their origin, but they did mention that they had bases on Earth. They also refused to discuss the purpose of their current visits with my friend, other than to admit that they were 'obviously not for entirely philanthropic reasons'. They did reveal, however, that on several occasions, over a long period of time, they had been responsible for genetically upgrading the human species. It was implied that other, less evolved beings were also visiting our planet.

Though highly evolved spiritually, these people were 'down to Earth' in the sense that they enjoyed creature comforts. And – thank heavens – they had a sense of humour.

Naturally, I am unable to prove that these events actually occurred, nor would I wish to do so in this particular case – even if I could. The extraterrestrials seem reluctant to establish contact with humanity at large, preferring to keep us at a safe distance. And who could blame them? Yet I am convinced that contact has been established with many individuals and groups throughout the world.

A Presidential Liaison?

A number of US presidents have made positive statements about the UFO subject, most notably Jimmy Carter and Ronald Reagan. In 1976, Carter admitted during his election campaign that he had seen a UFO while he was Governor of Georgia in 1969. 'If I become President,' he added, 'I'll make every piece of information this country has about UFOs available to the public and the scientists.'[11] Carter, a graduate in nuclear physics, was thwarted in his attempts to reopen investigations, and it is also likely that he may have changed his mind when presented with a presidential briefing on the subject (see Chapter 6).

If extraterrestrials are visiting Earth, many ask, why do they not land on the White House lawn and establish direct contact with the President? They have not landed on the White House lawn, of course, but there is circumstantial evidence that some presidents may have had contact.

One of the earliest contactees is Daniel Fry, a former pioneering rocket engineer who claims to have been taken for a flight aboard an unmanned craft on 4 July 1949, when he was working with the Aerojet General Corporation at White Sands Missile Range, New Mexico.

Communication was established via an intercom with an alien who claimed that some of his ancestors had lived on Earth tens of thousands of years ago, and that his race was now essentially independent of planetary existence, preferring to spend most of their time in huge, fully equipped spaceships. Their life expectancy was said to be about two and a half times that of ours.

In 1976 I spent several days with Dan Fry at his home, then in Tonopah, Arizona. He told me that he was contacted physically by the visitor in 1954, five years after the initial encounter (perhaps coincidentally, the year of the alleged Edwards AFB incidents). According to 'Alan' (the name he used), it had taken five years to become acclimatized to our environment and to establish certain terrestrial credentials, including, of course, a birth certificate and passport, which had supposedly been acquired with the aid of a co-operative official. Alan assumed the identity of an 'international businessman' and subsequently established a liaison with a number of high officials – including some US presidents.[12]

These claims are outrageous, of course. But Dan has shown me letters from two former presidents which at least provide circumstantial if tenuous evidence. One letter (Appendix, Fig. 4.2), dated 2 December 1968, is from President-elect Richard Nixon:

Dear Mr Fry:

    As you may know, I have pledged to bring into this Administration men and women who by their qualities of youthfulness, judgement, intelligence and creativity, can make significant contributions to our country. I seek the best minds in America to meet the challenges of this rapidly changing world. To find them, I ask for your active participation and assistance.

    You, as a leader, are in a position to know and recommend exceptional individuals. The persons you select should complete the enclosed form and return it to you. I ask that you then attach your comments. My staff will carefully review all recommendations for inclusion in our reservoir of talent from which appointments will be made.

I will appreciate greatly, Mr Fry, your taking time from your busy schedule to participate in this all-important program.

Sincerely,
[signed]
Richard M. Nixon

Three months later, following his letter of recommendation (for Thomas Yale Hurt), Fry received a letter from Harry Flemming, Special Assistant to the President:

'Thank you for your thoughtful recommendation for appointment to the Administration. Your comments concerning the applicant are particularly helpful to us. We want you to know that the President is grateful for your participation in this important program and that your views will be considered in making future appointments.'[13]

Nothing in the letters suggests that Nixon was in contact with a spaceman, of course. But what it does show is that, for whatever reason, Fry's opinion was respected.

Another letter to Dan Fry that I have seen is from President Reagan, and again, although there is no mention of flying saucers or spacemen, it is evident that the two men were on very friendly terms. It is also known that Reagan has a keen interest in the subject, having observed UFOs on two occasions.

One incident took place when Reagan was Governor of California, during a flight one night in 1974. 'I was the pilot of the plane when we saw the UFO,' reported Reagan's pilot, Bill Paynter. 'Also on board were Governor Reagan and a couple of his security people. We were flying in a Cessna Citation. It was maybe 9 or 10 o'clock at night.

'We were near Bakersfield when Governor Reagan and the others called my attention to a big light flying a bit behind my plane. It appeared to be several hundred yards away. It was a fairly steady light until it began to accelerate, then it appeared to elongate. Then the light took off. It went up at a 45-degree angle . . . from a normal cruise speed to a fantastic speed instantly.'

Reagan himself described the incident to Norman Miller, then Washington bureau chief for the *Wall Street Journal*. According to Miller, Reagan ordered his pilot to follow the object. 'We followed it for several minutes,' said Reagan. 'All of a sudden, to our utter amazement it went straight up into the heavens. When I got off the plane I told Nancy all about it. And we read up on the long history of UFOs . . .'

Miller then asked Reagan if he believed in UFOs. 'When I asked him that question, a look of horror came over him. It suddenly dawned on him what he was saying – the implications, and that he was talking to a reporter. He snapped back to reality and said, "Let's just say that on the subject of UFOs I'm an agnostic . . ."

'I didn't report the conversation at the time,' said Miller. 'Reagan didn't go into detail about the research he and his wife had done, because it was at that point that I asked him if he believed in UFOs, and he clammed up.'[14]

During a screening of the film *E.T.* at the White House in the summer of 1982, President Reagan is reported to have whispered to producer Steven Spielberg: 'There are probably only six people in this room who know how true this is.'[15]

In addition, Reagan has publicly stated on at least three occasions that a threat from outer space would have a unifying effect on the world's nations, and he has raised the matter with both President Gorbachev and Edvard Shevardnadze, the former Soviet Foreign Minister. According to Fred Barnes, senior editor of the *New Republic*, during a luncheon with Shevardnadze in the White House in September 1987, Reagan wondered aloud about what would happen if the world faced an 'alien threat' from outer space. 'Don't you think the United States and the Soviet Union would be together?' he asked. Shevardnadze said yes, absolutely. 'And we wouldn't need our defence ministers to meet,' he added.[16]

Since Reagan's comments have been dismissed as purely hypothetical speculation, let me quote from a speech given by Mikhail Gorbachev at the Kremlin, during which he commented on the 1985 summit conference:

At our meeting in Geneva, the US President said that if the Earth faced an invasion by extraterrestrials, the United States and the Soviet Union would join forces to repel such an invasion. I shall not dispute the hypothesis, though I think it's early yet to worry about such an intrusion . . .[17]

As mentioned in Chapter 1, Gorbachev has acknowledged the reality of the UFO phenomenon. Could it be that the new era of co-operation between the superpowers is due in part to the UFO intrusion?

'The Boys Upstairs'

Major Hans Petersen, who was in charge of air traffic control for the Royal Danish Air Force from 1949 to 1976 – the first such military controller in Denmark – has seen UFOs on a number of occasions, including some that were remarkably similar to those photographed by contactee George Adamski and others. And on one occasion, in about 1960, he tracked up to twenty-two unknown targets on radar and personally gave the order to scramble four jets to intercept.

But of relevance here is a letter that Petersen received from a US Army brigadier general (now deceased) describing his alleged liaison with extraterrestrials, whom he called 'the boys upstairs'. Although I have had a copy of the text of the letter for many years, it was only in 1990 that Hans kindly sent me a copy of the original, with the name, address and date deleted. The relevant extracts are as follows:

. . . What I am about to impart to you, I am asking you as a fellow Veteran not to divulge the source of – you are free to repeat it, but not the source . . .

I was contacted late one night 11 years ago, while working late in my shop to finish a printing job. True, like most intelligent beings, I was interested and curious, but had no expectation of a contact. They came to my shop door, insisted on my opening it, came in, looked around a bit, spoke no word, motioned me to come outside. As I did so I became aware of a large object, a few feet overhead.

I was taken aboard, and had my first experience of positive telepathy; a very informative few minutes. They left saying they would return soon. They kept their word and they returned, I think I can honestly say a few hundred times since, in the past 11 years.

They have requested that I act as their physical earth-man contact with quite a number of our national and religious leaders, and my identity and nationality must remain a strict secret, except with their permission as in your case. You can understand, that if my identity and work were to become known, I would never have a single moment's rest, and would soon become worthless to both them and the problems I attempt to handle . . .

Among their own people they use thought only, but . . . they have learned to speak our language so perfectly that if one of them was to step up and speak to you . . . you would not recognize him from one of your own people, and in appearance, probably the greatest difference you would note would be his handsome features and perfect proportions physically . . .

The brigadier general explained that 'the boys upstairs' had mastered the languages of those they contacted by means of their close proximity to Earth over a period of 2,000 years, but in cases where difficulties arose they made use of a translating device, which they were helping us to develop. 'In this manner too,' he explained, 'they can speak to us . . . if they are near to their ships; the difference being that they can transmit by thought to their machines and have it speak vocally. I know these things work, because I have used them . . .'

The remainder of the letter contains material similar to that disseminated by the typical contactees of the 1950s, some of which I have difficulty accepting; for example, that our solar system (comprised of twelve planets) is fully populated! This would tend, of course, to discredit everything else in the letter. Maybe the retired general had simply 'lost his marbles' – or maybe he was lied to. I don't know. If it were not for the fact that I have spoken to so many apparently honest witnesses who have made similar claims, I would have discarded the story long ago.

Human-looking aliens are not currently as fashionable as the little bug-eyed beings most frequently associated with abductions. Partly because of the association with contactees, reports of encounters with the human variety tend to be discarded or overlooked. In addition to the sometimes ludicrous points of origin given, the banal and evangelical tone of the 'messages' sometimes (but not always) dispensed to many of the contactees is another reason why we tend to discard such reports. Yet the difference may be only academic. Plenty of abductees have been given silly messages by the bug-eyed beings and numerous witnesses claim to have been abducted by the more human variety. Both types (as well as other beings) continue to be reported, and in some cases have been observed simultaneously during a close encounter. In the Colorado ranch case, we learned how the 'Bigfoot' entities were associated with human types. Let us now look briefly at the case of Travis Walton, who encountered both human-appearing and other beings – a contact involving no communications at all.

An Alien Co-operation?

The initial stages of Walton's alleged abduction in an Arizona forest on 5 November 1975 were witnessed by six people, when he was knocked senseless to the ground by a beam of light from a hovering UFO. The others fled from the scene in terror, and on returning later found no trace of Walton. When he recovered consciousness, in considerable pain, Walton found himself in a strange room with three humanoids a little under 5 feet in height, dressed in one-piece coveralls.

The beings had bald, oversized heads, with almost chalk-white, slightly translucent skin. 'They had bulging, oversized craniums, a small jaw structure, and an undeveloped appearance to their features that was almost infantile,' Walton reported in his book. 'Their thin-lipped mouths were narrow and I never saw them open. Lying close to their heads on either side were the tiny crinkled lobes of their ears. Their miniature rounded noses had small oval nostrils.'

The most noticeably different features were the eyes. 'Those glistening brown orbs had irises twice the size of a normal human eye . . . The iris was so large that even parts of the pupils were hidden by the lids, giving the eyes a certain cat-like appearance. There was very little of the white part of the eye showing. They had no lashes and no eyebrows . . . Their sharp gaze alternately darted about and then fixed me with an intense stare – a look so piercing that it seemed they were seeing right through me.'

No communication of any sort took place as Walton wondered how to make his escape, having already struck one of the beings. Eventually, as he was on the point of attempting to throw himself at them, they turned and hurriedly left the room.

Walking around the craft, Walton came across an unusual chair, with a console and screen on the arms. The closer he approached this chair, the darker the room it was in became, apparently showing the darkness of space through an increasingly translucent wall. (Dan Fry reported that the entrance of the craft he travelled in was rendered opaque by a beam of light, enabling him to see outside.) After playing around with the console, which caused apparent movements of the craft in relation to the stars, Walton was confronted by what he took to be a human being standing in the doorway.

The man was about 6 feet 2 inches tall, muscular, with a tight-fitting bright blue one-piece suit and a transparent helmet. Walton felt a sense of relief, assuming the man to be from NASA or the Air Force, and remonstrated with him, begging him to explain what was happening. But the man remained silent.

'He had coarse, sandy-blond hair of medium length that covered his ears,' Walton wrote. 'He had a dark complexion, like a deep, even tan. He had no beard or moustache. In fact, I couldn't even see stubble or dark shadows of whiskers. He had slightly rugged, masculine features and strange eyes. They were a bright, golden-hazel colour – but there was still something else odd about those eyes that I could not quite place.'

The man then took Walton on a guided tour, merely smiling tolerantly in response to further questions. They came out of the craft into a large hangar-like enclosure, where two or three other craft were parked, slightly smaller than the one he had presumably arrived in. On entering a room beside the hangar, Walton was surprised to see two more men and a woman, dressed identically to the first man but without helmets.

'The woman also had a face and figure that were the epitome of her sex,' said Walton. 'They were smooth-skinned and blemishless . . . They looked alike in a family sort of way, although they were not identical. They all had the same coarse, brownish-blond hair. The woman wore hers longer than the men, past her shoulders. She did not appear to wear make-up. They seemed to all be in their mid-twenties, perhaps older. They all had the same intense, golden-hazel eyes. Whether it was the brightness of their eyes or some other feature, something was definitely odd about their eyes; I just could not tell what it was.'

Walton was put on a table, the woman approached him with what looked like an oxygen mask without tubes, and the next thing he remembers is waking up on a pavement west of Heber, Arizona, watching a circular object rising from the road and departing silently. As it transpired, five days had elapsed since the initial encounter.[18]

Walton's case inevitably led to considerable controversy – as all such cases do – but a number of psychiatrists and polygraph examiners testified that he had been telling the truth. 'Our conclusion, which is absolute, is that this young man is not lying, that there is no collusion involved, and no attempt to hoax,' concluded Dr Rosenbaum, one of three psychiatrists who examined Walton.[19] A Minnesota Multiphasic Personality Inventory conducted by Lamont McConnell indicated 'no deviations that would point to psychosis'.

In October 1978 I interviewed Walton in his home town of Snowflake, Arizona, and was impressed by his sincere and reserved manner. I also spoke with a few neighbours (including a priest) who told me that Walton was totally truthful and had suffered from the ridicule heaped on him.

It is important to emphasize that everything Walton describes as having happened to him during the five days was recalled fully consciously, and although he was subsequently hypnotically regressed, no further information has come to light so far (or at least, up to 1978).

'Do you think that the time will ever come when the subconscious memories will come out,' I asked him, 'or would you rather they remained buried for ever?'

'Someday, maybe,' he replied. 'I just know that I'm not ready now. The knowledge to be gained, curiosity to be satisfied is one thing, but then, you know, there is the difficulty of what I *may* have to deal with – the memories or whatever . . . I'm open to any possibility, and I don't claim to be an expert on it. All I know is what happened to me.'[20]

The inference from Walton's experience is that there is some kind of liaison between human-type aliens and others that look like nothing on Earth. Whether or not the others are related in any way, or are biological robots, is open to debate.

'Who was co-operating with whom?' Walton asks. 'I saw nothing to indicate the answer to that question. In fact, I never saw the two types together in one place at the same time. There was nothing to indicate that one type was a bred-up slave of the other. Further, there was nothing that would indicate friendly co-operation either . . . But then again, the aliens and the human type might have been co-operating with each other in my abduction from the very start. There might exist an interaction and co-operation of all intelligent life-forms in space . . .'[21]

An Air Force Contact

A description of aliens remarkably similar to the non-human types reported by Walton was given by a US Air Force mechanic, Sergeant Charles Moody, who claims to have been taken on board a craft near Alamogordo, New Mexico, on 13 August 1975, three months prior to Walton's experience.

'The beings were about 5 feet tall and very much like us except their heads were larger and had no hair, ears very small, eyes a little larger than ours, nose small and the mouth had very thin lips,' he consciously recalled later. 'There was speech but their lips did not move . . . It was like they could read my mind, and I believe they did because the elder or leader would speak sometimes before I would ask something.'

At one stage, the 'leader' touched Moody's back and legs with a rod-type device. 'When I asked what he was doing he said there had been a scuffle when they first made contact with me and he only wanted to correct any misplacement that might have happened,' Moody explained.

The contactee was told that our radar interferes with their navigational system (a claim also made by William Herrmann, who was abducted by similar beings in a series of incidents commencing in 1978[22]). During the two hour and forty minute encounter, Moody was allegedly shown the drive unit, contained in a room about 25 feet across. 'In the centre was what looked like a huge carbon rod going through the roof of the room; around the rod were three what looked like holes covered with glass. Inside the glass-covered holes or balls were what looked like large crystals with two rods, one on each side of the crystal. One rod came to a ball-like top, the other one came to a 'T'-type top . . . There were no wires or cables.'

Moody then observed what looked like a large black box on the side of the room. 'I asked about it and was told what it was but then was told not to ever reveal what the black box was for. I have really tried to remember but I can't remember about the black box, only that it was there.'

It will be recalled that a 'black box' features in the story of multiple phenomena on the Colorado ranch (Chapter 3), although it would be pure speculation to ascribe a similar application to the one mentioned here.

Moody was told by the aliens that the craft they were on was not their 'main craft', which was then 400 miles above the Earth and utilized a different drive unit.

'It's not only just one advanced race that is studying this planet Earth, but a group of them,' Moody was supposedly informed, 'and within three years from now they will make themselves known to all mankind. I can also say that it will not be a pleasant type of meeting for there will be warnings made to the people of the world. Their plan is for only limited contact, and after twenty years of further study and only after deeper consideration will there be any type of close contact . . . Their intent is a peaceful one and if the leaders of the world will only heed their warnings we will find ourselves a lot better off than before, and at this time it's not up to us to accept them, but for them to accept us!'[23]

As with many similar contact accounts, such prophecies usually turn out to be false. But does this necessarily mean that the contactees are lying? A psychological stress evaluation (PSE) of Charles Moody by Charles McQuiston (co-inventor of the PSE) indicated that the witness was telling the truth. Moody held a high security clearance at Holloman AFB and was involved in the Air Force's Human Re- liability Program (HRP) where he had been carefully screened by a psychiatrist and declared free of emotional disorders. Moreover, his supervisor at the base, Sergeant Wright, confirmed that Moody was reliable and trustworthy.

A Government Liaison?

In *The Philadelphia Experiment*, co-author William Moore cites the interesting case of Robert Suffern, of Bracebridge, Ontario, who, on the night of 7 October 1975, encountered on the road ahead a dark saucer-shaped object about 12 to 14 feet in diameter.

'I was scared,' he later told a reporter. 'It was right there in front of me with no lights and no signs of life.' Before he stopped the car, the object ascended vertically and disappeared.

No sooner had Suffern turned his car round to head back home when a 4-foot-tall human-like figure with very wide shoulders, 'out of proportion to his body', and wearing a silver-grey suit and a globe-like helmet, walked right out in the road in front of the car. Suffern braked and skidded, coming to within inches of a collision with the figure, who immediately dodged, ran to the side of the road and disappeared effortlessly over a fence, 'like he was weightless'.

After arriving home, he again saw the UFO, flying slowly close to the road before disappearing vertically.

The following year, during a lengthy interview with Harry Tokarz of the Canadian UFO Research Network (CUFORN), Suffern disclosed that two months after the encounter, on 12 December, he and his wife were visited by three officials, who arrived in an Ontario Provincial Police car by pre-arranged appointment. The three men, in full uniform, bore impressive credentials from the Canadian Forces in Ottawa, the US Air Force, Pentagon, and the US Office of Naval Intelligence.

The officials allegedly showed Suffern a number of gun-camera photographs and other data on UFOs, and implied that the United States and Canadian Governments had known all about UFOs since 1943 (supposedly as a result of a US Navy experiment involving radar invisibility – the so-called 'Philadelphia Experiment'), stating that they had been co-operating with the aliens ever since that time. They said the incident witnessed by Suffern was 'a mistake', claiming that a malfunction in the craft had brought it down. Furthermore, the officials knew the precise time of the landing, which had not been revealed to anyone at that time.

The Sufferns were also impressed by the fact that the three officials answered all their questions unhesitatingly and authoritatively, and insisted that the men were legitimate government agents whose identities could be proven. Suffern was unwilling to disclose further details, however, preferring to comply with the governments' desire for secrecy.[24]

A Medical Examination

Dr Leopoldo Díaz Martínez, a pediatrics and anaesthesia specialist, was executive director of the Hospital del Ferrocarril del Pacifico in Guadalajara, Mexico, when the following incident is alleged to have occurred.

On 28 October 1976, Dr Díaz noticed an unusual man waiting in his office. He was short – about 5 feet 2 inches – with extraordinarily white skin, 'almost the colour of milk'. The stranger requested a physical examination – blood pressure, heart, lungs and so on – because, he said, he 'travelled a lot' and therefore required regular medical examinations. Dr Díaz asked the man to take off his clothes.

The man was normal in every way apart from being hairless, with the exception of his head – where a small growth of black hair encircled the temples – and the eyes. As the doctor approached him, he noticed that the colour of the man's eyes was 'almost impossible to describe . . . like violet', and that the iris was wider than normal.

Since it is necessary to relate blood pressure to age, Dr Díaz asked the man how old he was and received the reply that he was eighty-four. The doctor was incredulous, because the man appeared to be in his forties or fifties, judging from the mature expression on his face, although no wrinkles could be discerned. He was, said Dr Díaz, 'a good-looking man . . . very well constructed.'

Heart and blood pressure proved to be normal (120/80 mm), as did the lungs and other vital organs.

Suddenly the man explained that the true purpose of his visit was to impart some important information:

'I am not from this planet, but don't be nervous,' he began. 'It is necessary that you people recognize that many of us are here intermingled with you, and trying to help, because you are very close to having tremendous problems on your planet . . . You are misusing energy sources and it is necessary for you to learn to find another source of energy. We are trying to give you this information because you are polluting the atmosphere: you are contaminating not only your planet but even space, and are very close to being destroyed . . .'

Dr Díaz questioned why he was being given this information, rather than government officials and scientists, and was told: 'We have approached your government people and your scientists, but many are very arrogant. They don't want to hear; they don't want to change. We are trying to help, but only in the way you want to receive this help. We cannot force you to accept . . .'

There followed a lengthy discourse on cosmology, theology and physics. The alien's comments on the energy crisis were particularly apposite.

'It is necessary for you to find another energy source,' he said, 'and it is very easy. For that which you call electricity is an eternal energy . . . it is free. It is possible to get tremendous energy if you know how to dissociate electrons, for in this way you can have the free energy you need, without contamination or pollution, and this is what we use to travel space . . .'

The stranger revealed that his people had discovered more sub-atomic particles than we had, hence their ability to tap this source of energy.

Before the man left the office, Dr Díaz attempted to learn his origin, but other than saying that our solar system has twelve planets, the alien merely stated cryptically: 'The only thing I can tell you is that I come from beyond the sun . . .'

At the conclusion of this conversation, held in Spanish, the stranger left the office. Dr Díaz attempted to follow, but by the time he reached the corner of the block the man had vanished.

At first, Dr Díaz only related this experience to a few close friends and relatives, but subsequently he was introduced to the UFO Education Center in California, where he learned that others had claimed to have had encounters with extraterrestrials. In the realization that he was not alone, he felt secure enough to make the story public – and even to make a special trip to New York, where he related the details to a United Nations delegation.[25]

There will be those who will arbitrarily reject this sensational account without further consideration. Others will cast aspersions on the doctor's state of mental health or integrity, accusing him of fabricating the story for self-aggrandizement. But it is hardly likely that a highly respected doctor, who up to that time had been in practice for over twenty-five years, would risk his professional reputation with such a story unless it had actually taken place.

When I spoke with Dr Díaz by phone in 1980, he struck me as being completely truthful, and gave me the names of some of the United Nations delegates with whom he had spoken in New York. The meeting had taken place in the office of Robert Muller, Under-Secretary of Economic and Social Development, and accordingly I telephoned him at the UN.

Mr Muller confirmed the meeting with Dr Díaz, but when I asked what the UN proposed to do about it, he replied: 'Nothing – nothing at all. I circulated it to some people who might be able to do something about it and I had not a single response.'[26]

A German Connection

'We find ourselves faced by powers which are far stronger than we had hitherto assumed, and whose base of operations is at present unknown to us,' Dr Wernher von Braun is alleged to have stated in 1959, in reference to the deflection from orbit of a US satellite. 'More I cannot say at present. We are now engaged in entering into closer contact with those powers, and in six or nine months' time it may be possible to speak with more precision on the matter.'[27]

Whether Von Braun had aliens in mind may never be known, but in view of information I have acquired over the years from reliable sources, indicating that contact has been established with a number of scientists, the possibility cannot be discounted.

A colleague of mine, for example, learned from a scientist friend in the 1970s that the director of a German/US space research centre (located in West Germany) was of allegedly extraterrestrial origin. This knowledge was restricted to a quorum of scientists at the base, and the information apparently supplied by the director proved to be invaluable in their research effort. Just another wild, unsubstantiated story? Perhaps. But I have to add that my colleague had the opportunity of meeting the director in London in the 1980s (together with his scientist friend) and is satisfied as to the director's 'credentials'.

Even Germany's great space pioneer, Dr Hermann Oberth, is reported to have endorsed the suggestion of alien liaison. 'We cannot take the credit for our record advancement in certain scientific fields alone; we have been helped,' he is quoted as having said. When asked by whom, he simply replied, 'The people of other worlds.'[28] To my great regret, I neglected to ask Oberth about this when I met him in 1972, but I recall that he did not reject the possibility that aliens might have established bases here on Earth.

Dangerous Liaisons

But alien liaison is infinitely more complex than the scenario suggested here. Having spent over thirty years interviewing many witnesses throughout the world, it is evident to me that we are confronted with a diversity of UFO occupants, and I see no valid reason for discarding one type of report on the basis of its failure to fit in with our preconceived notions of alien appearance and behaviour. Neither are all the contactees lying. The aliens themselves are not averse to spreading disinformation, as I have remarked elsewhere.

Many UFO incidents are so puzzling that they will probably remain beyond our comprehension for centuries to come. And many reports suggest that not all the visitors have our best interests at heart.

The American journalist Bob Pratt has investigated some disturbing cases, including abductions, that took place in remote areas of north-east Brazil during the 1970s and 1980s and involve witnesses who typically claim to have been struck by beams of light from UFOs, in some instances causing serious injury.

In an incident that occurred on 23 April 1976, Luis Fernandes Barros, a businessman and rancher from Quixadá in the state of Ceará, was struck by a beam of light from a hovering aerial object. Initially, Barros suffered from nausea, diarrhoea, headaches and vomiting, and doctors and psychiatrists who examined him could only conclude that he had a brain lesion. His speech began to deteriorate, and three months after the incident his hair turned white. Six months later, he had lost all his mental faculties and regressed to the age of a one-year-old child.[29]

Dr Jacques Vallee, the distinguished researcher and astrophysicist, has also interviewed a number of witnesses in north-east Brazil, and concludes that most are truthful, though he rules out an extraterrestrial source for the UFOs.[30]

It is also in Brazil, of course, where Antônio Villas-Boas was apparently twice seduced by a 4.5-foot-tall alien female aboard a spaceship in October 1957.

The space-suited humanoids who kidnapped Villas-Boas very sensibly took the precaution of taking a blood sample before presenting him to the naked female, who was described as 'beautiful, though of a different type from the women I had known', with very fair, almost bleached hair reaching halfway down her neck. Her eyes were 'large and blue, more elongated than round, being slanted outwards'. She had high cheekbones, making the face look wide, but narrowing sharply and terminating in a pointed chin. Her lips were thin and barely visible. The ears, though small, were no different from ours. Her body was more beautiful than that of any woman Antonio had seen, with 'high and well-separated breasts, thin waist and small stomach, wide hips and large thighs'. Interestingly, the hair in the armpits and pubic area was described as very red.

'Obviously, I would not exchange our women for her,' said Antônio. 'I like a woman with whom you can talk and converse and make yourself understood, which wasn't the case here. Furthermore, some of the grunts that I heard coming from that woman's mouth at certain moments nearly spoiled everything, giving the disagreeable impression that I was with an animal.'

Following intercourse, the woman pointed at her stomach and then at the sky, and Antônio was escorted off the craft by the other aliens. Subsequently, he began to suffer from what can only be described as a type of cosmic 'clap': severe headaches, burning and watering of the eyes, then excessive sleepiness followed by the appearance of various lesions on his body.

Dr Olavo Fontes, who later examined and interrogated Villas-Boas, concluded that he was completely truthful. The physical symptoms described, he said, 'suggest radiation poisoning or exposure to radiation, but unfortunately he came to me too late for the blood examinations that could have confirmed such a possibility beyond doubt.'[31]

Unlike the majority of abductees, Villas-Boas's experience was recalled fully consciously. Other abductees, whose experiences are normally brought to light during hypnotic regression, believe that blood, ova or sperm have been extracted from their bodies.

While in Brazil in September 1988, Dr Richard Haines and I interviewed Elias Seixas, a witness who claims to have been abducted with two other men (one of whom was his cousin) in the state of Goiás, north-west Brazil, on 25 September 1980. Although only able to recall consciously the initial and final stages of his abduction (the witnesses managed to get some film of the craft, though the quality is poor), the more disturbing memories only emerged under hypnotic regression. Certain key elements in this lengthy and complex story are worth recounting here.

Seixas told us that the beings he encountered were 2 metres tall, with slightly Asiatic, violet-coloured eyes; the white part more grey than normal. They had no eyelashes or facial hair and their heads were covered with tight caps.

Not content with twice pulling Seixas's hair painfully to get samples, the sadistic spacemen apparently shoved needles (attached to thin wires) in his fingertips and between his fingers. They claimed that in addition to a genetic purpose, they needed Seixas to educate people about their visits, and said they would plant something inside his skull that would later help them to locate and communicate with him.

The naked Seixas was allegedly placed on a table where the aliens proceeded to arouse him sexually by provoking erotic images in his mind, and then introduced a tube over his penis and extracted semen. So disturbing was this experience that Seixas told me he was unable to have sexual relations for months afterwards, and that both he and to a lesser extent his wife, whom I also met, hear strange noises in their heads at certain times.

Despite the outrageous nature of this story – which of course guarantees that it will not be believed – Dr Haines and I remain impressed with Elias Seixas's integrity and intelligence.

Alternative Realities

Some of the more bizarre encounters, such as those reported by Whitley Strieber and others, have prompted researchers to argue that the aliens are extradimensional rather than extraterrestrial in nature. Such arguments are predicated on the false, in my view, assumption that the two hypotheses are mutually exclusive.

Gordon Creighton, one of the most learned scholars in this field, suggests that some aliens are interdimensional beings indigenous to planet Earth, and may have co-existed with us for thousands of years. In many ways, this is an attractive hypothesis which could explain the inconsistencies inherent in the phenomenon. Many of the reported abductions, for example, seem to take place in a different level or dimension of reality, seemingly making a nonsense of the physical examinations, extractions of blood, sperm and ova that are said to have taken place, and are more in line with the subject of demonology (particularly encounters with incubi and succubi).

While I accept that parallels can be drawn in many cases, there is no way such a theory can be applied in all cases. Firstly, it is impossible to reconcile the hypothesis with reports of recovered vehicles and bodies, as well as with those accounts involving an ongoing physical interaction. Secondly, although many encounters may seem 'supernatural' to us, we should never underestimate the mental and technological potential of advanced extraterrestrial species, who in my opinion may be able to manipulate space and time in such a way that they can function in other dimensions.

Unbelievable? Of course! So was manned flight, television, the atom bomb, space travel, microchip technology, and many other terrestrial achievements which we now take for granted. By the same token, extraterrestrial abilities may be unbelievable and indistinguishable from magic. But there is evidence that some of our scientists have already gained an insight into alien technology at least, thanks partly to the acquisition of extraterrestrial craft.

Notes

1 Information supplied to the author by William Moore.

2 *Flying Saucers at Edwards AFB, 1954*, published by Borderland Sciences Research Foundation, P.O. Box 548, Vista, California 92083; Berlitz, Charles and Moore, William: *The Roswell Incident*, Granada, London, 1980, pp. 119–28.

3 *Valor* magazine, 9 October 1954, and confirmed to the author by Desmond Leslie.

4 Picton, John: 'Eisenhower was visited by UFO, British lord claims', *Toronto Star* (undated, but story confirmed to the author by Lord Clancarty).

5 'Anchor' [Ann Grevler]: *Transvaal Episode*, The Essene Press, Corpus Christi, Texas, 1958, pp. 19–21.

6 Creighton, Gordon: 'The UFO Landings at Voronezh', *The UFO Report 1991*, edited by Timothy Good, Sidgwick & Jackson, London, 1990, pp. 67–8.

7 Beckley, Timothy Green: *MJ-12 and the Riddle of Hangar 18*, Inner Light Publications, P.O. Box 753, New Brunswick, New Jersey 08903, 1989, pp. 13–14.

8 Good, Timothy: *Above Top Secret: The Worldwide UFO Cover-Up*, Sidgwick & Jackson, London, 1987, p. 376.

9 Letter to Lou Zinsstag from Waveney Girvan, 17 September 1962.

10 Letter to Lou Zinsstag from John Lade, 11 July 1963.

11 Ball, Ian: 'Flying saucer seen by down-to-earth Carter', *Daily Telegraph*, London, 2 June 1976. For further information on Carter's attempt to reopen official investigations, see *Above Top Secret*.

12 Interviews with the author, August 1976.

13 Letter to Daniel Fry from Harry S. Flemming, Special Assistant to the President, The White House, Washington, DC, 13 March 1969.

14 The Reagan sighting was first mentioned in *Landslide: The Unmaking of the President*, by Jane Mayer and Doyle McManus, Collins, London, 1988, p. 402, and a follow-up report, based on interviews with Bill Paynter and Norman Miller, appeared in an article by Alan Smith and Ken Potter in the *National Enquirer*, 11 October 1988.

15 Information supplied to the author by Michael Luckman.

16 Barnes, Fred: 'Reagan reaps arms-control harvest', *The Plain Dealer*, 11 October 1987.

17 Speech by Mikhail Gorbachev at the Grand Kremlin Palace, Moscow, 16 February 1987, published in *Soviet Life* (supplement), May 1987, p. 7A.

18 Walton, Travis: *The Walton Experience*, Berkley, New York, 1978, pp. 105–26.

19 ABC News, 18 November 1975.

20 Interview with the author, 24 October 1978.

21 Walton, Travis: op. cit., pp. 160–1.

22 Stevens, Wendelle C. and Herrmann, William J.: *UFO: Contact from Reticulum*, UFO Books, Box 1053, Florence, Arizona 85232, 1981/89.

23 *APRO Bulletin*, Vol. 24, No. 12, 1976.

24 Berlitz, Charles and Moore, William: *The Philadelphia Experiment: Project Invisibility*, Souvenir, London, 1990, pp. 173–7.

25 Interview with Michael Packer, WOAI Radio, San Antonio, Texas, 1978; interview with the author, 5 May 1980.

26 Interview with the author, 6 May 1980.

27 *Neues Europa*, 1 January 1959.
28 Collyns, Robin: *Did Spacemen Colonise the Earth?*, Pelham Books, London, 1974, p. 236.
29 Pratt, Bob: 'Disturbing Encounters in North-East Brazil', *The UFO Report 1991*, edited by Timothy Good, Sidgwick & Jackson, London, 1990, pp. 117–18.
30 Vallee, Jacques: *Confrontations: A Scientist's Search for Alien Contact*, Ballantine, New York, 1990.
31 Creighton, Gordon: 'The Amazing Case of Antônio Villas-Boas', *The Humanoids*, edited by Charles Bowen, Neville Spearman, London, 1969, pp. 200–38.

· 5 ·

Hardware

In the last few years, a considerable amount of new information relating to the retrieval of crashed UFOs and their occupants has come to light, adding weight to the growing body of evidence that there is a factual basis for what has hitherto seemed a fantastic improbability.

Above Top Secret includes details of the following cases: Roswell, New Mexico (1947); Paradise Valley, Arizona (1947); Aztec, New Mexico (1948); Mexico (1948 or 1949); Kingman, Arizona (1953); New Mexico (1962); and examinations of alien bodies and craft at Wright-Patterson AFB in 1959 and 1962, as well as at an undisclosed base in Arizona during the 1970s. Leonard Stringfield and other researchers have published additional cases which have been reported not just from the United States, but also from countries such as France, Germany, Puerto Rico, South Africa, and Spitsbergen (Arctic Ocean).[1] Later in this chapter I shall relate new stories describing the recovery of anomalous devices in Australia and the Soviet Union, although in these cases – as with some of those listed above – there were no bodies.

In the majority of cases where bodies are recovered, the aliens are described as being of the small variety, and of all such reported incidents, the so-called Roswell incident of July 1947 has become one of the best-documented and thoroughly investigated cases in UFO history. Stanton Friedman and William Moore have now contacted over 160 witnesses who were directly or indirectly associated with the incident, and other researchers, such as Leonard Stringfield, Kevin Randle and Don Schmitt, have located additional witnesses, including aircrew members who transported the wreckage, bringing the total number of witnesses to 200.

The evidence now suggests that there were two separate crashes in New Mexico during the first week of July 1947, and that both possibly involved the recovery of alien bodies. In the best-known incident, scattered wreckage was discovered on 'Mac' Brazel's ranch near Corona, 75 miles north-west of Roswell, as has been confirmed by Major Jesse Marcel, the intelligence officer from Roswell Army Air Field who was in charge of the recovery operation. Marcel found no bodies at this location, but stated emphatically that the material he handled was like nothing on Earth. One piece of a metal foil-like material was so durable, he said, that it could not be dented with a 16-pound sledgehammer, despite its incredible lightness.[2]

Marcel's son, Jesse Marcel MD, also handled some pieces of the wreckage that his father had brought home with him, as he described to Lee Graham in 1981:

... the crash and remnants of the device that I happened to be present to see have left an imprint on my memory that can never be forgotten. I am currently undergoing training as a Flight Surgeon in the Army Air National Guard, and have examined the remnants of many conventional aircraft that have undergone unfortunate manoeuvres, and what I saw in 1947 is unlike any of the current air-craft ruinage I have studied.

This craft was not conventional in any sense of the word, in that the remnants were most likely [of] what was then known as a flying saucer that apparently had been stressed beyond its designed capabilities. I'm basing this on the fact that many of the remnants ... had strange hieroglyphic-type writing symbols across the inner surfaces ...[3]

Strange 'hieroglyphic-type' symbols have been reported in other cases, such as the incident involving the recovery by the military of an unidentified object that was found half embedded in the ground near Kecksburg, Pennsylvania, on 9 December 1965, following sightings by numerous witnesses of a UFO heading towards that vicinity. The case has been thoroughly investigated by Stan Gordon and other researchers, and one of those who observed the object at close quarters described a ring or bumper-like structure about 8 to 10 inches wide that seemed to cover the circumference of the 'acorn-shaped' object, and had what looked like Egyptian hieroglyphics on it: characters of broken and straight lines, dots, rectangles and circles. Asked by Leonard Stringfield if the symbols could possibly have been Russian, the witness, Jim Romansky, replied, 'No way! I'm of Russian-Polish descent and can read Russian. It was not Russian, nor American. I'll stake my life on it: the object was not man-made.'[4]

Slowly but surely the evidence is accumulating that the various extraordinary incidents associated with the Roswell case have a basis in fact. Following publication of *Above Top Secret* in 1987, I have been contacted by several people who have provided me with new information. One of my informants is former Air Force Lieutenant Colonel Robert Bowker, who at one time had been with the Communications Division of the Air Technical Intelligence Command at Wright-Patterson AFB.

'Over the years,' he wrote, 'I have heard rumours galore, fully substantiating my belief in the reality of UFOs and the sometimes pitiful efforts of the Establishment to cover them up, and I have seen two myself. Recently, I sent a copy of the MJ-12 document [see Chapter 6] to a friend in Arizona, who showed it to another agent there [whose] uncle worked at Wright-Patterson AFB as a welder at the time that artifacts from the 1947 NM crash were being analyzed, and was given a piece of it to melt with his equipment. He was unable to produce a flame hot enough for the task!'

The much-maligned Frank Scully, author of the 1950 book, *Behind the Flying Saucers*, described how he had handled some 'gears' that had come from a recovered craft. 'More than 150 tests had failed to break down the metal of the gears,' he wrote. 'The gears themselves were of a ratio unfamiliar to engineers on this earth; had no play, no lubrication.'[5]

It is therefore illuminating to learn of corroborative evidence supplied to me by Robert Bowker. 'Years ago, I had an engineer at Wright-Patterson AFB approach me while I was on Active Duty and tell me all about an investigation he was involved in of a gear fragment that turned out to entail Rare Earth elements in a quantity impossible on this planet for gear manufacture, and [was] not of the mathematical (cycloid) design our gears use, but one using a strange 3-level digital form.'[6]

The New Mexico Aliens

Alien bodies from one of the 1947 crashes were allegedly recovered near Magdalena, on the Plains of San Agustin, west of Socorro, New Mexico, about 150 miles west of Brazel's ranch near Corona. One witness was Grady L. Barnett, a civil engineer with the US Soil Conservation Service who was on a military assignment at the time. Barnett claimed to have come across a metallic, disc-shaped aircraft, about 25 or 30 feet in diameter, together with apparently dead bodies.

'They were like humans but they were not humans,' he reported. 'The heads were round, the eyes were small, and they had no hair. The eyes were oddly spaced. They were quite small by our standards and their heads were larger in proportion to their bodies than ours. Their clothing seemed to be one-piece and grey in colour. You couldn't see any zippers, belts or buttons . . .'[7]

A number of photographs of alleged alien bodies have surfaced from time to time, but most are either too indistinct to make a proper evaluation, or patently bogus. The photograph reproduced in this book shows a model of a deceased alien which was allegedly exhibited in Montreal, Canada, in 1977. The photograph was circulated to a number of researchers in 1990 by a retired Soviet Air Force colonel, Dr Marina Popovich, who seems to believe that it shows a real alien. I make no claims for the model's accuracy, but in view of the description given by a witness in the following story, we should perhaps keep an open mind.

Sergeant Melvin E. Brown was stationed at Roswell Army Air Field at the time of the crashes in July 1947. Not only did he stand guard outside a hangar where the recovered material was temporarily stored, but also claimed to have observed some alien bodies, as Beverley Bean, one of his daughters, related to me.

'Dad was reading this article in the *Daily Mirror* in the late 1970s, I think, and he said, "I was there!", pointing to this article. He said it was all true apart from one fact. He told us afterwards that any men available were taken to this site. They had to form a ring around whatever it was they had to cover, and everything was put on trucks. They were told not to look and to take no notice, and were sworn to secrecy.

'I can remember my Dad saying he couldn't understand why they wanted refrigerated trucks. And him and another guy had to sit on the back of a truck to take this stuff to a hangar. They were packed in ice. And he lifted up the tarpaulin and looked in, and saw three (or possibly two) dead bodies.

'He told us they were nothing to be scared of. They were friendly-looking and had nice faces. They looked Asian, he said, but had larger heads and no hair. They looked a yellowy colour. He was frightened a bit, because he knew he shouldn't be doing it, so he only had a quick glimpse. But he said they could have passed for Chinese – they had slanted eyes.

'And he had to stand guard duty outside this hangar, and his commanding officer came up and said, "I want to have a look in. Let's both have a look inside!" So they both went into the hangar, and they didn't see anything, as everything was packed away for storage to be flown out the next day.'

Melvin Brown only occasionally discussed the incident with his wife and three daughters, and always regretted having done so. 'He'd shut up if we questioned him about it,' Beverley told me. 'He wanted to tell people about it, but when you started asking questions he was completely off it. He was in a state about it when he was dying in 1986. Even when he was asleep he was mumbling about it . . . Dad was absolutely no liar. He was a smashing bloke and loved his country.'[8]

The family was initially reluctant to allow me to publish the story, in case of official reprisal, but in the last few years they have become more comfortable about discussing it openly, as additional military witnesses have come forward to confirm various details of the Roswell story.

Beverley kindly gave me copies of her father's military records, which prove that he was stationed at Roswell at the relevant period. They do not prove, of course, that he saw alien bodies, but they do at least show that he had an unblemished career in the US Army and Air Force. His World War II Army awards included the American

Fig. 5.2
Membership card proving that Sergeant Brown was a member of the Non-Commissioned Officers Club at Roswell Army Air Field during the time he claimed to have been involved in the recovery operation.

Defense Service Medal, American Campaign Medal, Asiatic Pacific Campaign Medal, Victory Medal and Good Conduct Medal (Appendix, Fig. 5.1). And in a letter of recommendation for promotion to staff sergeant in the Air Force, dated 7 May 1948 (Appendix, Fig. 5.3), Lieutenant Colonel Jack J. Catton wrote that:

> . . . Sergeant Brown has diligently and industriously performed all duties assigned to him while on duty with Task Unit 7.4.1. During the peculiar and tedious circumstances resulting from this project, he clearly demonstrated the qualities and abilities desired of a Staff Sergeant. Sergeant Brown's Service Record indicates no record of previous conviction by Courts-Martial . . .[9]

Melvin Brown was additionally engaged in espionage work, according to a relative, although no details are currently available. He also knew both Major Jesse Marcel and General Nathan Twining, Commanding-General of Air Matériel Command at the time of the Roswell incident.

According to the controversial Majestic-12 document (see Chapter 6), which purports to be a 1952 preliminary briefing document for President-elect Eisenhower, four bodies from the Corona crash were recovered 2 miles east of the wreckage site at Brazel's ranch, and all were described as 'dead and badly decomposed due to action by predators and exposure to the elements during the approximately one-week time period which had elapsed before their discovery . . .'

Given the rather spurious nature of the MJ-12 document, this may well be disinformation to cover up the more sensational reports. Alternatively, it is possible that four 'badly decomposed' bodies were indeed recovered by the military, especially since the evidence indicates that two such incidents occurred, and that Eisenhower was not fully appraised of these facts until later. Page two of the MJ-12 briefing paper emphasizes that the document 'has been prepared as a preliminary briefing only. It should be regarded as introductory to a full operations briefing intended to follow.'

Survivors?

In 1989, former NASA mission specialist Bob Oechsler interviewed Samantha De Los Reyes, a step-daughter of a now-deceased civilian employee who had been assigned to one of the New Mexico retrieval operations. Following a dispatch from Roswell Army Air Field, Burl Cassity, who held a Top Secret clearance with the Army Corps of Engineers at the time, was ordered to take heavy transport equipment to the site (location not known, but presumably near Magdalena), where a craft and alien bodies had been discovered.

'There were a lot of people around, including press and photographers, with the military running around trying to prevent them from taking pictures,' Bob recounted to me. 'There were four aliens − two dead ones and two live ones. One of them who was alive was walking erratically and apparently had internal injuries. The other one was apparently unharmed. And they had a bus and several trucks and a bulldozer, and he helped to put the two dead aliens on the bus, followed by the live ones.'

Cassity was ordered to paint the windows of the bus with black paint, and assisted in retrieving some components from the craft, one of which was what looked like a control panel made out of an un-known clear material. 'He said it was not glass and it was not plastic,' Bob told me. 'I don't know what it was made of, but it apparently took two of them to lift it – they really had to strain to put it on the bus. They collected as much as possible of the small debris and loaded it on to the trucks.'

The larger pieces, of which there were about fourteen, were all cata-logued, Bob was told, and Cassity was ordered to dig a trench with a bulldozer and bury them on site, presumably for recovery later. In the process, he inadvertently drove over a piece. 'It didn't do *any* damage,' Bob said.

'They were totally awed and shocked by what they saw. He learned that the alien that was injured died either before or shortly after arrival in Alamogordo [possibly Alamogordo Army Air Field]. They were unable to save him. The other one apparently survived for a few years at Los Alamos' (see Chapter 6).

Eighteen years later, Bob was informed, Cassity died in an unusual accident at the White Sands, New Mexico, Missile Test Range. He was found on a ravine where he had been digging a long trench for one of the tests. 'They found him laying down, with his arms at his side, face up, with his glasses on, and he had been run over by the tracks of the bulldozer – feet first. Samantha's husband, who was a state police trooper, had gone to White Sands and managed to get a look at the sealed file. The coroner's report indicated that he had died of a heart attack.'[10]

The death may have been entirely coincidental, of course, however puzzling the circumstances. And in some other respects the story seems unlikely. If there were reporters and/or photographers at the site, for example, why has no one yet come forward? Samantha told Bob that one of the cameras was confiscated by the military, so it is possible that others were confiscated too, and the photographers silenced. Twenty-five years have elapsed since Cassity died, and it is likely that Samantha may have forgotten or confused some of the details.

But another witness has now come forward who claims to have observed the craft and bodies, as well as the military presence, near Magdalena. Although only five years old at the time, Gerald Anderson has a vivid memory of the incident, now enhanced by hypnotic regression. Researchers John Carpenter and Stanton Friedman are both impressed with the sincerity of this witness and the amount of corroboration he has provided. Anderson, a former police chief and deputy sheriff, was visiting the area to look for moss agate stones, together with his father, brother, uncle and cousin (all now deceased), on 5 July 1947, when the incident took place.

'We came around a corner and right there in front of us, stuck into the side of this hill, was a silver disc. We all went up there to it. There were three creatures – three bodies – lying on the ground underneath this thing, in the shade.' The creatures were about 4 feet tall, with disproportionately large heads and almond-shaped, coal-black eyes.

'Two weren't moving, and the third one obviously was having trouble breathing, like when you have broken ribs,' Anderson reported. 'There was a fourth one next to it, sitting there on the ground. There wasn't a thing wrong with it, and it apparently had been giving first aid to the others. It recoiled in fear, like it thought we were going to attack it.'

The adults repeatedly tried to communicate with the creature, but there was no audible response to greetings spoken in English and Spanish. A few minutes after the Andersons arrived, five college students and their teacher (reported by Grady Barnett to have been from the University of Pennsylvania), who had been on an archaeological dig a few miles away and had been alerted the previous night to what they thought was a meteor fall, came on the scene. The professsor, a Dr Buskirk, tried several foreign languages in a further unsuccessful attempt at communication.

'It was 115 degrees out there that day,' Anderson recalled. 'But around the craft, when you got close to it, it was cold. When you touched the metal, it felt just like it came out of a freezer.' Anderson also touched one of the creatures lying motionless on the ground, and it too was cold.

A pick-up truck then arrived on the scene, and a person believed to be Barnett joined the onlookers.

Anderson approached the creatures once more, and as he did so became aware of a strange sensation. The upright creature 'turned and looked right at me, and it was like he was inside my head, as if he was doing my thinking – as if his thoughts were in my head.'

Anderson remembers a sensation of falling and tumbling. 'I felt that thing's fear, felt its depression, felt its loneliness. I relived the crash. I know the terror it went through. That one look told me everything . . .'

A contingent of armed soldiers then arrived. The creature, which had calmed down after its initial fright, 'went crazy'. Anderson lost sight of it as the soldiers surrounded the craft, which was described as being about 50 feet in diameter (at variance with Barnett's estimate). Anderson recalls shouts and threats by the military. 'The soldiers ushered us out of there very unceremoniously. Their attitude, to say the least, was very uncivilized. They told my dad and my uncle, who also worked at Sandia [Laboratories], that if they were ever to divulge anything about this – it was a secret military aircraft, they said – then us kids would be taken away and they'd never see us again . . . These people had machine-guns and you listened to what they said.'

The soldiers did not appear unduly surprised by the craft and bodies, Anderson recalls. 'They were very cognizant of what they were looking at. They knew what it was.'

There was a battalion of soldiers on the scene by the time Anderson and his group arrived back up on the hilltop where they had left their car. 'There were trucks, there were airplanes – they had the road blocked off and they were landing on it. They had radio communications gear set up. There were ambulances, and more soldiers with weapons.'

Anderson believes there is a link between the scattered wreckage found at Corona and the barely damaged craft found on the Plains of San Agustin. 'There was a gash in the side of the disc we saw, like it had been crushed in,' he reports. 'The contour of the craft would fit into that gash perfectly, like another one of these things had hit it. I think two of these discs had a mid-air collision. One exploded and fell in pieces near Roswell, and the other crash-landed where we found it.'[11]

The Jackie Gleason Story

It is not widely known that the great American comedian Jackie Gleason, who died in 1987, had a serious interest in UFOs. He possessed an extensive library on the subject in his Florida home and subscribed to a number of journals, including *Just Cause*, the newsletter of Citizens Against UFO Secrecy.[12] He even named his Peekskill, New York, residence 'The Mothership' and designed it to resemble a flying saucer.

According to Beverly McKittrick, Gleason's second wife, her husband came home one night in 1973, visibly shaken. He told his wife that he had just returned from a visit to Homestead AFB, Florida, where, thanks to his friend President Richard Nixon, who arranged the trip, he was shown a top secret repository where the bodies of aliens were stored. The visit was conducted under extremely tight security.

Larry Bryant (of Citizens Against UFO Secrecy) sent a Freedom of Information request to Homestead AFB to gain access to all official records pertaining to the repository and to the visit, but was told that no such records existed. While waiting for a response to his FOIA request, Bryant sent a draft affidavit to Gleason, asking him to execute it as further support for the growing body of evidence then being gathered as part of a forthcoming FOIA lawsuit to force the Government to release its records on UFO crash/retrievals.

'Though I never heard from Gleason,' Bryant reported, 'I did learn that he had been approached by a third party in the film industry. At this confrontation, Gleason chose neither to confirm nor deny the story, saying that he'd prefer not to discuss it at all. The way I see it, Gleason easily could have set the record straight in a reply to my proposal or in an explanation to the inquisitive film-industry representative. If the story was a fabrication or misinterpretation on the part of his wife, he now had every opportunity to say so. That he chose not to merely deepens the mystery.'

Larry Bryant, who is a civilian employee editor of the Army News Service, also sent an advertisement to the Homestead AFB newspaper, soliciting the testimony or evidence of anyone who could shed light on the Gleason story. The base's public affairs officer denounced the advertisement, however, and forbade its publication.[13]

Scientific and Military Confirmation

However absurd the stories of recovered flying saucers and alien bodies may seem, it is important to mention that in a letter to William Steinman in 1983, Dr Robert Sarbacher, a highly respected scientist who was a former consultant to the Research and Development Board and President and Chairman of the Board of the Washington Institute of Technology, acknowledged that the United States had indeed recovered both craft and bodies, and confirmed names of some of those involved at a high level. 'About the only thing I remember at this time,' he added, 'is that certain materials reported to have come from flying saucer crashes were extremely light and very tough ... There were also reports that instruments or people operating these machines were also of very light weight . . .'[14]

In his handwritten notes (reproduced in *Above Top Secret*), made after a meeting at the Canadian Embassy in Washington in September 1950, Canadian Government scientist Wilbert Smith wrote that Dr Sarbacher had confirmed that the facts reported in Frank Scully's book were substantially correct; that the authorities had been unable to duplicate the performance of the discs, and that 'it is the most highly classified subject in the US Government at the present time'.[15]

General George C. Marshall, US Army Chief of Staff in World War II, is also reported to have confirmed that, as of 1951, there had been three incidents involving accidents that had proved disastrous for the occupants, and that communications had been established with the aliens.[16]

In July 1990, a group of investigators and witnesses involved in the Roswell incident were invited by the Fund for UFO Research to a meeting in Arlington, Virginia, in order to discuss the latest developments and to record videotaped depositions for selected Members of Congress and the media. At the time of writing, the staff director of an important congressional committee has expressed interest in reviewing evidence associated with the Roswell case. The objectives of this endeavour are to seek immunity from prosecution for current and former military employees who are naturally reluctant to discuss their involvement, and to explore the possibility of closed-door hearings.

Among the ten witnesses interviewed were Jesse Marcel MD; Walter Haut, the public information officer at Roswell Army Air Field who issued the original press release confirming the recovery of a flying disc; Robert Shirkey, a flight operations officer at the base who recalls seeing the wreckage loaded on a B-29 with Major Marcel, headed for Carswell AFB in Fort Worth, Texas; John Kromschroeder DDS, and William Lounsberry, close friends of Captain O. W. ('Pappy') Henderson, the pilot who flew both wreckage and alien bodies to Wright Field, Dayton, Ohio; and Verne Maltais, a close friend of 'Barney' Barnett, who reported finding a crashed saucer and alien bodies on the Plains of San Agustin.[17]

USSR 1988–9

Nikolai Lebedev, a leading Soviet researcher, informed me during a visit to London recently that there have been a number of incidents relating to recovered UFOs reported in the USSR. In one incident, said to have occurred in the late autumn of 1988, military witnesses flying in a helicopter near Dalnegorsk, Dalniy Vostok, observed a strange object on the ground, and landed in order to investigate. The object, described as cylinder-shaped and approximately 6 metres in length, was definitely not part of a conventional aircraft. After an unsuccessful attempt to lift the device, the team decided to return early the following spring with proper equipment, by which time the object had disappeared.

According to Valeri Dvuzhilni, who has investigated the case, Soviet Navy personnel observed a glowing object enter the sea off the coast in the Dalniy Vostok area in the spring of 1989. A naval officer disclosed to Dvuzhilni that a recovery operation was immediately initiated, and a device, described as egg-shaped and about 6 metres long, was retrieved from the seabed and brought ashore.

'They tried to penetrate the device with an oxyacetylene flame, but without any result,' Nikolai told me. 'The naval officer informed Valeri that the object was later transferred to Vladivostok and then Moscow. I asked Valeri to try and obtain more information, but he told me that the officer refused to speak any more, as it was a top secret matter.'

Nikolai informed me that the Soviet Navy has specific instructions for reporting anomalous objects. In the case of landing traces, damage to military equipment, and so on, details must immediately be telegraphed to the following units: Leningrad, military unit 62728; Mytishchi, military unit 67947.[18]

Australia 1958/59

The following first-hand account was related to me by a witness who has requested anonymity. Employed as a radio technician at the Weapons Research Establishment, Salisbury, South Australia, from 1956 to 1960, the witness made a number of trips to the Woomera Test Range, which had been set up jointly with Britain in 1946 to test military missiles, and subsequently the Blue Streak, Black Arrow and Black Knight launchers.

'My class was unique,' the witness wrote to me in 1990. 'We were the first trained in Australia in transistor theory, and so were often the only ones able to work on missile equipment under trial. I was cleared for access to all parts of the range, and to all but a few projects. I was predominantly employed on Black Knight telemetry.'

Numerous sightings of UFOs were made at Woomera during this time, apparently, but were seldom reported for fear of persecution. 'I made a sighting and never reported it because of the pressures that existed as a result of sightings that had been reported by others,' my informant continued. 'A point of interest is that the sighting frequency rose dramatically whenever high-altitude trials were in preparation and readiness.

'While I was at Woomera the Americans were there in force for a number of reasons: we wanted them to use the range more, they wanted to sell us the Sidewinder [missile]. One particular man who I saw regularly in the plotting room was never seemingly employed on the actual trials, he was just there, perhaps, as an observer. I one day broached the subject of UFOs with him. He said in part (my quotes, but actual words were very close to the following):

' "We lost a pilot to one recently. It was sighted over Fort Knox and he was sent to intercept. He reported that he was diving on it, reported opening fire, and then the aircraft was seen to crash in flames. We have no idea of the cause . . ."'

While working at Woomera in 1958 or 1959, my informant revealed, an object was recovered on the range, outside any trials zone, by a helicopter involved in a search for a missing girl. 'The object eventually turned up in the workshop I was employed in at the time, because of its presumed ancestry. *I am telling you that I saw this, touched it, worked on it,*' he emphasized.

'It was a sphere about 2 feet 9 inches in diameter. Its colour was a mid-grey metallic, somewhat darkened, perhaps by extreme heat. It was very light. I have never been a good judge of weight, but it was disproportionately light, easily lifted by one person, easily supported from underneath by one hand.

'The initial assumption was that it was part of Black Knight, for that was the only missile here at the time that could have contained anything of the size, and it was left to languish uninvestigated for several days until one of the Black Knight experts disclaimed it. We then assumed it to be Russian or American, and had a closer look.

'Quite simply, there was not then the technology to produce what we had in our hands, and I frankly doubt that there is yet. We tried to cut it, and could not even mark it with hand tools – saws, drills, hammers, chisels – nothing. We heated it with an oxy torch, and could put a hand on it the minute the torch was removed. I did, several times. Oxygen applied at cutting volume made no difference – not that one would expect it to as we could not get it anywhere near oxidizing heat.

'By this time we were curious, to say the least, and examined it much more closely. Please remember that while we were dealing with an unknown, we had no doubt at this time that it would be explained by investigation.

'To the naked eye, and in any way we could measure, it was a *perfect* sphere. No dents or bumps, however tiny. It appeared as one piece. There were no joins, no rivets, no weld marks, no sign of weld marks having been polished off. There was nowhere that pipes could have been connected, no sign of any opening. It had no radiation – a Geiger counter registered zero – not even background, although we were later told it was a faulty instrument, and background was normal. Disinformation, perhaps?

'At this point we sought advice from on high – I don't know who; that was handled by an engineer. The next thing I knew was that it was removed by the Range Security staff, along with the American I mentioned earlier.

'Some weeks after it had been removed I asked the engineer what the object had been. He told me that the Americans had claimed it as part of their space debris, and that it had been returned by them to the States – to Wright-Patterson AFB. Some years later, I encountered by chance another of the people who had seen the object, but who unlike me was still employed at Woomera. I asked him about it. He told me that as far as he was concerned there had never been such an object, and strongly advised (i.e. warned not threatened) me to adopt the same line if ever I was asked.'

The finding of the sphere was briefly reported in the *Adelaide Advertiser*, and some months later another similar find in South Australia was mentioned in the same newspaper, the witness recalls, although he cannot remember the dates. And during the 1960s yet another sphere was apparently discovered in South-West Queensland and reported in the *Brisbane Courier-Mail*. The latter finding was not linked with the other two, he remembers.

The witness left the electronics industry and joined the police force, rising to the rank of inspector, and was put in charge of the Governor-General's security until retirement due to injury in 1982. 'I put it to you that my specialities of VIP security and counter-terrorism must suggest that I am both a skilled observer, and stable,' he emphasized.

'Perhaps this is foolish, but for many years now I have believed that what we held in those several days was not merely space debris, was perhaps not even some material left by a UFO, but that it was perhaps some form of UFO itself . . .'[19]

Pine Gap

Located twelve miles from Alice Springs in Australia's Northern Territory, Pine Gap is a highly secret communications base run by the National Security Agency. Ostensibly a 'Joint Defense Space Research Facility' sponsored by both American and Australian Defence Departments, Pine Gap serves principally as a downlink for geosynchronous SIGINT (Signals Intelligence) satellites.[20]

There are rumours that the NSA, which has a long history of involvement in monitoring the UFO phenomenon and is withholding many documents on the subject at an above Top Secret level, also monitors communications from UFOs, as we shall learn later. Interestingly, there have reportedly been a number of sightings in the Pine Gap area. In December 1989, for example, the American researcher John Lear received a letter from a university professor in Australia, in which it was stated that three witnesses, returning from an all-night hunting trip at 4.30 a.m., observed a camouflaged door open up in the grounds of the base, and a metallic, circular disc ascend vertically and soundlessly into the air before disappearing at great speed.

'The three witnesses are reliable,' the professor reported, 'though understandably rather reluctant to discuss what they saw. I am trying to arrange for a polygraph test for them, as well as getting sworn statements . . . We have an immense tract of empty territory ideal for UFO activity. In fact, this state has more UFOs coming and going, I guess, than anywhere else in Australia.'

I have subsequently been in touch with the professor, and he has reaffirmed the reliability of the witnesses.

From another reliable source, a friend who claims to have had contact with a group of extraterrestrials in England during 1963–4 (related in Chapter 4), I learned that communications had been established by that time with a number of scientists worldwide and that bases had been constructed in several countries – including Australia. The purpose of the liaison was not disclosed, nor the precise location of the bases, but the description of the camouflaged door and UFO at Pine Gap raises the possibility that such a base could be or may have been located there.

Let us now turn our attention to the various attempts by the US Government, during the period from 1973 to 1988, to indoctrinate the public about these complex and controversial matters. The incredible revelations which follow are necessarily diluted with disinformation, yet nevertheless incorporate a significant amount of truth, as we shall discover.

Notes

1 Stringfield, Leonard: 'UFO Crash/Retrievals: Is the Cover-Up Lid Lifting?', *The UFO Report 1990*, edited by Timothy Good, Sidgwick & Jackson, London, 1989; Five status reports on UFO crash/retrievals, available from Mr Stringfield at 4412 Grove Avenue, Cincinnati, Ohio 45227; Moore, William: *Crashed UFOs: Evidence in the Search for Proof*, 1985, William L. Moore Publications & Research, 4219 W. Olive Street, Suite 247, Burbank, California 91505; Steinman, William and Stevens, Wendelle: *UFO Crash at Aztec*, 1987, UFO Books, P.O. Box 1053, Florence, Arizona 85232.

2 Berlitz, Charles and Moore, William: *The Roswell Incident*, Granada, London, 1980, pp. 67–72.

3 Letter to Lee Graham from Dr Jesse Marcel, 21 October 1981.

4 Stringfield, Leonard: op. cit.; Gordon, Stan: 'The Kecksburg UFO Crash', *MUFON UFO Journal*, Nos. 257/8, September/October 1989, MUFON, 103 Oldtowne Road, Seguin, Texas 78155-4099; Gordon, Stan and Cooper, Vicki: 'The Kecksburg Incident', *California UFO*, Vol. 6, No. 1, January/February 1991, California UFO, 1536 S. Robertson Boulevard, Los Angeles, California 90035.

5 Scully, Frank: *Behind the Flying Saucers*, Henry Holt, New York, 1950, p. 137.

6 Letter to the author from Lieutenant Colonel Robert F. Bowker, USAF (Retd.), 22 November 1987.

7 Berlitz, Charles and Moore, William: op. cit., pp. 57–63.

8 Interviews with the author, January/March 1988.

9 Letter of recommendation from Lieutenant Colonel Jack J. Catton, USAF, Commanding, Headquarters Task Unit 7.4.1., 7 May 1948.

10 Interview with the author, 6 April 1990.

11 O'Brian, Mike: 'Noted Expert Finds Account Convincing', *The News-Leader*, Springfield, Missouri, 9 December 1990.

12 *Just Cause*, CAUS, P.O. Box 218, Coventry, Connecticut 06238.

13 *The Journal*, Alexandria, Virginia, 9 July 1987.

14 Letter to William Steinman from Dr Robert Sarbacher, Washington Institute of Technology, Palm Beach, Florida, 29 November 1983 (reproduced in *Above Top Secret*).

15 Good, Timothy: *Above Top Secret: The Worldwide UFO Cover-Up*, Sidgwick & Jackson, London, 1987, p. 393.

16 Ibid., pp. 410–11.

17 Summary Report, Fund for UFO Research Inc., P.O. Box 277, Mount Rainier, Maryland 20712, 19 September 1990.

18 Interviews with the author, December 1990.

19 Letter to the author, 27 June 1990.

20 Burrows, William E.: *Deep Black: The Secrets of Space Espionage*, Bantam Press, London, 1988, p. 190.

· 6 ·

Project Aquarius

In late 1972 film producers Robert Emenegger and Allan Sandler were considering various subjects for a documentary on defence-related programmes when they were approached by US Air Force officers who asked if they would be interested in making a documentary on a secret Government project. The producers were surprised to learn that the subject matter dealt with UFOs, since they had assumed that the matter had been resolved with the closure of Project Blue Book in 1969.

Having expressed serious interest, Emenegger and Sandler were invited to the Pentagon, where they met with a few high-ranking Air Force personnel, including Colonels William Coleman and George Weinbrenner, who had both been involved with Blue Book. The Air Force was now ready to release all the facts, the producers were told.

To their astonishment, Emenegger and Sandler were shown photographs and film not just of UFOs but grey-skinned alien beings – alive and dead. Bob Emenegger told me that he saw a 16 mm film of an alien in the company of an Air Force officer. The alien had supposedly survived a crash in 1949 and subsequently had been kept at a 'safe house' in Los Alamos, New Mexico, until his death of unknown causes in 1952.

In early 1973 Emenegger and Sandler were invited to Norton AFB, San Bernardino, California, where they met with the then head of the Air Force Office of Special Investigations (AFOSI) and Paul Shartle, former head of security and chief of requirements for the audiovisual programme at Norton. It was learned at this meeting that in April 1964 (or in May 1971, according to what Emenegger told me) a space-craft had landed at Holloman AFB, Alamogordo, New Mexico, by prior arrangement. Alien beings supposedly came out of the craft and communicated with a team of scientists and military officers. All this had been filmed, and Emenegger and Sandler were promised 800 feet of film for inclusion in their documentary, as well as several thousand feet of additional material.[1]

Emenegger told at least one investigator that he was allowed to take some of the film home, but denied this to me during one of our several conversations in Los Angeles. In any event, permission to use the film was suddenly withdrawn by Colonel Coleman. The timing was politi-cally inappropriate, it was explained, due to the Watergate scandal. However, permission was given to proceed with the documentary – *UFOs: It Has Begun* – on condition that the Holloman story was pre-sented only as a hypothetical case.

In Emenegger's 1974 book, *UFOs Past, Present & Future*, the Hollo-man incident is described as follows:

At about 5.30 a.m. on an unspecified date, the phone rang in the control room at Holloman AFB and 'Sergeant Mann' was informed that an unidentified aircraft was approaching the base. In the radar hut, several 'blips' appeared on the screen. 'I'll repeat again,' the radar operators announced. 'Unidentified approaching objects – on co-ordinate forty-niner – 34 degrees south-west following an erratic approach course.'

Back in the control tower the radio operator attempted to com-municate with the unknown aircraft. 'This is Holloman Air Force Base control tower. Identify yourself. You are encroaching on military airspace. Warning . . . What is your tail number? You are in a re-stricted military air corridor.'

There was no response. The base commander, 'Colonel Horner', issued orders for a red alert to be sounded and checks were made with Wright-Patterson AFB and Edwards AFB in an attempt to discover if there were any experimental aircraft in the vicinity. Two interceptor jets were sent up to escort the intruders out of the area.

By chance, cameramen, a technical sergeant and a staff sergeant of the base photographic team happened to be in an airborne base helicopter at the time, and took movie film of three strange objects as they approached Holloman. One of the objects broke away and began descending. Another photographic team, using high-speed cameras that had been set up to film a test launch, shot about 600 feet of 16 mm film as the craft came into land.

The object (shaped like a 'bathtub' in the real film, Emenegger told me) hovered about 10 feet off the ground, 'yawed' like a ship at anchor for nearly a minute, then landed on three extended legs. The base commander and two officers, as well as Air Force scientists, had by now arrived on the scene.

A panel in the side of the craft slid open and out stepped three 'men' dressed in tight-fitting jump suits, and described as 'perhaps short by our standards, with an odd blue-grey complexion, eyes set far apart. A large pronounced nose ...' (In conversation with Linda Howe, Emenegger recalled that the three aliens were 5 feet 2 inches in height, with eyes that had vertical pupils like those of a cat.[2]) They wore headpieces of what resembled 'rows of a rope-like design'.

The commander and two scientists stepped forward and communicated with the visitors, who appeared to be using some type of translation device. The group then retired to an inner office in the King 1 area before being led to the end of Mars Street to west area building No. 930.[3]

The Holloman scenario, as described in the book and documentary, is of course a reconstruction of the 'real' events, omitting and distorting certain allegedly factual details. But what about the actual Holloman film? It is tempting to dismiss this as a staged production, either for official training purposes or perhaps as part of an official public indoctrination programme. Yet there is now evidence that it could well be the 'real thing'.

Confirmation?

'What I saw and heard was enough to convince me that the phenomenon of UFOs is real – *very* real,' Bob Emenegger commented during the 1988 documentary, *UFO Cover-Up? Live*, a conviction he has reaffirmed to me.

In the same documentary, Paul Shartle also emphasized that the film seemed real enough:

> I saw footage of three disc-shaped crafts. One of the craft landed
> and two of them went away . . . It appeared to be in trouble because
> it oscillated all the way down to the ground. However, it did land
> on three pods. A sliding door opened, a ramp was extended, and
> out came three aliens . . . They were human size. They had odd
> grey complexions and a pronounced nose. They wore tight-fitting
> jump suits, thin head-dresses that appeared to be communication
> devices, and in their hands they held a translator, I was told. The
> Holloman base commander and other Air Force officers went out to
> meet them . . .

'I was told it was theatrical footage that the Air Force had purchased
to make a training film,' Shartle continued. '*It was too real* . . . If it were
a theatrical film, why didn't they have a record of this? It was my job
to keep accurate records of all audiovisual purchases . . .'[4]

While researching material for a projected documentary on UFOs
in April 1983, Linda Howe visited Kirtland AFB in Albuquerque and
interviewed Richard C. Doty, a counter-intelligence agent with the
Air Force Office of Special Investigations. Doty's military records
(provided for me by Victoria Lacas) do not tell the story of his covert
intelligence work, for obvious reasons, and it is probable that they
contain disinformation (it has even been suggested to me that his real
name is not Doty). He retired from the Air Force in the grade of
master sergeant in 1988, but was assigned to Retired Reserve for ten
years.

Linda was astonished when Doty confirmed the Holloman incident,
which had occurred on 25 April 1964 – not May 1971 – he insisted;
twelve hours after the famous UFO landing at Socorro, New Mexico,
witnessed by Deputy Marshal Lonnie Zamora.

The Socorro landing was a mistake, Doty claimed, explaining that
communications had been established but that either the aliens or our
own military personnel had mistaken the time and co-ordinates. 'We
got it corrected and they came back to where they were supposed to be
at Holloman the next morning at 6 a.m.', Doty said. Thus prepared
for the event, cameramen had taken film with five cameras, some from

airborne helicopters. One of three UFOs landed while the other two remained in the air as if for protection. Linda was told that the US Government returned some preserved dead bodies to the aliens and that 'something' was returned in exchange.

'I was to be given the film for inclusion in the [Home Box Office] documentary with support by official government confirmation,' Linda recalls. 'Doty said he would call me and use a code-name "Falcon". His call would be followed by others, including a "Tom". Arrangements would be made for me to screen all the footage on the east coast.'

As time passed, Linda grew worried. Doty phoned to say that release of the Holloman film had been delayed for 'political reasons', but that he had received the go-ahead for Linda to interview a colonel who, he claimed, would talk on camera about his contact with an 'Extraterrestrial Biological Entity' (EBE-1) who had survived a crash in 1949. Doty asked Linda to provide photographs of herself and the film crew, so that security clearances could be obtained. But it was to no avail. Appointments for the interview were repeatedly made, then cancelled, and the interview never took place.

The Presidential Briefing Papers

During the initial meeting at Kirtland AFB, which lasted three hours, Doty told Linda that he had been asked by his 'superiors' to show her a certain document, but that she was not allowed to make a copy or take notes. 'I took the papers and read the top page,' she describes. 'It was entitled "Briefing for the President of the United States of America" on the subject of unidentified and identified aerial craft or vehicles. I don't remember a president's name or date.'

The document included brief information on a number of UFO crashes that had happened in the US. The 'Extraterrestrial Biological Entities' were allegedly taken to various secure Government facilities, such as Los Alamos National Laboratory, New Mexico (in a facility designated YY-11, some claim), and Wright-Patterson AFB, Ohio. The bodies were grey in colour, between 3 to 4.5 feet tall, with long arms, four long fingers, claw-like nails and webbing between the fingers. Instead of a nose and ears, there were only holes, Linda remembers reading.

Following a crash near Roswell, New Mexico, in 1949 (not to be confused, apparently, with those in 1947), six aliens had been recovered, one of whom survived. An Air Force officer, later promoted to colonel (the one with whom Linda had been promised an interview), established communications with the creature (EBE-1) at Los Alamos until its death, of unknown causes, on 18 June 1952. Later, contact was established with other beings (EBE-2 and EBE-3). EBE-3 was allegedly living in secret at a certain base. It was learned that the alien civilization originated from a planet in a binary star system about fifty-five light years from Earth, and that we had been visited for at least 25,000 years.

Doty told Linda that there was a group called MJ-12 – 'MJ' meaning 'Majority', he claimed – whose function was to act as a policy-making committee, and whose twelve members comprised high-ranking scientists, military and intelligence personnel.

The briefing paper also listed a number of US Government projects that had been established in order to study the alien question. These included Project Garnet, which had studied (and apparently resolved) all questions relating to the evolution of mankind; Project Sigma, an ongoing project, initiated in 1964 (presumably following the Holloman landing), dealing with alien communication; Project Snowbird, a continuing research effort into the development and implementation of alien spacecraft technology; and Project Aquarius, an overall project devoted to the accumulation of all available information about alien life-forms.

Linda recalls that the briefing paper alluded briefly to another alien group, referred to as the 'Talls', which she believes are the more human-type species frequently reported. Pressed for further information, Doty explained that there was some kind of 'friction' between the small grey species and the taller ones. 'They tolerate each other', was his only comment.

According to the paper, the aliens have on various occasions manipulated DNA in terrestrial primates – and perhaps in other species as well. 'To the best of my memory,' Linda recalls, 'the time intervals for this DNA manipulation specifically listed in the briefing paper were 25,000, 15,000 and 2,500 years ago.'

One paragraph, Linda recalls, mentioned that 2,000 years ago the aliens had created a being who was placed on Earth to teach mankind about love and non-violence.[5]

In a letter to researcher Barry Greenwood, Doty admitted to the meeting with Linda (which, he said, was 'monitored' by his 'supervisor') to discuss material for her projected documentary, but denied having shown her the briefing paper or promising any film material:

> . . . I can tell you, without a doubt, that I never showed her any such document. First of all, I was not in a position to obtain any presidential briefing documents. Secondly, I would not allow a person without a security clearance to see any such document . . . I do not recall mentioning any Government plans to release documents or film to Ms. Howe for her documentary. I would not have been in a position to authorize or even discuss such a release . . . Finally, I know of no secret Government investigation of UFOs . . .[6]

Linda subsequently signed a notarized declaration testifying that Doty did indeed show her the document, and in our many conversations on the matter she has left me in no doubt who is telling the truth about the Kirtland AFB meeting. But we are agreed that this does not necessarily validate the information given by Doty or seen in the briefing paper. Doty was a counter-intelligence specialist, and it is my opinion that Linda was fed disinformation – along with *some* factual information – as had been done with Paul Bennewitz. But for what purpose?

At the beginning of the interview at Kirtland, Doty made an interesting comment regarding Linda's documentary on the animal mutilations, which may shed light on the reason. 'You know,' he said, 'you upset people in Washington with your film *A Strange Harvest*. It came too close to something we don't want the public to know about.' (Yet Emenegger's documentary – which presumably was officially vetted – included extensive material on the UFO/mutilations link.) Pressed for further information on the mutilations, Doty (who held a Top Secret clearance) remarked that the subject was classified beyond his 'need to know'.[7] Was there a determination on the part of AFOSI and others to ensure that Linda's next documentary never got off the ground? If so, the plan succeeded.

In 1983, only weeks before Linda's meeting at Kirtland AFB, researcher William Moore, who has developed a number of high-level contacts in the US Intelligence Community since 1978 (including Richard Doty), received a phone call telling him that some information was to be made available to him but that he would have to go and collect it in person. 'You will be receiving some instructions,' the caller said. 'You must follow them carefully or the deal is off.'

The instructions were convoluted, involving directions given on the phone at various airports as Bill made his way across the United States from Arizona. At the final destination, a motel in upstate New York, Bill was instructed to be ready at 5 p.m. At precisely that time, an individual came to the door carrying a sealed brown envelope. 'You have exactly nineteen minutes,' the man said. 'You may do whatever you wish with this material during that time, but at the end of that time, I must have it back. After that, you are free to do what you wish.'

Inside the envelope were eleven pages of what purported to be a 'TOP SECRET/ORCON' document, entitled 'Executive Briefing. Subject: Project Aquarius', and dated 14 June 1977 (i.e. during the Carter Administration). Bill asked if he could photograph the document and read its contents into a tape recorder. 'Both are permitted,' replied the courier. 'You have seventeen minutes remaining.'

Bill adjusted the table lampshade and photographed each page, placing a 25-cent piece on the lower left corner of each page for scale, then read the text (including punctuation marks) into his pocket tape recorder, in case the photos did not come out well. (The pictures did come out, but unfortunately all are of low contrast and some are out of focus.) When the prescribed time had elapsed, the courier collected and counted the pages, then replaced them in the original envelope.

The document appears to be a transcription of notes, either intended for use in preparing a briefing for President Carter or taken down during one and typed later. Bill is inclined to the view that it contains some important elements of truth, but that it was probably shown to him for purposes of disinformation. With this in mind, let us examine a few short extracts. The portions marked thus '–' have been censored by Bill and his colleague Jaime Shandera, pending further research.

From page 1:

TOP SECRET
PROJECT AQUARIUS

(TS/ORCON) (PROWORD: –) Contains 16 volumes of documented information collected from the beginning of the United States Investigation of Unidentified Flying Objects (UFOs) and Identified Alien Crafts (IAC). The Project was originally established in 1953, by order of President Eisenhower, under control of – and MJ12. In 19–, the Project's name was changed from Project – to Project Aquarius. The Project was funded by – confidential funds (non-appropriated). The Project – Dec 1969 after Project Blue Book was closed. The purpose of Project Aquarius was to collect all scientific, technological, medical and inteligence [sic] information from UFO/IAC sightings and contacts with alien life forms. This orderly file of collected information has been used to advance the United States Space Program.

From page 9:

TOP SECRET
SUB PROJECTS UNDER –

1. (TS/ORCON) PROJECT – : (PROWORD: –). Originally established in 19–. Its mission was to collect and evaluate – . This Project – provided United States – researchers with certain answers to – . (OPR: –) Terminated in 19–.

2. (TS/ORCON) PROJECT SIGMA: (PROWORD: –). Originally established as part of Project – in 1954. Became a separate project in 1976. Its mission was to establish communication with Aliens. This project met with positive success when in 1959, the United States established primitive communications with the Aliens. On April 25, 1964, a USAF intelligence officer met two Aliens at a prearranged location in the desert of New Mexico. The contact lasted for approximately three hours. Based on the Alien's language given to us by – , the Air Force officer managed to exchange basic information with the two Aliens (Atch 7). This project

is continuing at an Air Force base in New Mexico. (OPR: –)

3. (TS/ORCON) PROJECT SNOWBIRD: (PROWORD: –). Originally established in 19–. Its mission was to test fly a recovered Alien aircraft. This project is continuing in Nevade [sic]. (OPR: –)

4. (TS/ORCON) PROJECT POUNCE: (PROWORD: –). Originally established in 19–. Its mission was to evaluate all UFO – information pertaining to space technology. PROJECT POUNCE continues. (OPR: –)

In *Above Top Secret*, I alluded briefly to the Carter document, mentioning that efforts to identify the projects listed therein had met with a limited degree of success, and citing a letter from the National Security Agency to an enquirer which confirmed the existence of Projects Aquarius, Sigma and Snowbird. The NSA acknowledged that it had a Project Aquarius, not related to UFOs, and requested a $15,000 search fee for records pertaining to the project! Later, when the enquirer had narrowed down his FOIA request, the NSA's Director of Policy replied that a document they had located 'is classified because its disclosure could reasonably be expected to cause exceptionally grave damage to the national security [and] no portion of the information is reasonably segregable.'

In fact, several projects named Aquarius have now been identified, although considerable confusion surrounds their purpose. In 1982, Bill Moore learned from one of his sources ('Seagull') that a Project Aquarius exists within 'Control Channel Baker' (i.e. a 'black' project, the existence of which is officially denied) and is classified above Top Secret. This particular project allegedly comes partly under the Naval Intelligence Support Center at Suitland, Maryland, and also under a branch of the Defense Intelligence Agency (see p. 115).

Although never officially carried into effect, there was a Project Pounce which was definitely UFO-related in that it was proposed by the Sandia Laboratories at Kirtland AFB in 1953 in connection with the 'green fireballs' which had been reported since the late 1940s,[8] but it is unlikely that it relates to the project referred to in the briefing paper since the date (deleted) is more than a decade after 1953.

Both Projects Snowbird and Sigma have been officially identified as having nothing to do with UFOs (Sigma involves a laser weapons project), but that does not necessarily rule out the possibility that other projects with the same name could be UFO-related, or that a branch of the official project houses a UFO research programme. Bill Moore and Jaime Shandera (a Hollywood film producer who is also in contact with highly placed individuals in the Intelligence Community) feel that there may well be a Project Snowbird to test-fly alien craft in Nevada. 'Information which has been accumulated on this matter to date *suggests* but does not prove that such a project exists,' they believe.

'ORCON', Bill has learned, means 'Dissemination and Extraction of Information Controlled by Originator', and is used mainly by the CIA, DIA, NSA and USAF intelligence. 'OPR' is an acronym for 'Office of Primary Responsibility', and the use of 'prowords' is the correct form for documents pertaining to Sensitive Compartmented Information (SCI). (There is also reported to be a category known as ESI – Extremely Sensitive Information.)

Bill and Jaime remain sceptical of the alleged Carter briefing paper, pointing out, for example, that it has a generally sloppy appearance and contains misspellings; hardly likely, therefore, to have been used for a presidential briefing. But they remain open to the probability that some truth is contained therein.[9]

Irrespective of the document's authenticity, Bill Moore told me that the individual who showed it to him got into trouble, and Bill himself was the subject of an FBI investigation; an investigation which intensified following the release of the alleged MJ-12 briefing document for President-elect Eisenhower. Of sixty-one pages relating to that investigation, only six have been released by the FBI, the remainder being exempt from disclosure.

Above Top Secret

In conversations with lawyer Peter Gersten in 1983, Richard Doty claimed to have been briefed on the UFO subject with briefing papers similar to those used for presidents-elect,[10] which, if true, suggests that he must have held a security clearance higher than the Top Secret clearance he undoubtedly held. Is it remotely possible that the document he showed Linda Howe – which seems to have been similar if not identical to the Carter briefing paper shown to Bill Moore by another source – was the 'real thing', and that there was a genuine desire on the part of the Intelligence Community at that time to introduce the public to some authentic material, just as there seems to have been in 1973, but that on each occasion the plug was pulled out – ostensibly for political reasons?

There is no question, after all, that Senator Barry Goldwater was informed many years ago by General Curtis LeMay, a former Air Force chief of staff and head of Strategic Air Command, that a plan existed to release information on UFOs to the public. As Goldwater remarked in a letter in 1975:

> . . . About ten or twelve years ago I made an effort to find out what was in the building at Wright-Patterson Air Force Base where the information is stored that has been collected by the Air Force, and I was understandably denied this request. It is still classified above Top Secret. I have, however, heard that there is a plan under way to release some, if not all, of this material in the near future . . .[11]

Although there have been no sensational revelations of an official nature to date, a great deal of long-denied information has now been released by the US Intelligence Community under provisions of the Freedom of Information Act. Thousands of pages of reports dealing with UFOs have been and are continuing to be released by agencies such as the CIA, DIA, FBI, NSA, and the Air Force, Army, and Naval intelligence branches. Even though the most sensitive reports are being withheld in the interests of national security, it is clear that Senator Goldwater was correctly informed.

Operation Majestic 12

In *Above Top Secret*, I took the risk of publishing an extraordinary document which purports to be a preliminary briefing paper prepared in 1952 for President-elect Eisenhower by former CIA director Vice Admiral Roscoe Hillenkoetter. The document, classified Top Secret/Majic/Eyes Only, summarized what the so-called 'Majestic 12' committee – established by President Truman in 1947 – had learned about the UFO problem up to that time, and included information on the 1947 Roswell crash and the subsequent recovery of four dead alien bodies. From an historical perspective, much information which suggests that the document could be authentic has now been uncovered, notably by scientist Stanton Friedman, who devoted a number of years to the project with the aid of a $16,000 grant from the Fund for UFO Research.[12]

My copy of the document was sent to me by an intelligence source in the United States in March 1987, specifically for inclusion in *Above Top Secret*. I published the document in the conviction that it was probably authentic. However, some valid objections have now been raised, including the fact that the signature on the memo from President Truman to MJ-12 member James Forrestal (dated 24 September 1947 and authorizing 'Operation Majestic Twelve') is practically identical to a known-to-be-authentic signature on a Truman memo to Dr Vannevar Bush, dated 1 October 1947. Although Stanton Friedman argues that there are some differences in length and ratio (which indeed there are), such differences could easily have been effected by a skilled forger. Furthermore, in the examples of Truman's signature that I have seen, the signature almost invariably overlaps the typed text, which is not the case with the Truman/Forrestal MJ-12 memo.

I do not propose to get bogged down in the pros and cons of the MJ-12 controversy in this book: those interested should read Stanton Friedman's painstaking report, which I have edited in *The UFO Report 1991*, or avail themselves of the full report by contacting Mr Friedman. Readers should also obtain the exhaustive study by William Moore and Jaime Shandera, including the results of their research into typefaces and security markings, and, for a balanced perspective, the papers by Barry Greenwood, Robert Hastings, Philip J. Klass, Joe Nickell and John Fischer, which I have listed in the references.[13]

Suffice it to say, for the time being, that even if the entire MJ-12 document turns out to be fraudulent, I am convinced that the information contained therein, at least, is *essentially* factual. Moreover, I have learned from other sources that there is (or was) an above Top Secret Majestic 12 committee dealing with UFOs, as will be revealed.

It is perhaps significant that the MJ-12 document was first received anonymously in the post in December 1984 by Jaime Shandera, and that the envelope was postmarked 'Albuquerque, New Mexico'. This has led many critics to assume that Richard Doty was the sender, particularly since he showed Linda Howe a similar document in 1983 – at Kirtland AFB in Albuquerque. Doty has personally denied this, not surprisingly, and has hinted that the MJ-12 document was 'originated' by a source in the Defense Intelligence Agency and was sent with the purpose of discrediting both Jaime and Bill Moore. Perhaps there is some truth to this scenario. Although the Albuquerque postmark does not necessarily mean that the MJ-12 document originated there, Bill Moore claims to have developed a number of intelligence contacts in the Albuquerque area (including 'Falcon') and has readily admitted to me the possibility that he (and Shandera) may have been fed false information.

Bill and Jaime have contact with about twelve highly placed individuals within the Intelligence Community, all of whom have been allocated code-names of birds. During the *UFO Cover-Up? Live* documentary, two such agents – 'Condor' and 'Falcon', with their faces blacked out and voices electronically modulated – came out with some sensational information – or disinformation, as the case may be. Among various topics, the agents confirmed the existence of MJ-12.

Established by President Truman, Falcon claimed, much of MJ-12's function entailed keeping track of all information pertaining to UFOs. 'MJ-12 functions as a policy-making group relating to extra-terrestrial activities and contacts and UFO activities within the United States,' Falcon began. 'They make the policy, obtain presidential approval, and then . . . implement the policies . . . Part of their job was scientific advancements, but their primary purpose was to keep track of the information coming in on UFOs, and to analyze the information both scientifically and in a way that would advance our technology.'

Falcon went on to explain that various Government officials and elected officials were aware of the MJ-12 programme. 'These officals include the President, the Vice-President, as elected officials; the Director of Central Intelligence; and the Director of the National Security Agency,' he said. MJ-12 headquarters were situated at the Naval Observatory in Washington, DC, he claimed. 'The United

Above: The Laguna Cartagena area, Cabo Rojo, Puerto Rico, where many strange events are reported to have occurred, including the disappearance of U.S. aircraft. (© *Timothy Good*)

Right: Drawing by Jeffrey Acosta, one of the witnesses to the incident over the Cabo Rojo area of Puerto Rico on 28 December 1988, when two U.S. Navy jets were apparently 'abducted' by a large, unknown aerial craft. (© *Enigma!*)

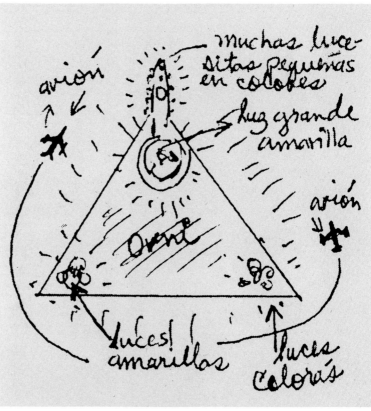

Above: 23 July 1989, Wayan, Idaho. Rancher Steve Somsen with a mutilated cow, from which the teats and part of the jaw had been excised with immaculate precision. (© *Ellen Carney/Idaho State Journal*)

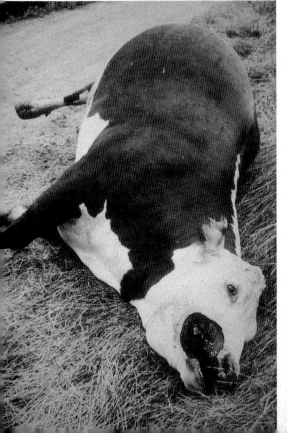

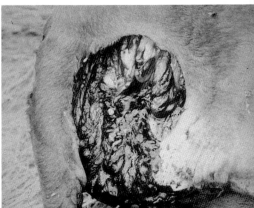

Above: Sergeant Melvin 'Brownie' Brown (left) on retirement from the U.S. Air Force, at RAF/USAF Chicksands Priory in 1964. Brown claimed to have been involved in a recovery operation in the New Mexico desert in July 1947, and his description of the alien bodies is remarkably similar to the photo below. (*U.S. Air Force*)

Right: Model of an alleged alien corpse in a zippered body-bag, from the New Mexico recovery in July 1947. The photo was in the possession of the late Dr Felix Zigel of the Moscow Aviation Institute, and has been acquired by Dr Marina Popovich, a former colonel with the Soviet Air Force.

Far left: 17 July 1989, Maple Valley, Washington. Six-year-old pregnant cow owned by Bill Veenhuizen, with oval excision of mouth and jaw tissue, teeth, tongue, vagina and rectum. (© *William Veenhuizen*)

Above left: Excision of rectum and vaginal tissue from Bill Veenhuizen's cow. (© *William Veenhuizen*)

Below left: 27 November 1989, Red Cloud, Nebraska. Excision across cow abdomen and removal of belly hide, udder, vagina, rectum, and internal organs. (© *Ron Bartels*)

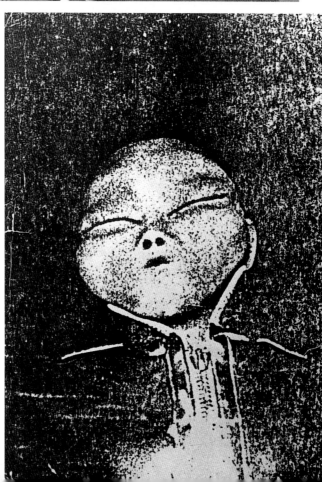

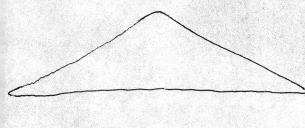

Above: Colonel William Coleman, who chased a UFO at low level above Alabama in 1955, flying in a B-25 Mitchell medium bomber. Years later, when Coleman worked with the U.S. Air Force's Project Blue Book he was unable to obtain the file on his report, and now admits that UFO reports affecting national security were not filed with Blue Book. (© *Timothy Good*)

Top left: A B-25 Mitchell medium bomber, similar to the type flown by Colonel Coleman and his crew. (© *Timothy Good*)

Above: Colonel Coleman's sketch of the side view of the UFO. (*William Coleman*)

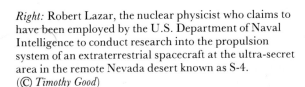

Right: Robert Lazar, the nuclear physicist who claims to have been employed by the U.S. Department of Naval Intelligence to conduct research into the propulsion system of an extraterrestrial spacecraft at the ultra-secret area in the remote Nevada desert known as S-4. (© *Timothy Good*)

Right: A 1968 satellite photo of Groom Dry Lake/Area 51, Nevada. S-4, where Robert Lazar worked, is located about ten miles south of this position, close to Papoose Dry Lake. (*U.S. Department of the Interior Geological Survey, Eros Data Center*)

Below and bottom: A rare photo of part of the Groom Lake/Area 51 complex, looking west, taken in 1978. In the enlargement below, a Soviet-built MiG-21 of the USAF's secret 4477th Test & Evaluation Squadron can just be seen, parked outside the central hangar at the north end of the facility. (© *John Lear*)

Above: The EG&G building at McCarran International Airport, Las Vegas, where Robert Lazar was interviewed for the job at S-4. (© *Timothy Good*)

Above left: A Boeing 737 of the Department of Energy, parked at McCarran Airport, one of several such aircraft that are used to fly employees to Groom Lake. (© *Timothy Good*)

Left: A bus with blacked-out windows in the Nevada desert (1986), similar to the type used to take scientists and security personnel from Groom Lake to S-4. (© *Timothy Good*)

Below: This photograph was taken in 1986 from the dirt road that leads to Area 51 ('Dreamland'), located behind the distant mountains. (© *Timothy Good*)

above: Dr Edward Teller, 'the father of the hydrogen bomb', responding in a private interview in 1990 to questions regarding his alleged recommendation of Robert Lazar for a job with the ultra-secret extraterrestrial research project at S-4.

above right: Robert Lazar in a private interview with George Knapp of KLAS-TV, Las Vegas, in 1989. (*KLAS-TV*)

right: Bob Lazar in court, August 1990. (*KLAS-TV*)

below: Sketch by Robert Lazar of the extraterrestrial craft he claims to have worked on at S-4. (*KLAS-TV*)

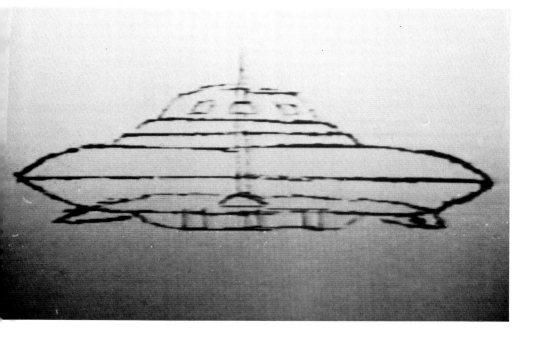

Above: Robert Oechsler, the former NASA engineer whose contacts with the U.S. Intelligence Community and the Cosmic Journey Project have led to a wealth of sensational information. (© *Timothy Good*)

Below: The National Security Agency's supercomputer facility for the Institute for Defense Analysis at the University of Maryland Science and Technology Center, where Bob Oechsler met Admiral Inman during the ground-breaking ceremony in May 1988. (© *Timothy Good*)

Above: Admiral Bobby Ray Inman, the former Director of the National Security Agency and Naval Intelligence, from whom Bob Oechsler obtained guidance on the acquisition of sensitive, information relating to extraterrestrial craft in possession of the United States Government. (© *Associated Press/Topham*)

States Navy has the primary operational responsibilities of field activities relating to MJ-12 policies. All information gathered in the field — not necessarily by Navy personnel — is transmitted to the Navy for analysis.'

The extent of alleged covert involvement by the US Navy is a subject I shall be returning to later. The dearth over the years of UFO-related documents released by the Navy under the FOIA has misled researchers into assuming that there has been little or no involvement. As we shall learn, this is far from being true.

Bill and Jaime, commenting on Falcon's disclosures, added that other Government agencies fed information to MJ-12 through a Top Secret cover project – Project Aquarius. 'MJ-12 connects selected individuals within the National Security Council, the Joint Chiefs of Staff, the White House intelligence unit, the National Security Agency, the Central Intelligence Agency, and the Defense Intelligence Agency,' Jaime reported. 'The research is conducted, the data classified and catalogued, all under the umbrella of strictest national security.'

In *Above Top Secret* I wrote a chapter on the involvement of the Defense Intelligence Agency in UFO investigations, based on information released under provisions of the FOIA. Further information has subsequently come to light which is of relevance to MJ-12 and Project Aquarius. One of the functions of Aquarius, Falcon claimed, was to act as a sort of communications umbrella through which various interested parties could pass and receive data, without revealing specifics about themselves in the process. At the apex of the umbrella was the MJ-12 group.

Some years ago Bill Moore learned of the existence of a special interest group within the DIA which comprised two distinct branches feeding data to Project Aquarius. One was lodged at the DIA's imagery division (DC5C) and operated from the Melpar Building in Falls Church, Virginia, with an additional presence at the Digital Imagery Processing Service (DIPS) in the Naval Intelligence Support Center (NISC), Suitland, Maryland. 'The group oversaw a small "black" budget appropriation and need-to-know access was maintained by probably not more than a dozen individuals at any given time,' Bill reports. 'Over a space of several years, I only ever heard three names of people reportedly associated with it. These were Colonel R. "Donny" Phillips, perhaps the leader of the group; Master Sergeant Theodore Zahrodney, who I understood did some of their field work; and John W. Westerman, an imagery specialist reputed to be DC5C's liaison with Aquarius ... I have been led to understand since then that the group, now referred to as a "working committee", underwent something of a reorganization in the latter part of 1986, and as far as I know, it continues to function. One of the results of that reorganization was the establishment of a computerized database and communications net known, curiously enough, as "MJ-SETI".[14]

In *Out There*, journalist Howard Blum identifies a 'Colonel Harold E. Phillips' of the DIA as being involved with a 'UFO Working Group' established in 1987, and claims that a 'Project Aquarius' was supervised by the DIA's Directorate for Management and Operations. Discussing the FBI's classified investigation into the authenticity of the MJ-12 document, Blum reveals that the FBI had supposedly looked into the possibility that the working group was 'responsible' for the document, but that this had been denied by the group. An FBI agent in Los Angeles expressed the agency's frustration at failing to find the source of the documents. 'We've gone knocking on every door in Washington with those MJ-12 papers,' he allegedly told Blum. 'All we're finding out is that the Government doesn't know what it knows. There are too many secret levels. You can't get a straight story. It wouldn't surprise me if we never knew if the papers were genuine or not.'[15]

I have to add that there are factual errors in Blum's book which do not inspire confidence in the reliability of his reporting, and the 'UFO Working Group', in the sense that he describes it as a top secret group established in 1987 to determine if there is life 'out there', seems unlikely to me, in view of all the accumulated evidence indicating that such a determination was made in 1947.

Falcon and Condor

Having checked and verified Falcon's credentials, Jaime and Bill are satisfied that the intelligence agent is indeed highly placed, with access to the MJ-12 infrastructure, and that his disclosures are officially sanctioned. Peter Leon, an executive producer for a Los Angeles TV station, has also met Falcon. 'I'm satisfied at this time that he is who he says he is,' he confirmed during the documentary. But who is Falcon?

It will be recalled that Special Agent Richard Doty used the code-name 'Falcon' when liaising with Linda Howe. Bill and Jaime insist that Doty's code-name is 'Sparrow', and that Doty acted as the go-between in arranging meetings with the real Falcon. Doty, too, denies the charge. 'I am not the person code-named "Falcon",' he wrote in 1989 to Robert Hastings, a researcher from Albuquerque. 'I have underwent [sic] two extensive Government investigations regarding this claim. I have been exonerated by the Government on both occasions. My name was connected with Falcon to cover up the true identity of Falcon. However, the Government knows the true identity of Falcon and that person (employed in Washington by DIA) is presently under investigation.'[16]

Michael Seligman, producer of *UFO Cover-Up? Live*, quite properly refused to break his promise by revealing the identity of Falcon to me when I questioned him in 1990. But co-producer Curt Brubaker told me without any hesitation (although he never met him) that Doty is indeed Falcon.

As to the identity of Condor, veteran researcher Leonard Stringfield claims to have been contacted by him several times in 1985, while Condor was stationed at Wright-Patterson AFB. 'Expressing interest in my research and sources, he claimed to know a colonel with sensitive information relative to my work,' Len reports, 'but his proposal for me to meet with this source fell through and I heard no more. Later I learned that he confided with a member of the Fund for UFO Research and after that with Bill Moore etc.'[17]

Robert Hastings is confident that Condor is Robert M. Collins, a former USAF captain who was assigned to the Plasma Physics group at Sandia National Laboratories, Kirtland AFB, until his retirement in 1988.[18] Significantly, Collins was actively involved in the promotion of *UFO Cover-Up? Live*. Although Michael Seligman refuses to disclose the identity of Condor, he nevertheless confirmed that he is a bona fide scientist. 'I know where he was working and did check that out,' Seligman told me. 'He was very credible, and I really believed everything he told me.'

Interestingly, Michael Seligman also informed me that it was evident from the way that Condor and Falcon were 'testing' each other that they had not met before.[19]

Project Blue Book

Interviewed on Seligman's documentary, Condor revealed that Project Blue Book was merely a low-level effort by the Air Force to gather information, with a minimal staff of one officer, an NCO, a secretary, and a scientist. 'The interesting and most exciting reports that came into Blue Book were often syphoned off by moles within the [MJ-12] organization. Those reports were pulled out of the files and never returned, and just simply sent forward . . . The effort of Blue Book was to minimize the effects of these reports and to try and explain away as many as they could. And of course, it worked [in that] it closed down Project Blue Book and terminated official Air Force involvement.'

Colonel William Coleman, who had served with Project Blue Book and had been an Air Force spokesman at the Pentagon, allowed me to interview him in Florida in 1989 regarding his own report of a UFO sighting which subsequently 'disappeared' from Blue Book files. The incident occurred in the summer of 1955 when Coleman was flying a B-25 Mitchell bomber from Miami, Florida, to Greenwood, Mississippi. Together with the rest of the crew, Coleman sighted an unidentified object in the sky, and eventually gave chase over Alabama.

'Finally, we were down about 200 feet off the ground, just going across the treetops,' he told me. 'I mean, in that section of Alabama, there is *nothing*. We crossed one farm and one highway . . . there wasn't a vehicle in sight. We saw no people. The only thing we saw was animals, which got disturbed – naturally, they would be, with that B-25! We were within an eighth of a mile of it, and there was this perfect round shadow of this thing, going over the treetops!'

Coleman and his crew lost sight of the object during a manoeuvre, so climbed to 1,500 feet to try and find it. Nothing could be seen at first. 'Then I looked over into a big field, freshly ploughed – southern Alabama has a clay-type loam, and it was very dry – and I saw it. It was going across this ploughed field, right on the deck. What made me notice it was that it was leaving twin vortices of this red dust swirling up.' Coleman immediately descended to a lower altitude to give chase, but at this stage only the trail could be seen. 'The trail continued all the way across the field. We made several turns out there, but never saw it.'

As the B-25 began its descent into Greenwood, the object was seen briefly, moving at speed without any contrail at 25,000 feet. On landing, the crew submitted independent reports of what they had seen. Some time later, when Coleman was about to be assigned to Project Blue Book, he asked Colonel Robert Friend to look up his report in the files. It was nowhere to be found, so another search was made. 'But it was not there, and there was no record that it had ever arrived there,' Coleman told me.

'You are aware,' I asked, 'that those UFO reports affecting national security were re-routed?'

'Yes,' he replied. 'I'm damn aware of that. Certainly.'[20]

In an interview with Jaime Shandera, Falcon described how MJ-12 decided towards the end of the 1960s that Project Blue Book had served its purpose and was to be discontinued:

'[MJ-12] were afraid at the time that if they continued with Project Blue Book, some of the information – some of the guarded secrets that the Americans obtained from the investigations of UFOs – would get out into the public, so they decided to end Project Blue Book. And they did that with an investigation by the University of Colorado – the so-called Condon Report – which basically stated that there wasn't anything to the sightings; that there were some unexplained, but basically everything was explained . . . The Government had decided to go underground with the investigation and that's when it was transferred from Blue Book by the US Air Force to another intelligence agency, which started a domestic investigation of UFOs in the United States.'

Covert Investigations

'We are continuing the investigation of UFO sightings and landings in an official capacity, sanctioned by the Government, but clandestinely, without the knowledge of the public, and, I must say, without the knowledge of a lot of other Government agencies,' Falcon continued, and went on to explain that the United States could ill afford to risk losing technological data that had been obtained from the sightings and landings, 'and the information that we have obtained independently from alien crafts'.

Another chief concern was fear of public reaction. 'In some ways,' commented Falcon, 'the United States is afraid that the public would panic if they knew the real story – the whole story.'

'But couldn't the Government just admit that this is a legitimate classified area of information?' asked Jaime.

'Because of our democratic society,' replied Falcon, 'everyone has a right to freedom of information, except for what's exempted under certain paragraphs of Title 5, US Code. But the public would continue to ask for information, continue to pry into the investigations, and eventually they would harm the process that the Government has taken to obtain the information from the aliens.'

Asked how the covert investigations were carried out, Falcon replied that the process was the same as that of an intelligence operation, involving the recruitment of various 'co-operating individuals', in much the same manner that an intelligence officer would recruit an agent of a foreign country. 'When they gave us information [on] a sighting or landing, then we would either use them or ourselves in a cover capacity, or identify ourselves as some other person, to investigate that sighting. We've used newspaper personnel, wittingly and unwittingly, and we've used scientists, or we have posed as scientists.'

The collected information is then passed to Washington, DC. 'It would go through the Director of Central Intelligence, who is of course the Director of the Central Intelligence Agency, but he is also the director of all the intelligence agencies within the United States Government. And then from there it's filtered to the appropriate individual for analysis and filing . . . If the information contained actual sightings and contacts, that's normally classified at a level of Top Secret that is specially compartmented.'

According to a source who worked for the Joint Chiefs of Staff's office at the Pentagon's National Military Command Center (NMCC), a secret, centralized command structure dealing with

UFOs has been in operation since the mid-to-late 1970s and continues to handle the UFO situation from the ranks of the NMCC, the level at which the Joint Chiefs of Staff, in conjunction with the White House 'war room', deploy US military forces worldwide. The UFO situation is apparently considered so serious that it warrants a 'consolidated oversight mechanism and planning force, on a par with management for global conflict'.[21]

How did Falcon feel about deceiving the public? 'Well, sometimes when you deceive the public, you're protecting the public,' he responded. 'And I would certainly protect the public in deception operations if it was for their own good. But some aspects of these UFO investigations that have occurred over the years have no reason to be withheld from the public. The general knowledge that there were aliens that landed on Earth back in the Fifties, late Forties, and that we have had some type of communication with them since, shouldn't be kept from the public.'

'You've said that one of the reasons the Government is conducting these ongoing investigations in a covert manner is their concern about the public reaction to this,' said Jaime, 'yet we've had a great number of science fiction movies that really address some of these critical key questions right now. In view of that, are we getting closer to the point where the Government is going to say, "We've been doing this, we want to come clean about it"?'

'I think, since the early 1950s, the first movie that I can remember about the subject, *The Day the Earth Stood Still*, until the most recent movie, *E.T.*, the United States Government is conditioning the public into just determining their reaction to aliens and the subject of extra-terrestrials. The Government wants to know how the people would react, and I believe that this information — or the Government believes that if this information is released over a period of time, the public would readily accept it more than they would if it was all shoved out at one time,' Falcon explained.

The EBEs

If Falcon and Condor are telling the truth, it is a safe assumption that they are principal collaborators in the Government's plan to release the facts gradually to the public. Disinformation is involved in this plan, of course, but there may well be good reasons for it. Supposing the facts are unpalatable; that some aliens are hostile, for example, and that we have no control over the situation? We can hardly expect our leaders to acknowledge openly such a scenario. Instead, would it not be easier to soften up the public by promoting the concept of co-operative little aliens with whom we have managed to establish friendly communications, but occasionally hinting that we are not in complete control?

With this in mind, let us examine the most controversial disclosures by Condor and Falcon: the alleged contact with 'Extraterrestrial Biological Entities' or 'EBEs', as revealed in the documentary and in additional interviews with Jaime Shandera and Bill Moore. Much of the information, it will be noted, is similar to that given and shown to Linda Howe by Richard Doty in 1983.

Falcon claims to have acquired most of his information about the EBEs from first-hand descriptions as well as films and photographs, but on one occasion he was shown an alien craft. 'It was in a security area,' he told Jaime and Bill. 'Even with a security clearance as high as I have, I did not have access to that, to the close proximity of it, but I was observing it from a distance. It was up on a platform. It was circular-shaped [and] had an opening on one side and had a battery of lights on the top. I was within maybe 150 yards of it.'

'Was there any indication of weapons on board?'

'No – not to the best of my knowledge. There was a – I should say the aliens have a defensive system but it's not an offensive weapon; it's a defensive system that would cause an electrical interference to any incoming rockets or missiles.'

'Has there ever been any indication that the aliens could be dangerous to mankind?'

'Earlier, in the Fifties, there had been some jets [that] chased aliens. The jets crashed, and there's reason to believe that it wasn't anything intentional on the part of the aliens, [who] were probably just as mystified as we were, and that they therefore made some type of defensive gesture which caused our aircraft to be destroyed.'

Falcon was shown a film of an alien that was supposedly 'exchanged' sometime in the 1970s. 'I don't know the exact date,' he said, 'but I saw a videotape of an interview being done by an Air Force colonel. It was shown to a group of us in Washington, DC.' The film showed an exchange of information with a particular alien given the name 'EBE-2' (EBE-1 having been the first to arrive in 1949). EBE-2, claimed Falcon, 'voluntarily came over to be examined and spoken with' for this purpose. But how was communication initially established with EBE-1?

'It took a year or so before the military intelligence personnel were able to communicate with him,' Falcon explained. 'But once they did communicate with him, he told them the basics of his knowledge of his planet's exploration of Earth. His knowledge wasn't totally complete, because he was basically a mechanic . . . I wouldn't say he knew it all, and I think that was the consensus of the intelligence personnel who were investigating and interviewing him.'

'And what planet did he come from?' asked Jaime.

'He was in the Zeta Reticuli star group – the third planet – and it had a binary sun [system] – two suns together.'

'Just how did they exchange information?'

'In 1951 or '52, sometime after the alien was recovered, this doctor devised a way of planting a device in the throat of this alien in order for him to speak words,' Falcon explained. 'He learned the English language, I'm told, very rapidly . . . Although it was not always recognizable, you could most of the time understand the words he was speaking.'

The EBEs wore clothing, 'but they apparently don't require the type of clothing that we would require.'

Falcon went on to describe how the entire history of the United States' communications with the EBEs is contained in a very special book, known as the 'Bible' in the Intelligence Community (and kept at the CIA headquarters in Langley, Virginia).

'It's a very, very thick, detailed account of the investigations that have been conducted from about 1947 . . . Every so often it's updated with additional information, and I read the document in 1977. I had access to it. I didn't read the entire document but I read extracts, and that's where I obtained this information from.' The 'Bible' contains information on 'everything that occurred from the Truman era up through to the three aliens being guests of the United States Government; technological data gathered from the aliens; medical history gathered from dead aliens that were found in the desert; autopsies; and information obtained from the extraterrestrials regarding their social structure and their information pertaining to the universe.

'As of the year 1988,' Falcon said, 'there is one extraterrestrial being [EBE-3] who is a guest of the United States Government, and he's remained hidden from public view.' Also part of an 'exchange programme', EBE-3 has been a 'guest' since 1982, Falcon claimed.

During the documentary, Falcon alluded briefly to another book, known as the 'Yellow Book', which supposedly had been written by EBE-2. 'The book relates to the alien's planet, the social structure of the aliens, and the alien's life among Earthlings. What was most intriguing, in my experience with the aliens, is, I believe, an octagon-shaped crystal, which when held in the alien's hand and viewed by a second person, displays pictures. These can be of the alien's home planet, or pictures of Earth many thousands of years ago.'

Asked by Jaime for a physical description of the EBEs, Falcon responded as follows:

'The ones that I saw pictures of and the videotapes that I observed, and the information they obtained from the medical examination of the aliens, describe the alien as a creature about 3 feet 4 to 3 feet 8 inches tall. Their eyes are extremely large, almost insect-style. Their eyes have a couple of lids, and that's probably because they were born on a planet that had a binary sun [system]. The days are extremely bright, probably twice to three times as bright as our sun, I think.

'They have just two openings where our nose would be,' Falcon continued. 'They have no teeth as we know it: they have a hard gum-like area. Their internal organs are quite simple. They have one organ which encompasses what we would refer to as a heart and lungs: it's one pulminary sac which does the job of our heart and lungs. Their digestive system is really simple. They only have liquid wastes and not solid wastes . . . Their skin structure is an extremely elastic skin, and hard, probably hardening from their sun[s]. They have some basic organs. Their brain is more complex than ours. It has several different lobes that ours have. Where our eyes are controlled by the back of the brain, theirs is [sic] controlled by the front of the brain. Their hearing is quite better than ours, almost better than a dog's, [and the ears are] small areas at the side of their heads . . . They have hands without thumbs – four fingers without thumbs. Their feet are small, web-like.

'Their sexual organs – they have males and females. The female has a sex organ similar to our females. There's some difference of the ovary system. And their kidney and bladder is one organ. They excrete waste. They have another organ which – I don't know if our scientists determined what it was for, but I believe it's to transfer the solid wastes into liquid wastes . . . They don't require very much liquid. They transfer all the food that they eat into liquids. The body extracts the liquids out of the food . . . but they have been able to eat some basic food products – vegetables and fruits – that we would eat. But I believe that they have problems digesting meat products, and I don't believe they eat meat on their planet.'

During the documentary, Falcon claimed that the EBEs' lifespan was approximately 350–400 years. 'It's my understanding that the aliens have an IQ of over 200,' he added. 'They have a religion but it's a universal religion. They believe in the Universe as a Supreme Being. The aliens enjoy music – all types of music – especially ancient Tibetan-style music.'

And then Falcon came out with a comment that must have amused but alienated millions of viewers. 'They like vegetables. And their favourite dish or snack is ice-cream – especially strawberry.'

At a stroke, credibility in Condor, Falcon – and the aliens – probably evaporated. The inclusion of such a comment was a serious misjudgement on the part of those behind the scenes. Unless, of course, one takes the view that it was all part of a disinformation programme to discredit the subject. In any event, the ice-cream comment provided light relief. And who knows, maybe the aliens *do* like strawberry ice-cream!

In the private interview with Jaime and Billy, Falcon claimed that more than one species of alien are visiting Earth.

'We have reason to believe there are more than one species. In the last ten years, there's been a number of sightings, landings and contacts with an alien that was quite different than the EBEns – the smaller ones. These were larger, and they had hair, whereas the EBEns had no hair on their body . . . They were still [of an] almost insect-like appearance, but they had hair and they were relatively tall . . . a number of sightings listed them as almost 5 feet tall . . . and this is one reason why the domestic collections people within the Intelligence Community [are] investigating sightings, because we have reason to believe – we have knowledge that there's at least one other alien race visiting this planet . . . One of the MJ-12 people told me that in the last twenty-five years they believed there had been nine different species of aliens visiting this planet. But that's basically all I know on the subject.'

NSA Communications

Nine different species visiting Earth? It seems preposterous, yet those of us who have studied the hundreds of reports from all over the world of encounters with UFO entities are well aware of the bewildering diversity of occupants described by witnesses. These range from creatures that look like nothing on Earth to beings remarkably similar to *Homo sapiens*, as we have learned earlier. And in 1990 I was informed independently via a National Security Agency linguist that the NSA has a signals intelligence (SIGINT) operation to monitor nine separate alien groups.

Interestingly, Falcon confirmed that the NSA is involved in a communications programme. Asked by Jaime Shandera to describe how communications were established with the aliens prior to landings (as part of an ongoing 'liaison'), Falcon made an intriguing reply.

'To the best of my knowledge – that's limited I must say – the National Security Agency has devised a system for communicating with the aliens [which is] some type of electronic or pulse sound system. [The aliens] send a signal to a certain location on Earth – and I'm not sure where that receiving point is. I believe one is in Nevada and one is in California. Anyways, the sound or the communication is translated in the computer and the aliens give the landing co-ordinates to us, so we know the location of known landings. Now, what we investigate are the *unknown* landings; the ones where they're not telling the United States that they're landing.'

'Do nations other than the United States communicate with aliens?' Jaime enquired.

'I have limited knowledge that the Soviets have communicated with aliens – at least attempted to communicate with them in the early Fifties, and also recently, in the early Eighties.'

'Would you say the United States is in the forefront of this communication?'

'I would say they were – many years ahead of them in communications with the aliens. Yes.'

Project Snowbird

I referred in my previous book to the extraordinary incident in December 1980 when three witnesses were irradiated by an unusual aircraft as it flew slowly above them near Huffman, Texas, escorted by over twenty helicopters. The witnesses subsequently sued the US Government for $20 million in damages, but the case was dimissed on the grounds that no such object was owned, operated or in the inventory of the Air Force, Army, Navy or NASA (experts from each were represented in court).[22]

'The craft that was observed was an alien craft piloted by military aircraft pilots,' Falcon claimed during *UFO Cover-Up? Live*, as the principal witnesses, Betty Cash and Vicki Landrum, listened attentively in the studio. 'Although they had been trained and were somewhat familiar with the craft, they found that the aircraft did not respond to certain controls. They radioed that they thought the craft was going to crash – standard procedures for the military in any situation where an aircraft was going to crash – the military would send up search-and-rescue helicopters. The helicopters were following the craft. The craft experienced severe problems. It was thought that the craft was going to crash. However, this craft did not crash . . .'

Both the alleged briefing papers seen by Linda Howe and Bill Moore, it will be recalled, contained brief references to Project Snowbird, which (according to the Carter document) had been established in order to 'test fly a recovered Alien aircraft'. The project was said to be 'continuing' in Nevada. Falcon claimed on the documentary that the aliens had 'complete control' of a base located in Nevada, while Condor explained further:

'From what we understand, an agreement was signed between our US Government and the extraterrestrials [which says that] we won't disclose your existence if you do not interfere in our society, and we allow you to operate from a designated piece of the United States. It's in the State of Nevada, in an area called Area 51, or "Dreamland" . . .'[23]

Notes

1 Howe, Linda Moulton: *An Alien Harvest*, Linda Moulton Howe Productions, P.O. Box 538, Huntingdon Valley, Pennsylvania 19006-0538, 1989, pp. 137–42; Clark, Jerome: 'UFO Crashes', *Fate*, January–June 1988; interviews with the author.

2 Howe, Linda Moulton: op. cit., p. 140.

3 Emenegger, Robert: *UFOs Past, Present & Future*, Ballantine Books, New York, 1974, pp. 127–9.

4 *UFO Cover-Up? Live*, produced by Michael Seligman and distributed by Lexington Broadcast Service (LBS), 14 October 1988.

5 Howe, Linda Moulton: op. cit., pp. 143–55

6 Letter to Barry Greenwood from Richard C. Doty, 3 March 1988.

7 Howe, Linda Moulton: op. cit., p. 147.

8 The mysterious 'green fireballs' are predominantly luminous green aerial objects of various sizes, moving at various speeds and sometimes exhibiting erratic flight patterns that have been reported over the years. An increase in sightings in the US South-West in the late 1940s led to official investigations (see *Above Top Secret*). See also 'Green Fireballs', by Erich A. Aggen, Jr, *MUFON UFO Journal*, No. 271, November 1990.

9 Moore, William L. and Shandera, Jaime H.: *The MJ-12 Documents: An Analytical Report*, The Fair Witness Project, 4219 W. Olive Ave., Suite 247, Burbank, California 91505, 1990.

10 From Barry Greenwood's notes on Peter Gersten's meetings with Richard C. Doty, January 1983.

11 Letter to Shlomo Arnon from Senator Barry Goldwater, 28 March 1975 (reproduced in *Above Top Secret*).

12 Friedman, Stanton T.: *Final Report on Operation Majestic 12*, Fund for UFO Research, P.O. Box 277, Mt Rainier, Maryland 20712, 1990. Also available from Mr Friedman, 79 Pembroke Crescent, Fredericton, New Brunswick, Canada, E3B 2V1.

13 Hastings, Robert: *The MJ-12 Affair: Facts, Questions, Comments*, 1989. Available from the author at 6200 Eubank Boulevard NE, Apt. 833, Albuquerque, New Mexico 87111; Numerous articles by Barry Greenwood in *Just Cause*, published by

Citizens Against UFO Secrecy (CAUS), P.O. Box 218, Coventry, Connecticut 06238; Klass, Philip J.: 'New Evidence of MJ-12 Hoax', *The Skeptical Inquirer*, Vol. 14, No. 2, Winter 1989, pp. 135–40, available from Box 229, Central Park Station, Buffalo, New York 14215; Nickell, Joe and Fischer, John: 'The Crashed Saucer Forgeries', *International UFO Reporter*, Vol. 15, No. 2, March/April 1990, J. Allen Hynek Center for UFO Studies, 2457 West Peterson Avenue, Chicago, Illinois 60659.

14 Moore, William L.: 'UFOs and the US Government: Part IV', *Focus*, Vol. 5, Nos. 1–3, March 1990, p. 18, published by the Fair Witness Project Inc., 4219 W. Olive Avenue, Suite 247, Burbank, California 91505.

15 Blum, Howard: *Out There: The Government's Secret Quest for Extraterrestrials*, Simon & Schuster, New York, 1990, pp. 265–7.

16 Letter to Robert Hastings from Richard C. Doty, 20 March 1989.

17 Stringfield, Leonard: 'UFO Crash/Retrievals: Is the Cover-Up Lifting?', *The UFO Report 1990*, edited by Timothy Good, Sidgwick & Jackson, London, 1989, p. 174.

18 Hastings, Robert: op. cit.

19 Interview with the author, 13 September 1990.

20 Interview with the author, 12 July 1989.

21 Neilson, James (pseudonym): 'Secret US/UFO Structure', *California UFO*, Vol. 4, No. 1, January/February 1989, California UFO, 1536 S. Robertson Boulevard, Los Angeles, California 90035.

22 Good, Timothy: *Above Top Secret: The Worldwide UFO Cover-Up*, Sidgwick & Jackson, London, 1987, pp. 297–8.

23 *UFO Cover-Up? Live*, produced by Michael Seligman with LBS, 14 October 1988. The Moore/Shandera interview with Falcon is available on videotape from The Peregrine Company, (The 'Falcon' Tapes), 12226 Victory Boulevard No. 207, N. Hollywood, California 91606.

· 7 ·

Dreamland

Is there any truth at all to the statements of Falcon and Condor? Diluted as they may be with disinformation, sorting the wheat from the chaff presents a daunting task. Yet I have been encouraged by the accumulation of corroborative evidence in support of some of the claims, at least, including significant and intriguing information relating to 'Dreamland'.

According to an increasing number of witnesses, the United States Government has been test-flying some very unusual aircraft for many years in the remote Nellis Air Force Range and Nuclear Test Site in Nevada, and particularly at the top secret Groom Dry Lake area and its environs, otherwise known by various names, but usually as 'Area 51' or 'Dreamland', located about 80 miles north-north-west of Las Vegas.

'Dreamland' is (or was) the radio call-sign for the Nellis AFB air traffic controllers who maintain the highly restricted airspace in this vicinity. Although it is known that 'stealth' and other unconventional aircraft are flown in the area – including two squadrons of the Lockheed F-117a of the 37th Tactical Fighter Wing, based at the Tonopah Test Range Airfield (TTR)[1] which abuts the north-west corner of the vast Nellis complex, about 150 miles north-west of Las Vegas – little is known about other more secret 'black' projects.

'We are test-flying vehicles that defy description', aviation writer and photographer James Goodall was told by an Air Force officer. Another of Goodall's informants, a retired colonel, concurred. 'We have things that are so far beyond the comprehension of the average aviation authority as to be really alien to our way of thinking', he reportedly stated. Furthermore, Goodall has heard rumours that these new projects involve 'force-field technology', 'gravity-drive systems' – and even 'flying saucer' designs.[2] But does anything substantial lie behind these rumours?

Jim Goodall has informed me that Ben Rich, the recently retired vice-president and general manager of Lockheed's Advanced Development Projects division (the 'Skunk Works'), who was largely responsible for the F-117 programme, has disclosed a belief in both extraterrestrial and man-made UFOs. 'I'm a believer in both categories,' he told John Andrews of the Testor Corporation. 'I feel everything is possible. Many of our Man-made UFOs are *Un-Funded Opportunities*.'[3]

Interestingly, there is a unit at Nellis AFB, 8 miles north-east of Las Vegas, called the 'Alien Technology Center'. This unit, I was told by aviation writer Bill Gunston, relates solely to the testing of foreign, but conventional aircraft. The Air Force's secret 4477th Test and Evaluation Squadron ('Red Hats/Red Eagles') has flown more than a squadron of Soviet-built aircraft from the Groom Lake and Tonopah test ranges. But is it possible that more advanced craft, of truly 'alien' origin or design, have been flown? The editor of the American military magazine *Gung-Ho*, Jim Shults, lends credence to the possibility.

'The [Alien Technology] Center is rumoured to have obtained alien (not Earth) equipment and, at times, personnel to help develop our new aircraft, Star Wars weaponry, etc.,' Shults wrote in 1988. 'Yes, I know I sound crazy, but the rumour is awfully solid! The Alien Technology Center is for real. Something remarkable has caused the Russians to suddenly want to play ball, and I personally believe this could be it . . .'[4]

Project Red Light

In the early 1960s Mike Hunt, who at the time held a 'Q' clearance from the Atomic Energy Commission and an inter-agency Top Secret clearance, claims to have seen a saucer-shaped aircraft in Area 51, while engaged in radio maintenance.

'I only saw the UFO one time', he related to researcher David Dobbs in a letter (a copy of which is in my possession). 'It was on the ground and partly hidden behind a building and at first I thought it was a small private aircraft until I noticed it had no wings or tail. I was probably half a mile or further from it but I would guess it was 20 to 30 feet in diameter and sort of a pewter colour rather than bright polished aluminium'.

Hunt claimed to have been present on a number of occasions when the 'flying saucer' was taking off or landing, although he was never allowed to observe it. 'The reason that I knew take-offs and landings were occurring was that I would be told something like "IT will be landing in [so many] minutes" or "We will be taking IT out of the hangar", etc. I remember that any referrals were to "IT" . . . I was always taken inside and out of view of the runway at these times', he explained, 'and at no time did I hear anything that sounded like a conventional or any other kind of engine . . .'

Hunt related that on a number of occasions the radio sets he was working on suddenly 'died' inexplicably, then just as suddenly began functioning normally. He paid little heed to this at the time. Richard Shakleford, a radar operator from the radar station at the north end of the test site near Tonopah, also mentioned to Hunt that he frequently tracked UFOs over the test site, but was told to ignore them.

Mike Hunt believed that a highly secret programme, known as 'Project Red Light' or 'Redlight', connected with flying discs, was in operation at Area 51 at the time, and that this area was not controlled by Nellis AFB. 'I always had the impression that the flight test area was from Area 51 north because there is a natural valley that runs in that direction for 200 miles or so,' he told David Dobbs. 'Also I entered Area 51 from the north and there were a couple of times that I was questioned about whether I had "noticed" anything on the way in . . . I was reminded constantly that no matter what I saw, I could be in serious trouble if I ever talked about any of it. I can't stress too much how tight the security was. . .'[5]

Additional rumours concerning 'Project Red Light' have surfaced over the years. In *UFO Crash at Aztec*, authors William Steinman and Wendelle Stevens (a former Air Force lieutenant colonel) cite a number of similar stories from independent sources. In one case, Stevens was approached after a lecture by a former medical corpsman who had been at a Navy Auxiliary airfield within the Atomic Energy Commission test site in 1951, at a time when all the base personnel, with the exception of the base hospital staff, had been transferred to other units. A Navy construction battalion was moved in and began extensive dismantling work, prior to constructing an underground facility.

By the end of 1951, Stevens was told, the battalion had completed their work and a Project Red Light team moved in. This team grew to 800 or 1,000 men, who remained on permanent duty at the base, which was reportedly protected by three separate perimeters and later guarded round the clock by a detachment of Blue Berets. According to Steven's informant, many leading scientists with top security clearances were involved in this maximum security research programme.

'Although no statements were released and nothing was said of this in official papers,' Stevens reports, 'the research was said to cover UFO propulsion, UFO weaponry, and examination and description of UFO hardware. There were even rumours of attempted repair or reconstruction of captured UFOs . . . and attempts to fly the captured craft or copies of them . . . The facility was said to have at least three captured UFOs, two nearly complete and one dismantled. One of the operational UFOs was said to have exploded in flight with two US test pilots aboard.

'As if that wasn't enough to swallow,' Stevens continues, 'he said that a special habitat had been prepared during the reconstruction of the facility, and that two human-like alien beings that had been kept alive in special environments were moved to the new habitat facility. At the time of this story one of them had died in the habitat shortly after being moved there . . . The aliens were described as small-size humans of a greyish-white to parchment-white colour . . .'

Wendelle Stevens cites two other instances when witnesses approached him following lectures, both claiming to have been employed at the Navy Auxiliary base south of the Tonopah Test Range. One witness said that during the reconstruction in 1951, parts of the existing runway were dug up and most of the new facility was installed underground, after which the runway was relaid to appear as it did before.[6]

Captain Nunnallee of the 27th Tactical Fighter Wing, Cannon AFB, New Mexico, has spoken to a guard who claims to have seen an extraordinary aircraft kept in a hangar at 'Dreamland'. The guard disclosed that all area lights were shut off when the hangar doors were to be opened, researcher Tom Adams was told. 'On one occasion he saw the doors open during the night and saw an unusual object come out and take off straight up.' Described as 'disc-shaped with dull tone lights', it was rumoured that the craft had been given to the US by aliens.[7]

A Saucer at Nellis AFB, 1953

Yet another story of a flying disc seen in the Nellis AFB/Area 51 vicinity is reported by journalist Robert Dorr, a former Air Force veteran, who claims to have been told about a recovered saucer witnessed by a member of an Air Technical Intelligence Center team assigned to the Nellis test base in April 1953. The saucer had reportedly been recovered on the east coast.

'It was a perfect saucer, 30.3 feet in diameter', Dorr was told, 'with thickness ranging from 1 foot around its circumference to 9 feet at its centre. It had a raised cockpit similar to that of a fighter plane and an enclosed area beneath, 5 by 5 by 7 feet. Its propulsion system had been totally destroyed, and most of the instrumentation and wiring, although involving familiar materials, was almost incomprehensible. No one ever seriously believed this was an interstellar starship. The feeling was, it was a small craft designed to operate from a mother ship in orbit around the Earth. Judging from its dimensions, and from the battered wreckage of acceleration couches, it was designed to carry two crew members, apparently with human-like limbs but considerably smaller than human beings. It took months of work to redesign the thing so a human pilot could fit into it.'

Dorr was informed that there had been lengthy debate at Nellis over whether or not the craft could actually be flown. 'Metallurgy experts understood the composition of the machine, and actually identified new alloys that we had under development. But nobody could figure out what held it "up" . . . Since there was no "airfoil" built into the saucer shape, it was assumed that it did not operate on the principle of "lift" but, rather, was moved solely by its propulsion source . . .'

The craft was supposedly fitted with two Wright J-65 jet engines, and Dorr was told by another source that it was test-flown at Nellis between 1953 and 1955. The tests, of brief duration and at low altitude, were said to have yielded little of practical value, since 'most of the alien technology had been lost in the original crash'.[8]

Since Robert Dorr worked for a certain intelligence agency before retirement, I asked him if perhaps the Nellis story had been concocted for purposes of disinformation. 'None of the information in the article is invented,' he replied. 'It is as accurate as it was possible to make it. Disinformation, as the word is used on this side of the Atlantic, means false information intentionally disseminated by someone in authority for the purpose of deceiving. It is against the law for a United States Government agency to put out disinformation and in my opinion there is no reason to do so. To the best of my knowledge, there is none in the article.'[9]

Disinformation, of course, is standard practice in the world of counter-intelligence, even if it is not legally sanctioned. But in view of additional evidence that the US Government has actually test-flown disc-shaped aircraft of exotic origin, there may well be an element of truth contained in Robert Dorr's report; indeed, it could even be factual. While conceding that some unexplained UFO reports have been made by trained military pilots and others, Dorr points out, however, that 'This does not make them spaceships and it does not mean the Air Force is holding a little green man in a bottle in Nevada.

'Above all,' Dorr continued, 'it does not mean that the United States Government is engaged in some massive conspiracy to hide the arrival of the little men from space. If you knew more about the Government, you would know that it is almost impossible for CIA, DIA, the Air Force, etc., to co-operate on anything – let alone to pull off a massive conspiracy. There is no organ of the US Government which possesses either a reason or the competence to conspire in such a manner.'[10] Even so, some of Dorr's comments in his article are at variance with these statements.

In *Above Top Secret* I alluded to the Avro-Car, a disc-shaped, jet-propelled vehicle designed by John Frost and built by A. V. Roe Ltd of Canada in the 1950s. The Avro-Car, or VZ-9, was first 'flown' in 1959, and following some unsuccessful trial hovering flights, was cancelled a few years later, despite extravagant claims made for its performance. A 1955 CIA memorandum includes the interesting statement that 'Mr Frost is reported to have obtained his original idea for the flying machine from a group of Germans just after World War II . . .'[11]

That the Germans were engaged in research into disc-shaped flying vehicles during World War II is undisputed, yet the available records suggest that they did not get very far – probably no further than the Avro-Car. But supposing that they did get further, and that subsequent research yielded positive results, as has been claimed by a number of sources, could it be that the stories of extraterrestrial flying saucers are no more than a cover for highly secret tests of terrestrial craft? I do not entirely discount the hypothesis, yet there is another possibility which I find more convincing.

Robert Dorr confirms that man-made saucers had been under consideration by the US Air Force for years, but had repeatedly proven impractical. He cites the opinion of Colonel Robert Gammon, an Army historian, who said that he had always wondered why a 'joint' Army–Air Force project was initiated in the mid-1950s to develop a new, man-made saucer. 'Neither service had a pressing need,' Gammon reportedly stated. 'In the aftermath of the Korean War, pursestrings were tight and funds were urgently needed for more practical aircraft. The Avro VZ-9 man-made saucer was an interesting idea, but there was no clear requirement for it'.

In his intriguing 1978 article, Dorr suggests that there could indeed have been a 'clear requirement':

Was the Avro VZ-9 . . . also known as 'Weapons System 606A' . . . intended as a smokescreen to shift attention away from the *real* saucer – the alien spaceship? If there was any *other* purpose behind the VZ-9, it has become obscured by questions this project raised from the start. Why the 'weapons system' designation, when the craft was never designed to be armed? Why, at a time when the US aerospace industry led the world, did Army and Air Force purchasers go to a Canadian firm? . . . Why was the VZ-9 extensively publi-

cized when first announced in 1955 (while the *real* saucer was allegedly being flown) and yet *not* publicized when it finally made its first
test flight on December 5, 1959? Why was the test program halted
after a few, unsatisfactory tests?

Did the Air Force need the VZ-9 only long enough to cover up its
testing of an alien spaceship, then lose interest when those tests
ended in 1955?[12]

Lieutenant Colonel George Edwards (USAF, retired) claims that
he and others involved in the VZ-9 project were aware from the outset
that it would never be successful. 'Although we weren't cut in on it,'
he reportedly stated, 'we knew that the Air Force was secretly test-
flying a real alien spacecraft. The VZ-9 was to be a "cover", so the
Pentagon would have an explanation whenever people reported seeing a saucer in flight.'[13]

Red Flag

Four times a year, Nellis AFB plays host to 'Red Flag', a six-week
mock air war between players from the Air Force, Navy, Marine
Corps, and NATO forces, in which pilots engage in 'combat' with
'enemy' aircraft. Researcher Tom Adams has been given a fascinating
account by an F-111D pilot who inadvertently flew over Dreamland
during a Red Flag exercise. The pilot, 1st Lieutenant Parrish, of the
522nd Tactical Fighter Squadron, 27th Tactical Fighter Wing, based
at Cannon AFB, New Mexico, claims that when his plane was picked
up on radar, interceptors were sent aloft and he was ordered to land
on the dry lake. Both pilot and navigator were detained for three days,
during which time they were repeatedly asked what exactly they had
seen. Parrish reportedly refused.[14]

Most of the aircraft and personnel involved in Red Flag exercises
are made up of 'Blue', or 'friendly' forces, while the 'Red' force con-
sists of 'enemy' aircraft and equipment. According to a January 1986
report supplied to me by John Lear, a part of Emigrant Valley near
Groom Lake – most probably the area known as S-4, which will be
described in the following two chapters – is strictly off limits to over-
flights, including those made by the Red/Blue teams that simulate

dogfights over the northern part of this area. These teams are only permitted to fly over the southern areas when there is heavy overcast, and even then under rigidly controlled conditions.

The report cites the case of a 'Red' pilot flying an F-5, simulating a Soviet MiG fighter, on an occasion in the mid-1970s – possibly 1976 or 1977 – when there was cloud cover. He decided to drop below the clouds and take a quick look before returning to Nellis AFB, only to be chased out of the area by what he described as UFOs, which seemed to have come up from below to meet him. On his return to Nellis, the pilot was met by an Air Force officer who took him away for a debriefing. The following day, the pilot reportedly acted as if the incident had never occurred.

Wendelle Stevens relates a similar story of an unnamed Air Force officer of a Tactical Air Command combat squadron, who in 1977 had been assigned to a Red Flag exercise and sent on a 'strike' mission against the 'enemy' airfield (Tonopah Test Range). The pilot headed out on a course designed to confuse the 'enemy' radar, and decided to bend the rules by giving himself an advantage, cutting across the forbidden AEC reservation area to make his approach to the 'enemy' airfield from an unexpected direction.

As the pilot entered the reservation area from what he considered to be below radar scanning levels, cutting across north of Area 51, he observed a disc-shaped aircraft, about 60 feet in diameter, flying to the south of his position. A voice on the emergency channel almost immediately ordered him to abandon his mission and land at Nellis AFB.

Taxiing to the parking place, the plane was surrounded and the pilot met by uniformed and plain-clothes personnel who escorted him to a security office in the bunker area. One of the civilian interrogators produced an FBI badge. The pilot was allegedly held for two days and questioned about everything he had seen. When he mentioned the flying disc, everything was done to persuade him that what he had in fact seen was merely a water tower. After signing a statement to this effect, the pilot was allowed to return to base. A few days later, the pilot was transferred to another squadron and warned not to discuss the incident. Later that year, however, he told his father, from whom Stevens obtained the story.[15]

Further Reports

Many other strange occurrences in the Nevada Test Site have been reported. The January 1986 report cites a claim by Colonel 'L', who in 1970 was involved with setting up seismic instrumentation in connection with underground nuclear tests west of Area 51. The assignment included placing seismometers in an old mine shaft. The security guard who accompanied 'L' warned him to be out of the area by 10 p.m. because, he said, unusual things had happened and a number of guards and technicians had simply 'disappeared'. On this particular night, a technician who did not return until sunrise the following day reported that at about 11 p.m. the lights and engine of his vehicle failed, and he was unable to drive back until 2 a.m.

During preparations for the next nuclear test, in a different location about 30 miles from the boundary of Area 51, 'L' was told by another security guard that UFO activity occurred in the area 'almost nightly', mostly between 10 and 12 p.m., and there had been several occasions when guards had simply disappeared during those hours.

According to 'L', a guard who after seven years was no longer able to take the strain of working under such conditions applied for a job in his unit, but discovered that all his employment records had vanished from official files. He had been working for 'L' on unclassified material while waiting for clearance for the job he had applied for, but clearance was refused, according to the Defense Investigative Service, owing to an unaccountable seven-year gap in his life. Shortly afterwards, the guard disappeared without trace.

Steinman and Stevens cite the case of a Navajo Indian who on an unspecified date in 1978, in a remote canyon area close to the AEC reservation, encountered a large military helicopter which at intervals broadcast warnings to anyone who might be in the vicinity that they should make their presence known, since a dangerous military test was about to take place. The witness decided to remain where he was, and sheltered among the rocks. The helicopter flew off, but returned fifteen minutes later, repeating the warning.

Half an hour later, two helicopters came into view, apparently escorting a large dark grey disc-shaped aircraft. 'It was smooth-skinned, metallic and circular in form, with a raised dome on top, and flew steadily in the formation', Stevens was told. All three aircraft then flew out of sight.

About ten minutes later the two helicopters returned, without the disc, and eventually flew back the way they had come. Suddenly, the disc reappeared, flying at great speed down the middle of the canyon, apparently following the same track as on the 'outbound' flight.

Later, the Indian related his experience to the tribal elders, who cautioned him to remain silent about it, and then to Mitchell Uribe (Stevens's informant), who had been recording a list of similar sightings reported by the tribe.[16]

There have also been reports of animal mutilations in the vicinity. Former State Senator Charles Lamm has lost two prize bulls to the mystery mutilators, according to a 1989 television report. 'Like many ranchers, he is self-reliant and didn't bother to file police reports,' the journalist commented. 'His Lincoln County ranch sits adjacent to the Nevada Test Site, so he's seen his share of unusual things over the years. But he hasn't got a clue about who is carving up cattle. Lamm has several neighbours who have also lost cattle. Most of these weren't reported either.'

One of the Nevada mutilations occurred just yards from the home of Jane Bradshaw. She saw nothing, and surmised that 'devil worshippers with dart guns' were responsible. 'We cut down into the animal,' an expert said. 'The ball joint was completely gone off the shoulder, and just a perfect flat cut inside – no bone chips. I don't know how it was cut.'[17]

The Groom Mountain Range

In early 1984 the US Air Force illegally seized 89,000 acres of public land, known as the Groom Range, in order to further restrict access to Area 51. The decision to control access was made after consultation with local Bureau of Land Management officials and after USAF Headquarters had conferred with the Air Force Secretariat. Following the seizure, briefings were arranged for the appropriate personnel in the Offices of the Secretary of the Air Force and the Secretary of Defense, as well as for members of the National Security Council.

In August 1984, during a hearing before the House Subcommittee

on Lands and National Parks at the House of Representatives, a
heated exchange took place between the Chairman, Mr Seiberling,
and the Honourable John Rittenhouse, representing the Air Force:

SEIBERLING: Is it true that the Air Force has already acted
                 to restrict public use of the Groom Range
                 area?

RITTENHOUSE: Yes, sir, it is true. We have asserted the right
                 to control the surface access and egress to the
                 extent of requesting people not to go in and
                 out. We have people posted on the roads and
                 at certain times we do not. We ask their co-
                 operation.

SEIBERLING: Under what legal authority was that done;
                 that right asserted?

RITTENHOUSE: As far as I know, sir, there is none; except de-
                 cisions were made at a much, much higher
                 level than mine that that be done.

SEIBERLING: There is no higher level than the laws of the
                 United States.

RITTENHOUSE: No, sir. I understand, and we can describe
                 that further if you would like, sir.

SEIBERLING: I would like.

RITTENHOUSE: In closed briefing.

SEIBERLING: . . . why would that have to be in a closed
                 briefing?

RITTENHOUSE: I can't discuss it, sir.

SEIBERLING: Shades of Watergate. All I am asking you is
                 under what legal authority this was done. I
                 am not asking you the technical reasons. That
                 certainly is not classified.

RITTENHOUSE: . . . as I stated earlier, originally we had no
                 legal authority but we asserted the right to re-
                 quest people not to enter that area.

SEIBERLING: How?

RITTENHOUSE: We legally did not have the authority.[18]

Outraged local residents gave vent to their feelings during a public hearing at Alamo, Nevada, in November 1985. 'If the public safety and the national security would be jeopardized,' asked a Mr Benezet, 'why did the Air Force not tell us so in 1981 when they withdrew the Nevada Test Site?'

'I'd like to know how the military can hide behind the guise of national security', another resident objected to the Air Force spokesman, 'when you have broken all of the rules that's supposed to ensure this country's freedom, denying our access, holding us at gunpoint when you feel necessary, not telling people you're withdrawing it for our own good . . . You can't tell me why you've broken all the rules? And you say it's national security.'[19]

Advanced Aircraft

Security surrounding Groom Lake is formidable. The area is protected by motion detectors, laser sensors, and highly mobile security personnel reputedly recruited from the Green Berets, Navy SEALs and police agencies, and trained by the élite Delta Force. I have been told by an informed source that even civil aircraft overflying the area can be shot down if warnings are not heeded. But what are the reasons? Is it merely to protect the airspace where secret 'stealth' aircraft, remotely piloted vehicles (RPVs) and cruise missiles, as well as Advanced Tactical Fighter (ATF) planes and the Aurora project, which includes Lockheed's hypersonic replacement for the SR-71 spy plane, are flown, thus ensuring that sightings of such aircraft, either in the air or on the ground, are kept to a minimum? There is no question that this is one reason behind the security, but I am convinced that the existence of other, less conventional aircraft is another reason for the high level of secrecy.

In October 1990, *Aviation Week & Space Technology* reported on a number of reliable observations of unconventional aircraft in Nevada and California, including a triangular-shaped, quiet aircraft seen with a flight of F-117a stealth planes, and believed to be a demonstrator or prototype of the General Dynamics/McDonnell Douglas A-12 Avenger for the Navy (now scrapped), as well as a high-speed aircraft that makes a very loud, rumbling roar, leaving a thick, segmented smoke or contrail in its wake (almost certainly the SR-71 replacement, believed to be 'nested' in the Aurora project).

But of particular interest here is *Aviation Week*'s commentary on reports of even less conventional aeroforms, including 'a high-altitude aircraft that crosses the night sky at extremely high speed. Normally, no engine noise or sonic boom is heard. The vehicle typically is observed as a single, bright light – sometimes pulsating – flying at speeds far exceeding any other aircraft in the area, and at an altitude estimated to be above 50,000 feet. Such aircraft have been reported by both ground-based and airborne observers . . .'

These types of 'black' aircraft appear to employ relatively conventional propulsion systems, although more advanced than those available to the 'white' world, *Aviation Week* commented, but added significantly that *'there is substantial evidence that another family of craft exists that relies solely on exotic propulsion and aerodynamic schemes not fully understood at this time*. Data pertaining to this type of vehicle are being studied by *Aviation Week* and several consultants.'[20] [My italics.]

Researcher William Hamilton III contacted the writer of the article, Bill Scott, who has a background as a flight test engineer and is a graduate of the US Air Force Test Pilot School. Scott admitted that the 'exotic propulsion' system he referred to could be an anti-gravity unit, and mentioned that he had heard of these crafts' ability to move from extremely low speeds (15–20 m.p.h.) to supersonic speeds.[21]

According to Mark Barnes, who works at the Federal Aviation Administration's long-range radar station at Angel Peak, strange radar echoes have occasionally been picked up over the Groom Mountain area, indicating the presence of an object hovering for periods of up to fifteen minutes. 'It mostly stays put,' said Barnes in 1990. 'It doesn't move in range or azimuth very much and uses a stationary code that we normally use for a test function.'[22]

Breakthrough

In March 1989 a physicist who claims to have been employed at a test site near Groom Lake revealed on a Las Vegas TV interview that not only had the US Government test-flown highly advanced disc-shaped aircraft, but that he himself had been involved in the research programme. Given the pseudonym of 'Dennis', the scientist, with his face darkened, spoke guardedly about his involvement in the super-secret project.

'Exactly what's going on up there?' he was asked by interviewer George Knapp.

'Well, there's several – actually nine, er, flying saucers – flying discs – that are out there that are of extraterrestrial origin,' the scientist replied. 'They're basically being dismantled. Some are, well, in various stages of completion, built from other parts, and they're being test-flown, and basically just being analyzed. Some of them are 100 per cent intact and operate perfectly. The other ones are being taken apart. I was involved mainly in propulsion and the power source . . . As far as I can remember, about half of them do operate, and the other half are just being torn down, basically to analyze the components.'

'Where did we get these saucers? How did they come into the hands of the Government?' asked the interviewer.

'I haven't the slightest idea, and you have to understand that the information is very compartmentalized, and I was only allowed information that pertained to what I was involved in.'

'But I mean, couldn't *our* government have made them, as opposed to getting them from some alien beings?' asked Knapp.

'Totally impossible,' replied Dennis. 'The propulsion system is a gravity propulsion system: the power source is an antimatter reactor. This technology does not exist at all. In fact, one of the reasons that I'm coming forward with this information [is that] it's not only a crime against the American people, it's a crime against the scientific community, which I've been part of for some time, actively trying to duplicate these systems. Yet they are in existence now and basically in the hands of the Government.'

'What would happen to you if the Government learned that you were giving us this information?'

'Anything could happen. I don't know . . .'

'Well, you referred to getting into trouble. Have you had some repercussions already?'

'Yeah. I've been threatened with being charged with espionage,

I've had my life threatened by them, my wife's life threatened by them, and I mean, I don't know where else you can go from there.'

'Will the Government ever tell us about the testing, and do the Soviets know about this?'

'The Soviets were involved at some specific point,' Dennis continued. 'They were kicked out of the programme rather abruptly – in the middle. I don't know why that was or what happened. They're not very happy about it, and as far as them revealing it, I'm sure that they have every intention of claiming that all the technology was developed here [on Earth], which it was absolutely not.'

'If the Soviets were kicked out of this testing programme, why wouldn't they tell us about it?'

'I have no idea. They weren't allowed all the information. Apparently, they had some, and we were basically trading with them. As far as whether they have discs or not, I don't know. I don't even know if they had knowledge that we actually had any there, but they were involved to some extent, and I don't know how much.'

'What about aliens? Any of those up there at Groom Lake?'

'Er, I really want to steer away from that right now.'

'Is the "Star Wars" programme in any way related to what's going on up there? I know some believe that maybe we're building Star Wars for something other than the Soviets.'

'This directly taps out of the Star Wars budget, which is very hard to follow because it requires huge amounts of money,' the scientist replied. 'It also taps out of a lot of other places too that would be very hard to track down. But yes, Star Wars is directly related to it. The United States Navy is the part of the Government that really maintains control over this.'[23]

Thus ended the preliminary interview with 'Dennis', who later revealed his real name. Is it a simple hoax, a fantasy – or Government disinformation? In another series of interviews in 1989, and with me in 1990, Robert Scott Lazar elaborated on his alleged involvement at the world's most secret test site in the remote Nevada desert.

Notes

1 The two squadrons of F-117a Nighthawk aircraft currently based at the Tonopah Test Range Airfield are scheduled to be moved to Holloman AFB in 1992. For fascinating information on this remarkable aircraft, see *Lockheed F-117a: Operation and Development of the Stealth Fighter*, by Bill Sweetman and James Goodall, Haynes Publishing Group, Sparkford, Nr Yeovil, Somerset BA22 7JJ, or Motorbooks International, 729 Prospect Avenue, Osceola, Wisconsin 54020; also *Lockheed F-117 Stealth Fighter*, by Jay Miller, Midland Counties Publications, 24 The Hollow, Earl Shilton, Leicester LE9 7NA, or Voyager Press, 123 N. 2nd St., Stillwater, Minnesota 55082.

2 Goodall, James C., (writing as 'Al Frickey'): 'Stealth – and Beyond', *Gung-Ho* magazine, February 1988, pp. 38–43.

3 Letter to the author from James C. Goodall, 9 February 1990.

4 Schults, Jim: 'Stealth – and Beyond', *Gung-Ho*, February 1988, p. 43.

5 Letter from Mike Hunt to David Dobbs, 20 April 1980.

6 Steinman, William S. and Stevens, Wendelle C.: *UFO Crash at Aztec: A Well-Kept Secret*, UFO Photo Archives, P.O. Box 17206, Tucson, Arizona 85710, 1986, pp. 426–7.

7 Report by Tom Adams on file.

8 Dorr, Robert F. (writing as 'Rufus Drake'): 'Air Force Tests Captured Saucer – Also Flies Own!', *Ideal's UFO Magazine*, No. 3, 1978.

9 Letter to the author from Robert F. Dorr, 27 February 1990.

10 Letter to the author from Robert F. Dorr, 26 January 1990.

11 Good, Timothy: *Above Top Secret: The Worldwide UFO Cover-Up*, Sidgwick & Jackson, London, 1987, pp. 220–1.

12 Dorr, Robert: op. cit.

13 *Ideal's UFO Magazine*, No. 4, 1978.

14 Steinman & Stevens: op. cit., pp. 568–9.

15 Ibid., pp. 383–4.

16 Ibid., pp. 384–5.

17 KLAS-TV, Channel 8, P.O. Box 15047, Las Vegas, Nevada 89114, November 1989.

18 Hearing before the House Subcommittee on Public Lands and National Parks of the Committee on Interior and Insular Affairs, House of Representatives, 6 August 1984.

19 Public Hearing for Renewal of Groom Mountain Range Land Withdrawal, Alamo, Nevada, 20 November 1985.

20 *Aviation Week & Space Technology*, 1 October 1990, p. 20.

21 Hamilton III, William F.: 'Flying Wings and Deep Desert Secrets', *MUFON UFO Journal*, No. 271, November 1990.

22 *UFOs: The Best Evidence?*, KLAS-TV, Channel 8, Las Vegas, 1990.

23 Interview on KLAS-TV, Channel 8, Las Vegas, March 1989.

· 8 ·

Alien Technology

Bob Lazar was introduced to me in Las Vegas in March 1990 by John Lear, who had met him in 1988 through his friend Gene Huff, a real-estate appraiser. I found Bob to be a soft-spoken, unassuming young man, who over a period of several days answered my questions patiently and politely.

I first queried him on how he came to be interviewed for the job at the test site known as S-4 near Groom Lake. The two interviews had taken place at the EG&G (Edgerton, Germeshausen and Grier) facility at McCarran Airport, Las Vegas, in late 1988. 'I had sent résumés to several places, and they returned my call and set up an interview. But it wasn't *with* EG&G,' Bob explained, 'it was just at the building.'

EG&G is a huge company employing tens of thousands of personnel at over 150 business establishments worldwide. On behalf of the US Government, EG&G manages many vital programmes for NASA, the Department of Energy, the Department of Defense, and many other agencies. Much of the work is top secret, especially the research conducted at the Nevada Test Site, which, I learned from another source, involves EG&G's Special Projects Division, now based at Nellis AFB.

'The first question, the first day when I went out to EG&G for my interview, was, "What is your relationship with John Lear?",' Bob continued. 'Thinking that that's going to be a problem right away, my answer was, "John is just an acquaintance." And he was. I had met him through Gene Huff. I said that he's a guy who sticks his nose in places where it doesn't belong. And that was the last time they ever asked about him or said anything about him at all. At that time John was just showing me pictures of stealth and SR-71 planes.'

John Lear, as mentioned in Chapter 1, is the only pilot to hold every airman certificate issued by the Federal Aviation Administration, and in addition to having flown in over 160 types of aircraft, he at one time flew many missions for the CIA. John has become a well-known figure in Las Vegas, particularly since he began giving a series of lectures which dealt with the more sensational aspects of the UFO subject, occasionally making rather extreme statements. Even so, I know that he has cultivated a number of legitimate sources of information in the military and intelligence communities.

It has been suggested that the S-4 story was 'set up' by Lear and/or Gene Huff, but I have yet to find evidence of this. 'Gene never heard of S-4 until I told him about it,' Bob Lazar said, and he made it clear that he does not subscribe to John's views, insofar as the 'big picture' is concerned. 'I didn't buy *any* of this stuff before I got into the programme,' he assured me. 'In fact, John Lear was giving a speech on UFOs and a friend wanted me to go. I just laughed and I told him what a waste of time it was.'

The Los Alamos Connection

The roots of Lazar's employment at S-4 go back to 1982, when he worked at the Los Alamos National Laboratory, conducting experiments with the Meson Physics Facility's medium energy linear particle accelerator, concentrating on polarized proton-scattering experiments. He was also employed in the Weapons Division, where his work centred on high-energy particle beam accelerators for use in space. Lazar quite rightly refuses to discuss this aspect of his work, since it involves the Strategic Defense Initiative – SDI, or 'Star Wars'.

(Following Lazar's disclosures on local radio and television, the Los Alamos National Laboratory repeatedly denied that he had ever been employed there. When proof of employment, in the form of Lazar's entry in the internal phone book (Fig. 8.1), was presented to the Laboratory by TV journalist George Knapp, they grudgingly admitted that Lazar had in fact worked there on 'non-sensitive' projects.

But Knapp told me that he has spoken with a number of Lazar's former associates who confirm his involvement in top secret SDI work.)

On 28 June 1982, Lazar met Dr Edward Teller, the 'father of the hydrogen bomb', during a seminar that Teller was giving at Los Alamos. 'I had built a jet car, and they put it in the local newspaper on the front page,' Lazar related to Knapp. 'And as I walked up to the lecture hall, I noticed Teller was outside sitting on a brick wall reading the front page. And I said, "Hi, I'm the one that you're reading about there," and he said, "That's really interesting." And I sat down and had a little talk with him.' The meeting turned out to be fortuitous, since Teller was one of those to whom Lazar sent his résumé in 1988. Teller gave Lazar the name of someone to contact, and this led to the interview at EG&G.

Confronted by a TV reporter, Dr Teller denied knowledge of Lazar and Area 51/S-4. 'Look, I don't know Bob Lazar,' he responded, but added rather ambiguously: 'All this sounds fine. I probably met him. I might have said to somebody I met him and I liked him, after I met

LAWRENCE JOHN W	7-9403	PA-10	P204	3	261	T242	
LAWRENCE JOHN W	7-9403	PA-10	P204	3	261	T242	
LAWRENCE RICHARD J	7-5525	WX-3	C934	16	260	122	
LAWRENCE THOMAS A	7-6726	MEC-5	C929	16	202	107	
LAYNE SCOTT PETER	7-1444	CNLS	B258	03	123	170	
LAZAR ROBERT	7-6735	K/M	H840	53	2	4	
LAZARUS GLORIA S	7-6339	O-11	K571	0	487	123	
LAZARUS MICHAEL E	7-4653	MST-14	G742	3	29	9116	
LAZARUS ROGER BEN	7-6943	C-3	B265	3	132	202	
LAZAZERA VITO J	7-3046	CHM-6	J564	46	1	5	
LAZZARD DOLORES M	7-6136	NSP-10	F670	3	43	A314E	
LAZZARO ERIC S	7-6359	M-4	P942	15	183	131	
LEA BENJAMIN C	7-4814	MEC-DO	D472	3	39	SHO5	
LEA BETTY MARIE	7-2087	ENG-3	M703	3	410	132	A150
LEA WALTER BYRON	7-6341	WX-3	C934	16	370	103	
LEACH TERRY	7-4820	MRL	H814	53	6	206	

Fig. 8.1
Robert Lazar's entry in the Los Alamos National Laboratory telephone directory, October, 1982. When Lazar's story broke, officials at the laboratory denied that he had ever been employed there.

him, and if I liked him. But I don't remember him . . . I mean, you are trying to force questions on me that I simply won't answer.'[1]

Majestic Clearance

At the first interview, Lazar was told that he was overqualified for the job they had in mind and would quickly get bored with it, but that they might have something in the near future that would really interest him.

'They continued questioning me, mainly on my interests outside of work,' Lazar told George Knapp. 'They seemed to be really concerned about that. They said, "You work on little projects?" and I said, "Yeah, I have a particle accelerator in my master bedroom, and things of that sort." That's what really impressed them. And some time went by and they called me back in. There was a senior staff physicist who was leaving this organization, and they basically interviewed me for that job.

'They didn't mention anything about flying saucers; they didn't mention anything specific as far as what was going on. We got on to a discussion of gravitation and things of that sort, and they kind of looked at each other and said, "You'd be interested in this". And I had a feeling that it had to do with some kind of field propulsion system, or just a very secret project that would be out in the middle of the desert.'

Lazar explained to me that as soon as the interviews began, his Top Secret 'Q' clearance, which had been deactivated when he left Los Alamos, was reactivated, and a more intensive investigation into his background ensued, prior to his being cleared to a higher level. 'It's a more in-depth personal look at your background and your life,' he said. 'The clearance, as far as any ties to any adversary of the United States or any strange things in your background, is already done on "Q" clearance. The rest is trying to determine whether or not you're a stable and sane person. And one of the reasons I didn't get my final clearance was disruptions in my family life.'

Lazar claims that following the interview he was given a security clearance thirty-eight levels above 'Q' clearance. The existence of such above Top Secret levels – or 'compartments' – is normal within the Intelligence Community and is considered the best way of re-stricting particularly sensitive information to those with a 'need to know'. Compartmented intelligence was introduced during World War II, and those involved in US space reconnaissance and related aerial activities, for example, work under a system known as Sensitive Compartmented Information – SCI. According to the writer William Burrows, there are more than thirty SCI categories used by the US Intelligence Community,[2] which renders Lazar's claim less fanciful than it might otherwise seem.

In spite of the lack of final clearance, Lazar began work at S-4, and claims he was given a white badge with a light blue and dark blue diagonal stripe and 'MAJ' on it – for 'Majestic'. This seemed too good to be true, especially since I had exposed Majestic clearance in *Above Top Secret*. But Lazar was insistent that everyone at the site wore badges with MAJ displayed, with the exception of his supervisor, Dennis Mariani (the inspiration for Lazar's 'Dennis' pseudonym), whose badge had 'Majestic' on the top. He nevertheless admitted to me that it could have been some kind of an inside joke. Whatever the case, Lazar's claim is substantiated on his W-2 Wage and Tax Statement for 1989, as is his claim to have been employed by the US Department of Naval Intelligence (Fig. 9.1).

Lazar states that even the President of the United States does not possess Majestic clearance. 'The President doesn't have the highest clearance in the United States,' he explained to George Knapp. 'There's no reason for him to know everything. Certainly, the President has clearance high enough to know about specific things that many people don't ... those that are involved in this project, of course, don't have a clearance to know what the President knows: everything's compartmentalized all the way up to the President.' Lazar nevertheless concedes that George Bush, as a former Director of Central Intelligence, does in fact have a lot of knowledge of the project at S-4.

'Do you get the feeling that this is a Government project, or is it a "Cabal" within the Government?' Knapp asked.

'No. It's not an overall Government project,' Lazar replied. 'It's not something that Congress appropriates money for – say two billion for this, fifteen billion for flying saucers, eight billion for Star Wars. It doesn't go like that. I don't believe [Congress has] any knowledge of it at all. And I believe that, from what I understand, this project, because of its potential magnitude, was given executive power in the late 1940s, and in itself they could appoint, seal off information, or whatever was necessary, and that's how it kind of ran on a parallel road by itself.'

'Obviously, Congress doesn't know about this. Do you believe perhaps that some of the money for this comes out of the Star Wars budget?' Knapp queried.

'Yes, that's my own personal belief.'

'Based on anything at all?'

'Oh, little hints here and there, but nothing that I can document and say, look, this is absolutely true.'

'But you also believe that to be true because of your previous experience with Star Wars?'

'Right. Which is classified, and should remain that way.'

S-4

There was no set routine for Lazar's job at S-4, and in total he spent no more than six or seven days there between December 1988 and March 1989. He would be called by phone and told when to go to McCarran Airport, where a Boeing 737 belonging to the Department of Energy would fly him and others to Groom Lake (Area 51). From there, after waiting briefly in a cafeteria, a bus with blacked-out windows drove the remainder of the journey along a dirt road to an area estimated to be approximately 10 miles south of Groom Lake, adjacent to Papoose (Dry) Lake in Emigrant Valley. To avoid confusion, I should point out that there is another S-4 area, located in the Nuclear Test Site proper.

On first arriving, Lazar was impressed by the extraordinary building within the S-4 facility, where he was to work. 'It's got a slope of about 30 degrees – which are hangar doors,' he said during an interview in late 1989, 'and it has textured paint on it, but it looks like sand. It's made to look like the side of the mountain that it's in, possibly to disguise it from satellite photographs. The hangars are all connected together and there are large bay doors between each one.'

The whole scene reminded him of a James Bond film set.

Lazar saw only this part of S-4 during the duration of his employment, and was escorted at all times by his supervisor and a security guard. 'The installation takes up a whole range of mountain,' he explained to me, 'and I'm allowed into a little office area here, and all I know is the corridor that connects it.'

About twenty-two scientists worked at S-4 and the number of security personnel was over three times that amount, Lazar told me. Security was formidable, and various methods of intimidation (including the possible use of drugs and hypnosis) were used to ensure that those who worked at the base kept their mouths shut. Even conversations were forbidden, except with the supervisor. On one occasion, guards pointed weapons at him and someone slammed a finger into his chest, screaming into his ear at close range. 'It's really not a good place to work,' he commented dryly.

Lazar was taken to an office beside the hangar and given about 120 briefing papers to read. The papers, in blue folders, covered many aspects of the UFO subject and contained a great deal of astonishing information, which Lazar pored over during his visits, trying to remember as much as he could. Owing to compartmentation, he did not learn everything, and doubts that anyone there was aware of the complete picture. 'They don't brief you on every aspect of what's going on, though they do give you a rough idea. But, specifically, I had to deal with propulsion and the physics of the intricate little workings of what was going on.'

Lazar learned that the United States has acquired a number of spacecraft, although exactly under what circumstances was not pointed out. He also saw autopsy reports as well as black and white photos of alien bodies (the typical 'greys', with large, hairless heads), some of which showed various organs spread on a table, listing weights and densities, and some that had been cross-sectioned.

Lazar believes that he was gradually being prepared for what was to follow: actual 'hands-on' experience with an extraterrestrial spacecraft, which first took place, he thinks, during his second visit to S-4.

The Craft

Lazar had been puzzled by a number of posters displayed at the site, showing a photograph of a disc hovering about 3 feet above the dry lake at S-4, with 'They're Here!' written below. As it turned out, the craft depicted was the one he was to work on.

'It was exciting. What else can you say?' Lazar said in 1989, commenting on his first sight of the craft. 'Of course, I couldn't say whether it was an alien device or just an interesting craft that we had been developing. So it was a little while before I ascertained that it was an extraterrestrial craft.'

The disc was approximately 30 to 35 feet in diameter and 15 feet high, resting on the ground inside one of the hangars. No landing gear of any sort was visible.

'When I was led in, I was told not to say anything and just keep my eyes forward and walk past the disc into the office area. And I did, and as I went by it I just stuck my hand on it, just to run it alongside the thing. I'm not a metallurgist; I don't know what the alloy was. It seemed brand-new – if I know what a new flying saucer looks like!'

The shape was similar to one of the craft shown in some of the dubious photographs taken by contactee Eduard (Billy) Meier in Switzerland,[3] and Lazar refers to it as the 'Sport Model', owing to its sleek shape. 'It's a slim disc with ridges in it, and bears an incredible resemblance to that [Meier's photo]. It's like it's pressed out of one piece of sheet metal. At the top there are some things that look like small square portholes' (see photo section).

'Were they portholes or something else?' I asked.

'It could have just looked like it because they were black,' Bob replied. 'I didn't see through them so I really can't say what they were. But there was certainly another level up there, but I don't know if there was an observation room or what. I always assume that was where the nerve centre was, as far as the electronics, control, navigation, and whatever else might be in there. I was always interested to see what was up there, but I was never allowed, and I had no idea how to get up that high.'

On another occasion Lazar was able to go inside the craft. 'It was all the same colour as the outside – I guess a dull aluminium finish is the best way I could describe it. There's a central column that goes right up the centre of the disc.[4] The wall inside – the inner skin of the ship – has archways in it, almost like Spanish-style homes, that go all the way round the wall. Whether that's bracing or not, I don't know. There were some components removed, like a console of some sort was taken off. There were just a few chairs and another console that was left inside, and the reactor.'

'How did you enter the craft?' I asked. 'Presumably there was a door or something?'

'No, the door was removed, and there were no hinges that were obvious. When you're entering a craft, you don't look and see how the door was attached; it's far more interesting what's in front of you! [The edges] were layered, so maybe something could fit in there. And there were a couple of steps leading up to it that were not provided by the craft. And when you first walk in the craft, that opening extends beyond the first floor. In other words, if you were looking straight into the door, you would see the honeycomb, bottom level, which you could grab on the side and lift up, and that provides access down.'

Lazar was puzzled by the internal structure, particularly the lack of any sharp edges. 'It was beyond being rounded,' he told me, 'it was like it was almost melted.' In an earlier interview, Lazar explained in more detail. 'It looked like it's made out of wax and heated for a time and then cooled off. Everything has a soft, round edge to it – there's no abrupt changes in anything. It looked like everything was cast out of one piece.'

Particularly puzzling were the chairs. 'The chairs are only like a foot or foot and a half off the ground. It looked like it was made for little kids!' Lazar reported.

Is it not more likely that the craft was manufactured here on Earth? Lazar is adamant on this point. 'The disc that I saw close up was not made by the United States,' he said in 1989. 'It was definitely extra-terrestrial. I don't know the exact history of them, but they're certainly alien craft, produced by an alien intelligence with alien materials. We were trying to see if we could duplicate what was there, with earthbound material and technology. You start with a finished product and you try and find out how it was built.'

According to some independent reports, the US has already succeeded in duplicating alien technology. A friend of mine, Ron Banuk, was driving to Minneapolis on the night of 30 December 1973, at the height of the second gas-rationing frenzy, when he heard an announcement on the radio that a recently retired Air Force general had stated that the US Government had unlocked the secret of UFO propulsion and had duplicated it. 'In vain did I search the newspapers on subsequent days to find a confirmation, explanation, or retraction of that statement,' Ron told me. 'The radio waves were also mute on the subject.'[5]

Lazar says he was never told how the craft arrived at S-4. 'I don't know where we got it from or how long ago it was, or anything. I don't know if they were flown here and given to us or if they were crashed and repaired. I don't think they crashed. I only had a chance to work on one, and it was in perfect operating condition. I don't know what the alloy was on the craft itself, but certainly we can manufacture something like that. [But] technical aspects, power source, and things of that sort; those we can't duplicate. And that's what we're most concerned with.'

Propulsion

Lazar learned that the power source of the craft he worked on is an 'antimatter reactor'.

'There's a [hollow] central column that goes right up the centre of the disc that's a wave guide – the gravity wave is channelled through there. The bottom of that connects to the antimatter reactor [which is] a half of a sphere on the floor of the craft.' The central column or wave guide extends to the top of the craft, and retracts upward to remove the reactor (Appendix, Fig. 8.2).

The reactor itself is about the size of a basketball, Lazar claims. 'It's half of a sphere on a small plate. It doesn't get warm. It produced a bizarre field around it when I saw it operating. You can push on it; it's almost like pushing together two magnets of like poles. Through some reaction, it produces a gravity field that's not completely understood, and one of the things they were teaching was the physics that connects all this together.'

The fuel element is even more bizarre, Lazar explained in this and another interview. 'On the periodic chart, it would be 115. It's always been theorized that up around Element 113–114, that they become stable again ... this is a stable element, and there are certain "magical" combinations of protons and neutrons which make up the elements, and this is apparently what is being used. On bombardment with protons it kicks it up to Element 116, and then releases anti-matter, and that's reactive with matter in [what is] called an annihila-tion reaction. And it appears they have something like a 100 per cent efficient thermocouple of sorts that produces power, and some sort of standing gravitational wave that propagates up through the wave guide, and then they use that excess power to do whatever they need.'

The craft does not create an 'anti-gravity' field, as some have sup-posed. 'It's a gravitational field that's out of phase with the current one,' Lazar explained to a listener during a 1989 radio interview. 'It's the same gravitational wave. The phases vary from 180 degrees to zero ... in a longitudinal propagation.'

Element 115 does not exist on Earth and cannot be synthesized, Lazar claims, because it is a 'superheavy' element. 'All indications are that it's found naturally, and it seems that it would have to occur naturally, in a place where there would be a much larger star – maybe a binary star, in an area where there's been a supernova – some place where there's been a sufficient energy release to synthesize such a heavy element ... To go so high up the chart, it really can't be pro-duced artificially in any way I can see. To make even a lighter ele-ment, like 103, takes a huge amount of money, and involves putting on a lighter element at the end of an accelerator and bombarding it with protons, trying to get them to plug into atoms, and you wind up with micrograms of the substance after an incredibly long period of time.'

The disc allegedly uses 223 grams of Element 115, and on one occa-sion, Bob told me, he tested a sample at his house. 'We put it in a cloud chamber, which is used to track the paths of nuclear particles – alpha particles in particular – over the top of the 115, showing that its gravitational force would change the path of the particle. We got that and filmed it on video. I didn't steal that from the site! That was not in fact even taken from S-4; that went through a different national lab that was actually machining the substance into a configuration neces-sary to power the craft, and it was offered to me.'

Five hundred pounds of Element 115 is alleged to be available for top secret research. The material is orange in colour and extremely heavy, Bob told me.

Manipulation of space and time is possible, Lazar claims, by virtue of the propulsion system. 'The crafts have three gravity amplifiers on the bottom of them. What they do – assuming they're in space – they will focus the three gravity generators on the point they want to go to. Now, to give an analogy: if you take a thin rubber sheet, say, lay it on a table and put thumbtacks in each corner, then take a big stone and set it on one end of the rubber sheet and say that's your spacecraft, you pick out a point that you want to go to – which could be anywhere on the rubber sheet – pinch that point with your fingers and pull that all the way up to the craft. That's how it focuses and pulls that point to it. When you then shut off the gravity generator, the stone (or spacecraft) follows that stretched rubber back to its point. There's no linear travel through space; it actually bends space and time and follows space as it retracts.'

There are two modes of travel, Lazar says. 'In the first mode of travel – around the surface of a planet – they essentially balance on the gravitational field that the gravity generators put out, and they can ride a "wave", like a cork does in the ocean. In that mode they're very unstable and are affected by weather. In the other mode of travel – where they can travel vast distances – they can't really do that in a strong gravitational field like Earth, because to do that, first of all they need to tilt on their side, usually out in space, then they can focus on the point they need to with the gravity generators and move on.

'If you can picture space as a fabric,' Lazar explained, 'and the speed of light is your limit, it'll take you so long, even at the speed of light, to get from point A to point B. You can't exceed it – not in this universe anyway. Should there be other parallel universes, maybe the laws are different, but anyone that's here has to abide by those rules. The fact is that gravity distorts time and space. Imagining that you're in a spacecraft that can exert a tremendous gravitational field by itself, you could sit in any particular place, turn on the gravity generator, and actually warp space and time and "fold" it. By shutting that off, you'd click back and you'd be at a tremendous distance from where you were, but time wouldn't even have moved, because you essentially shut it off. It's so far-fetched It's difficult for people to grasp, and as stubborn as the scientific community is, they'll never buy it that this is in fact what happens.'[6]

While Lazar's claims may not be acceptable to many scientists, some nevertheless believe that time travel into the past and instantaneous journeys by spaceships to distant parts of the universe by means of 'worm holes' may be feasible for a sufficiently advanced technological civilization. In November 1988, Dr Michael Morris, together with Professors Kip Thorne and Ulvi Yurtsever, speculated that 'worm holes' – holes in the structure of space and time – exist at a submicroscopic level but could be 'enlarged' by an advanced technology as a means of travelling instantaneously, bypassing the speed-of-light limit.[7]

NASA physicist Alan Holt also firmly believes in the feasibility of 'hyperspace' travel. He speculates that with the frequency of UFO sightings and the different types of beings that have been observed, one must assume that a number of different civilizations are visiting us, but this makes no sense whatever unless the speed of light is exceeded. He has proposed several hypotheses for surmounting this problem. By artificially generating a certain electromagnetic pattern, for example, a gravitational field could be generated that could nullify the Earth's own gravitational field. 'You'd select an energy configuration that has a resonance with the location you wanted to go, and travel through a type of hyperspace, or a higher dimensional space,' he stated in 1980.

Asked if the shape of the spacecraft would be a determining factor, Holt made an interesting reply: 'I think the shape of the spacecraft can be quite important. Elliptical or saucer-shaped would be the shapes I'd start out with. I hate to use those words because of the connotations. But what you're trying to do with the artificial energy pattern is overwhelm the natural mass energy pattern and exist in the material of the spacecraft itself. So a saucer is probably best. I don't think it's an accident that the UFO phenomena we see are, by and large, saucer-shaped.'[8]

In his *Field Resonance Propulsion Concept*, published by NASA, Alan Holt further speculates on hypothetical UFO propulsion systems:

If the speed of light is a true limit of velocity in space-time, then the potential extraterrestrial visitors must utilize a form of transportation which transcends space and time to keep the trip times short. UFOs are often observed to disappear instantaneously. In a subset of these cases, the UFO later reappears at a nearby location, implying a disappearance from and a reappearance into space-time.

The high-speed, right-angle turns, abrupt stops or accelerations of UFOs, and the absence of sonic booms despite calculated speeds of 22,000 m.p.h. or more, suggest that UFOs may generate an artificial gravitational field or otherwise use properties of space-time which we are not familiar with. UFO propulsion systems appear to involve electromagnetic or hydromagnetic processes, as evidenced by radiative effects on the environment, such as burns, dehydration, stopping of automobile engines, TV and radio disruptions, melting or alteration of ground and road surfaces, power disruptions, and static electricity effects . . .[9]

The propulsion system installed in the saucer at S-4 gives rise to certain peculiar effects, Bob Lazar claims, *including invisibility of the craft*.

'You can be looking straight up at it, and if the gravity generators are in the proper configuration you'd just see the sky above it – you won't see the craft there. That's how there can be a group of people and only some people can be right under it and see it, and there can be people 100 feet off to the left and not see it. It just depends how the field is bent. It's also the reason why the crafts *appear* as if they're making 90-degree turns at some incredible speed: it's just the time and space distortion that you're seeing. You're not seeing the actual event happening.'

Lazar is reluctant to release further details of the propulsion system. 'The entire concept I have no problem bringing forth, but the inner workings and details I still believe should remain classified. You have to understand that a lot of the reason these systems are being kept quiet is that everything is being looked at from a weapons point of view. I have no intention, and never have, of releasing precisely how everything works.'

Lazar suggests that possibly the main reason for maximum security about the craft is the potential for construction of a superbomb, as well as an advanced propulsion system. With regard to the latter, his work at S-4 involved an attempt to duplicate the reactor, using terrestrial materials, something which, he believes, is impossible. Several unsuccessful attempts had been made in the past. 'They were trying to use a normal nuclear generator, fuelled with plutonium, and that was really a futile attempt,' he said. (Perhaps the Snowbird project was one such attempt.)

Element 115 is not antimatter itself, but under certain nuclear reactions becomes highly explosive, Lazar explains. 'Essentially, all you need to do is bombard it with protons, which is an easy device to make, something to accelerate protons. It would be extremely easy to make a very, very powerful bomb. You're talking about hundreds of megatons off a small piece of it. It sounds incredible, but a total conversion of matter to energy does release that amount of power. So it's not something that you'd want to fall into someone's hands.'

Lazar believes that he was recruited to work at S-4 in order to replace one of three scientists who lost their lives in a tragic experiment that had taken place at the Nevada Test Site in May 1987. 'I guess they were proceeding along with tests on the antimatter reactor, and for some reason they decided to cut the reactor open while in operation,' he told me. 'They brought this down to the nuclear test site and did it in a vertical tunnel, with the blast doors, because they thought there might be an explosion. Something went wrong and the thing just detonated, killing all three guys. From what I understand, it took out the first door, which rarely ever breaks, and vaporized a couple of hundred thousand dollars of equipment.'

'So this is why you were brought in?' I asked.

'That's exactly what they said. And it was almost tongue-in-cheek, like, "Maybe you can find a little bit better way to investigate what's going on here than cutting it in half with a chain-saw!"'

Test Flight

During the third visit, all the connecting bay doors inside the hangar at S-4 were opened, allowing Lazar a distant view of nine different types of craft (including the one he worked on).

'You said in your initial interview that you thought about half of them were functional?' I reminded him.

'Now, that's a rough guess. You have to think of the great distance here that is involved, because those hangars are big and stretch out fairly far, and just at a quick glance it would really be tough to see what would operate and what wouldn't. I'm just counting the one that kind of looked like a top hat, which had a large hole in the side. I'm assuming that that didn't fly because it was in a non-functional condition. There was a 4- or 5-inch hole in the "brim" of the "top hat" section, and the metal was bent upwards like a projectile had gone through it. It is possible it could have been something else, but that's what it looked like to me; like it was shot from underneath. That's the only thing that ever put the seed in my mind that perhaps they weren't all *given* to us, because that looks like a fairly offensive move. Unless they just stood it up on its side to see how impenetrable the metal was and fired at it, or some other ridiculous test!'

But the most spectacular experience was the actual test flight of the craft that Lazar was familiar with.

'It was just about dusk,' he related to George Knapp. 'I came out of the door that was inside the hangar, which led to a hallway, came out of there, and the disc was already outside. Whether they carted it out or flew it out, I don't know. It was sitting on the ground. Right off to the side there was a guy with a scanner [radio]. The first thing I was told [was] to stand by him and not go anywhere else. And he was in communication with the disc. I said, "That's strange: it looks like you're on a normal frequency on a 200 MHz band", and he said, "Yeah". And I said, "Isn't it encrypted or coded or something?" and he said "No". And that just surprised me and I said, "What a breach of security, because you could just stand outside the base and listen to what's going on".

'The disc sat out there for a period of time, then the bottom of it glowed blue and it began to hiss, like high voltage does on a round sphere. It's my impression that the reason they're round and have no sharp edges is to contain the high voltage . . . It lifted off the ground, quietly, except with that little hiss in the background, and that stopped as soon as it reached about 20 or 30 feet. It shifted over to the left, shifted over to the right, and set back down. I mean, it doesn't sound like much, but it was incredibly impressive, just — mind-boggling. It's just magic!'

But who was on board?

'I don't know,' Lazar told me. 'I saw the radio set up when they were in communication with the craft, but I only heard instructions being *given*; I never heard anything come back, because I wasn't there for a long enough amount of time. So I assume there were people in the craft.'

'Sitting on those little seats?' I asked incredulously.

'Or they could have been on the upper section of the craft. It was amazing enough to see it operate; you really didn't care what was going on inside, just the fact that it was operating!'

Lazar elaborated on what he had learned about, and to a limited extent witnessed of, the bizarre effects produced by the propulsion system.

'If the crafts look like they're flying at 7,000 m.p.h. and they make a right-angled turn, it's not necessarily what they're doing. They can *appear* that way because of the gravitational distortion. I guess a good analogy is that you're always looking at a mirage — [it's only when] the craft is shut off and sitting on the ground, *that's* what it looks like. Otherwise, you're just looking at a tremendously distorted thing, and it will appear like it will be changing shape,[10] stopping or going, and it could be flying almost like an airplane but it would never look that way to you.'

'How close do you think you have to get before time distortion takes place?' I asked.

'It's tough to say, because it depends on the configuration of the craft. If the craft is hovering in the air, and the gravity amplifiers are focused down to the ground and it's standing on its gravity wave, you would have to get into that focused area. If you're directly underneath the craft at any time there's a tremendous time distortion, and that's in proportion to the proximity of the craft.'[11]

The disc is allegedly capable of erratic manoeuvres, and '2- to 3-mile drops in a second to zero velocity'. Great caution is exercised during the test flights, which are restricted to the Earth's atmosphere.

At that time, the tests were only conducted on Wednesday nights, Lazar revealed, because statistically it was the night of least traffic in that area. And so it was that on a Wednesday night in March 1989, Lazar took his wife Tracy, John Lear and Gene Huff, to an area about 15 miles from the remote test site, hoping to prove the reality of at least some of his sensational claims.

Notes

1 Private videotape made available to the author by Gene Huff.

2 Burrows, William E.: *Deep Black: The Secrets of Space Espionage*, Bantam, London, 1988, pp. 22–3.

3 Meier's photographs can best be seen in *UFO . . . Contact from the Pleiades*, Vols. I & II, Genesis III Publishing, Inc., P.O. Box 32067, Phoenix, Arizona 85064. Gary Kinder's *Light Years: An Investigation into the Extraterrestrial Experiences of Eduard Meier*, published by Atlantic Monthly Press (New York 1987), also includes a few of the photos. I remain unconvinced by much of Meier's material, but do not doubt that he has had some genuine experiences and that *some* of his photographs could be genuine. When I first spoke with him in 1965 (having heard about him in India the previous year), he seemed sincere, but on meeting him at his home in Switzerland in 1977 and examining the evidence that he had since accumulated (including film and photographs), I became suspicious.

4 Many contactees have reported a central column running down the centre of flying discs, the most notable being George Adamski. A more recent example is that reported to me by Alfred Burtoo, who in 1983 was taken aboard a craft in Aldershot, England (see *Above Top Secret*).

5 Letter to the author, 1 November 1987.

6 Bob Lazar has made additional information available on videotape. Write for details to: The Lazar Tape, 1324 S. Eastern, Las Vegas, Nevada 89104.

7 Berry, Adrian: 'Time travel may be possible via "worm holes" say scientists', *Daily Telegraph*, London, 23 November 1988.

8 Stewart, Connie: 'Star Wars travel might be only 12 years away', *Herald Examiner*, Los Angeles, 5 June 1980.

9 Holt, Alan C.: *Field Resonance Propulsion Concept*, NASA, Lyndon B. Johnson Space Center, Houston, Texas, August 1979, p. 3.

10 A perfect example of such changes of shape is visible in the 8 mm movie film taken by George Adamski and Madeleine Rodeffer in February 1965, at Silver Spring, Maryland (for details, see *Above Top Secret*). In addition to the film having been authenticated by former Kodak senior project engineer William Sherwood, ex-NASA mission specialist Bob Oechsler has recently stated his conviction that the film is genuine.

11 Interviews with the author, March/April 1990. Additional interviews were with George Knapp of KLAS-TV (mostly in private) and Billy Goodman on KVEG Radio, Las Vegas, in 1989.

· 9 ·

Containers

On Wednesday, 22 March 1989, the team, travelling in John Lear's recreational vehicle, arrived a little later than anticipated and parked on a road with a commanding view. I have been out to this vicinity on two occasions (in 1986 and 1990) and the landscape is truly awe-inspiring and majestic. Unfortunately, I have never seen anything unexplainable, probably because I was there at the wrong times. But John, Gene, Bob and Tracy – with advance knowledge of the test-flight time – were luckier.

While John was in the process of setting up his telescope, a light came very slowly over the horizon from the direction of the test site. A plane or satellite perhaps?

'Then the object *jumped*,' Gene told me. 'It jumped a long way to the right. Then we got the telescope on it. At that time, John was the only one who viewed the elliptical-shaped light through the telescope. The disc just flew around and then went down back to the mountains, south of where we were looking.'

The sighting, lasting about seven minutes, was hardly conclusive proof, although Bob had predicted that the craft would appear to make 'jumps', owing to the bizarre nature of the effects produced by the propulsion system. But the following Wednesday night, 29 March, Bob went out to the same viewing point, together with his wife, Gene and another friend, and this time they were all rewarded with a more substantial sighting.

'We were looking to the mountains to the south,' Gene recounted, 'and it came up very slowly and glided around very gently, in a strange movement. Through the telescope it was an elliptically shaped light. And then it did some very, very strange moves, like a "step" move. It would be sitting there and it would go, then sit, then drop down to mountain level. And it came up the mountain range, and glowed. Bob told me that the glow of the disc is just by virtue of the way it's energized: it's not like you can turn this light on and off. And it came up towards us, stopped and hovered, and not only did it glow, it glowed brighter and brighter. Finally, it glowed so bright that we started backing up behind the car. We thought it might explode, but it didn't. It went back down, went back above the mountain range gently, went down and hovered for a while, and went down as slowly as it came up.'

Gene had never seen any object move like that before, he told me. 'When it came up the mountain range it covered some distance to get to us. It's not the same as if there's a car coming on the highway, and there are the lights and you know it's coming. It'll just be there and all of a sudden it's a lot closer, then a *lot* closer. That's kind of an alarming thing.'[1]

The group had a video camera, and some of these manoeuvres are clearly visible on the film. Bob Oechsler, who has a lot of experience in analyzing video films (including Ed Walters' remarkable film taken in Gulf Breeze, Florida, in 1987), is convinced that the film provides powerful evidence in support of Lazar's claims, as he explained to me:

With a VCR, you're looking at an electronic reproduction of what the eye sees. In other words, you're looking at it through a series of horizontal bars, so essentially half the image is cut out. What you're looking at in this particular video of 29 March is a [light] that moves perhaps one third of the total distance of the screen, but it does so in a series of jumps. In other words, the light's on, it's off: you can do it frame by frame, which I've done, and you'll find that the light actually disappears then reappears at another location to the left of the original location, has a luminosity-characteristic signature, then it goes out again and jumps to another location.

The point is that it absolutely verifies the principle that Bob Lazar offered as to how the system works. It adds great integrity to his allegation that if you focus the gravity-wave amplifiers on a specific point in space, you intensify a gravitational field, 'pull' that point of space to you, in essence, and when you shut off the amplifier, you snap back to that point with it. In other words, you disappear and reappear at that point, as far as the eye would see, looking at it from any distance. So what you're seeing is a series of 'hyperspace' jumps on the videotape. And to me it is the most extraordinary piece of video footage that I've ever seen in terms of UFO films. Unfortunately, there are no reference points. You only have the witnesses' perspective to go on, and that perspective gives only some definable characteristics; that . . . the light came up from below a mountain range a certain distance away . . .[2]

Threats

Bob Lazar was taking enormous risks by bringing friends to an area where they would have an opportunity of viewing the test flights. And finally, on the night of 6 April 1989, they got caught.

While Lazar, together with his wife, sister-in-law, John Lear and Gene Huff, were waiting for another expected test, a security vehicle approached. 'Bob didn't want to get caught with us, so he went out in the desert,' Gene related. 'We . . . turned around, and we pulled up that dirt road and we stopped. So then they started up again and we went up further, stopped, and pulled the telescope out.' They pointed the telescope at Jupiter, hoping to allay suspicion, but it was to no avail.

'The security guys came up, all dressed in camouflage, but with no markings. They had pistols on them, and machine-guns, which they left in their vehicle. And they radioed back to the base security station that we said we were out there looking at the stars. They just told us that they would prefer that we weren't there, but that it was public land; they couldn't make us leave but they wanted us back up on the highway.

'So we didn't leave for a while, and Bob came back over and we were joking around. As it turned out, they were watching Bob and us all the time through night-vision binoculars. So then we pulled up on the highway and went the other way to watch for a while. As we understand it, we actually stopped the test this night because they had so much trouble with us.'

As they began the long drive back to Las Vegas, the sheriff stopped them, having been alerted by the security personnel, and asked each member of the group for identification.

'Lear had left his wallet in the trunk, and he opens the trunk, and there's a video camera, a big telescope, and a Geiger counter, of all things! And the sheriff says, "What are you doing out here with all this stuff?" Well, we wouldn't say anything. He tried to bluff his way into allowing the car to be searched. We didn't want it to be searched, because we had a gun in the trunk – for no other reason than that there are rattlesnakes out in the desert. So he radioed the base station and took all our IDs and it was put into a computer base at Area 51. He detained us for about fifty minutes, and it's only legal to detain you sixty minutes if they don't arrest you or tow your car in. So he let us go and said not to come out there any more.'[3]

The following day, Lazar was ordered to go to Indian Springs Air Force Auxiliary Field, about 35 miles north-west of Las Vegas, for a debriefing, which was attended by an FBI agent. 'Needless to say, they weren't happy that I had told a group of people what was going on and brought them down to show it!' he told George Knapp. 'They threatened me, put a gun to my head, and went over the security – the level of security that they had originally briefed me with. They did everything but physically hurt me [and said things like], "We have the power to kill you right now. No one's going to know about it – we can come up with a thousand excuses". I mean, just picture a guy with his face this far away from you, just screaming at you. It's bizarre.

'We had a story all made up as to why I was out there, about me being dropped off at the stop sign at the top of the hill, and that I really didn't go out there, and I didn't want to, and all that. And the first thing that they said when I got in was, "Forget about the stop sign story". We had only talked about that on the phone, and it's all too obvious it was tapped.'

During the interrogation, the guards from Area 51 who had caught the group were brought in. 'It was kind of funny,' Lazar told Knapp, 'because obviously they didn't know what was going on; they didn't know about the existence of the crafts or anything. I purposely made a point of saying, "What? Are you referring to the flying discs?" And the two guys – their eyes got really big, and they were shocked at what was going on. The FBI guy hussled them out of the door and was kind of upset that I had mentioned it.'

It was during this period that Lazar decided to go public with his story and give the interview, in silhouette, with George Knapp on KLAS-TV, Las Vegas. 'I used the name Dennis, which was my supervisor's name. He called immediately after that, and was really pissed off. "Do you have any idea of what they're going to do to you?" he said. "Well no, I don't," I said. Since then I've had other threatening phone calls, saying they're going to kill me. The chances are they're going to do nothing. I mean, I'm no hero or anything of that sort; I'm not foolhardy either, but if you're really going to kill someone, you don't tell them.'

Lazar described for me an alarming experience he had when someone took a shot at his car, following the initial television broadcast.

'I was getting on the Interstate 15 freeway, north from Charleston Boulevard [Las Vegas], and when I turned the corner, a white car drove up alongside, pulled down the window and fired a shot. At the time I had to go into a turn to get on to the freeway, but instead chose to keep going straight, and just hoped that he would go away and take the turn, so I just drove off into the dirt and kept going. The shot hit the brake section in the wheel and snapped part of the rear brake and shot the tyre. I just continued on and stopped in the dirt, and he continued driving and rolled up the window.'

In January and February 1990, Nippon Television filmed interviews with Lazar in Las Vegas. Further interviews in Japan were planned, but the day before Lazar was due to leave, he apparently received a call from his ex-boss. 'You'll never make it back', he was told. One of the many rumours circulating about Lazar is that he had pocketed the cash for the interview in Japan and that Nippon TV had sued him for breach of contract. The truth of the matter is that Nippon TV had agreed to pay him $2,000 on arrival in Japan, $3,000 having already been paid for the extensive interviews in Las Vegas. After the alleged threat, Lazar decided that he could not risk his life. Nippon TV were accordingly informed that he would not be able to make the scheduled visit, and the final payment was therefore never made.

Breaking Security

Why did Bob Lazar decide to risk everything by going public with the secrets of S-4?

'One of the reasons I'm coming forward with this information,' he said in 1989, 'is that it's not only a crime against the American people, it's a crime against the scientific community, which I've been part of for some time. It's just unfair not to put it in the hands of the overall scientific community. There are people who are much more capable of dealing with this information, and by this time would have got a lot further along than this select, small group of people working out in the middle of the desert. They don't even have the facilities, really, to completely analyze what they're dealing with.'

Lazar was also frustrated at being unable to discuss the sensational nature of his work. 'You really can't say anything. Like when you get home and your wife says, "Hi. What happened at work today?" You can't say you worked with some stuff from another planet! It's ridiculous. You need someone to talk to – it's just a tremendous thing to keep on your shoulders. How anyone else does it is beyond me.'

Another reason was the working environment, which Lazar found oppressive and restricted. He particularly resented the harassment that he underwent as part of the security procedure, which of course increased once it became evident that he had broken his security oath. Following the debriefing at Indian Springs, he was asked to go to work at S-4 but refused. 'Are you officially refusing?' he was asked, to which he replied in the affirmative. 'And that was the end of it. I left on a sour note. I was never officially fired and my clearance was never officially taken away. At that time there was a lot of tension, a lot of worry, and the last place I wanted to get trapped was where no one could get to me, so I officially refused to go back. There was no communication after that.'

But Lazar's main purpose in coming forward, he claims, was to protect himself. 'I tried to protect myself in several ways. One of them was going on the air and getting some of the information out, because that would be the only thing they would want to try and prevent. And once that was done — unless they do things for revenge, and I don't believe that they operate that way — there would be no reason to hassle me any more. Any action on their part right now would guarantee what I'm saying is true, so I think it's going to be a "hands-off" policy.

'I've essentially accomplished what I wanted to. I don't want to run out and prove everything to everyone, because frankly I don't really care if anyone believes anything I say at all. The only thing is to confront them with things they can't deny. No matter what I say, no matter how much proof comes out, more people from S-4 need to come forward, because we have to come forward as a group. Just one person doesn't cut it.

'Where are the limits to national security? There has to be some sort of moral guideline where you have to draw the line and say, you know, it's our responsibility to let everyone know about this, and we have to let national security kind of hang in the balance ... I did not believe that this should be a security matter. Some of it, sure, but just the concept that there's definite proof and that we even have articles from another world, another system, you just can't not tell everyone.'

Asked if he felt comfortable about breaking security, Lazar replied, 'No. To some degree I regret it, but it's tough to backtrack now.'

Support

During one of the interviews with Bob Lazar on KVEG Radio in November 1989, a man claiming to be a construction worker from a company based in Mercury, at the southern part of the test site, nervously offered some support.

'We're all kind of fed up with what's going on,' the anonymous caller began. 'We are the construction workers: we put things together and take them apart. We heard about your situation. People are meeting in small groups and we're trying to organize support for you to back you up. At the meeting we had yesterday of seven people, two will come forward and support you in what you saw, or what they're involved with, but the other guys are just scared to death. And I'm a little scared myself ... It's kind of hard to talk to you like this, but the guys are for you. Everybody wanted to do something a long time ago, but nobody knew what they had to do.'

'Do you think these people would come forward if there was some sort of Congressional amnesty for them?' Lazar asked.

'Well, I don't know. But we all know a lot ... Like when you walked into those hangars there. I mean, somebody had to put them up, right? It's frightening. It scared the heck out of a lot of us. We've just got together now to see whether we're going to do something. We could form some sort of a picket, or make some kind of announcement on the street ...'

'You start making a ruckus like that,' Lazar said, 'and these guys can lose their jobs right away. There's a ten-year jail term and $10,000 fine for divulging information like that. There's an awful lot to lose.'

Lazar told me that he had no idea how genuine the caller was, since a number of cranks had called him during the radio interviews. In any event, nothing came of the offer of support.

Polygraph Tests

The results of polygraph tests undertaken by Bob Lazar are generally encouraging, if inconclusive. According to examiner Ron Slay, for example, Lazar appeared to be truthful on one test and deceitful on another. Slay recommended that a second examiner be brought in, and Terry Tavernetti, a former Los Angeles police officer, put Lazar through four tests and concluded that there was no attempt to deceive. Tavernetti sent the results to a third polygrapher, who corroborated the findings, and to another examiner, who did not, stating his belief that Lazar might have been relating information that he had learned from someone else. Tavernetti, however, remains convinced that Lazar was telling the truth, as he explained during a television interview in 1990:

He gave absolutely no physiological indications of attempted deception ... My personal thoughts [on] the pre-test interview of three and a half hours, the test itself, and the post-test interview, showed absolutely nothing to deter my thought that Bob Lazar was truthful. Unfortunately, we're dealing with a subject matter here where fear, on behalf of Mr Lazar, of reprisal, might far exceed just the threat of losing his credibility as a scientist, which would make polygraph tests maybe totally ineffective.

Significantly, Tavernetti's boss received a telephone call from a certain Government agency wanting to know why Tavernetti was getting involved in 'something he shouldn't be'. 'I asked what agency and what [they] said that identified themselves, and that I'd be happy to talk,' said Tavernetti. 'And I was refused this information, and told that he didn't know.'

Perhaps coincidentally, Tavernetti, who has retained the tapes and printouts from Lazar's polygraph tests, had his home broken into in January 1990.[4]

Corroborative Evidence

During my visits to Las Vegas, I met with a number of Bob Lazar's friends and associates, including George Knapp, who had first interviewed Lazar in March 1989. George is a TV journalist and anchorman for KLAS-TV, Channel 8, Las Vegas, and after he had interviewed me in March 1990 for his second UFO documentary,[5] he talked about his impressions on meeting Lazar and the subsequent evidence he has uncovered which tends to support Lazar's extraordinary claims.

'I felt real impressed,' he began. 'The first meeting that we had of any substance was when I took my news director to John Lear's house to meet him. My boss was ultra-sceptical going in. Coming out, we just looked at each other and he said, "OK. Ten minutes a night, and as much time as you need. Go for it!" He was that impressed with him.

'It's just a story that's made the rounds here in Nevada for a long time that nobody has really bothered to look into. We know a lot of secret stuff goes on in Area 51; we know the nature of some of those programmes, and there's been this lingering, nagging voice floating around at the test site for many years that something else, something alien, was up there, but no one's ever bothered to check it out. But Bob is the first to come forward to say anything about it – to have inside knowledge.

'I've spent almost a year on the Lazar story. We've gone over every aspect of the story again and again. Knowing him really sells a lot of it, because he's not out to impress anyone and he's not trying to make a million dollars with this. He's not trying to spill the secrets of the universe or blow himself up to be more important than he is, and he tells you when he doesn't know something. The story has been consistent again and again, and we've gone over it many times. The checks into his background have been difficult. If you know Bob, you realize how lackadaisical he is about these things: he's like your typical absent-minded professor. Details of his life he just disregards. We've talked to his co-workers and the guy he used to work with at Los Alamos, who took us into these top secret areas.

'A number of people have come forward with little bits and pieces of information,' George continued. 'There was a security guard at the test site. I pursued him for a couple of months, but he would not talk to me. There was another security guy, who claimed to have seen Lazar up there. He thought Lazar hadn't seen the whole picture, and he agreed to meet with me and he was going to provide some material. The meeting didn't come off. I got a call at home, and he said, "Something's wrong with your phone, because my house was broken into. The materials were the only things that were taken".

'A second guy called me who claimed to have done the tax returns over a number of years for people that worked at 51, and he'd picked up a number of bits and pieces about the saucer programme up there. Well, the morning after he calls, he gets a visit by two guys saying they're Secret Service and they want to ask him about some old records. He related to me that it was pretty clear to him that it was an attempt of intimidation; that they just wanted to get a look at him, get a photograph, and let him know they didn't appreciate him talking to me.'

'Have you spoken to people who've seen craft up in the area?' I asked.

'Sure. There was another fellow – actually, a guy who used to work here at this station as an engineer. Before he worked here, he worked at 51. He inadvertently walked into a hangar and saw one of these discs under a big tarp. I called him to arrange an interview, to do it in limbo, and the morning after he agreed to do the interview, there's two guys sitting out at the front of his house in a car, with a radio. They follow him to work and follow him home again. And that's the last I heard from him. He communicated with me through another party that he wouldn't do the interview.'[6]

George Knapp has learned that it is common knowledge among those with high security clearances that extraterrestrial craft are kept at the Nevada Test Site. A Las Vegas man who was once stationed there claimed to have seen a flying disc land outside the boundaries of Area 51. And an airman who worked at one of the Nellis AFB radar installations said that he and his fellow servicemen watched unusual objects flying over the Groom Mountains for a period of five nights. The radar images indicated that the objects zoomed into range at 7,000 m.p.h. and would then 'stop on a dime'. When word of the sighting leaked out, the airman was told to keep quiet about the matter and that 'it didn't happen'.[7]

Another highly placed informant who was going to give George information on crashed discs, recovered bodies, and alien technology, was visited at her home by a man who identified himself as a Government agent, warning her that any release of information would lead to trouble, and reminding her that she did a lot of travelling and that 'accidents can happen'. Her family could also be harmed, he warned.

The existence of an S-4 area on the Nellis Test Range has been confirmed to George Knapp by a spokesman for the Nellis AFB Public Affairs Office, who admitted that the military 'operates certain equipment at S-4', but refused to divulge where S-4 is located or what equipment is tested there. (It is quite probable, in my opinion – which is shared by Bob Lazar – that the 'equipment' has been transferred to another location, S-4 having been exposed.)

During his extensive research into the stealth programme, Jim Goodall, the well-known aviation photographer and writer, has spoken with a number of sources who have added substance to the growing body of stories about Area 51/S-4, including a master sergeant who did three tours of duty at Groom Lake.

'He said that the United States Government and the military have things out there that you can't describe as airplanes, that are literally out of this world,' Goodall revealed in 1990. 'He emphasized "out of this world" and said, "And they're alien to anything that you've ever seen". And I tried to press him some more and he says, "Look, I can't comment. I've gone much further than I should already".[8]

Controversial Background

An inevitable consequence of Lazar's revelations was that attempts were made to discredit him. To begin with, it has proved extremely difficult to substantiate his educational background. This is due partly to the fact that he left many of his papers at his house in Las Vegas, following the tragic death of his first wife, Carol Strong, and also because Lazar himself tends to be absent-minded at the best of times. But there is also evidence that certain officials have gone to great lengths to ensure that as few records as possible are located.

When George Knapp contacted the hospital where Lazar says he was born, in Coral Gables, Florida, no records could be found. And when Knapp contacted the schools and universities where Lazar claims to have studied, he was informed that they had never heard of him.

Lazar told me that he attended Pierce Junior College, California, then the California Institute of Technology (Caltech) and California State University at Northridge. A period of employment at Fairchild was followed by a return to Caltech. He claims to have obtained Masters degrees in physics (his thesis was on Magnetohydrodynamics) from the Massachusetts Institute of Technology (MIT) and in electronics from Caltech. To date, no proof for these has been forthcoming. Although physicist Stanton Friedman has been able to verify that Lazar did indeed attend both Pierce College and California State University, he has so far drawn a blank about MIT. 'There's no trace of him at MIT and no record of him having attended any course. Maybe he took a lot of courses but didn't get a degree – that's a possibility.'

As we have seen, Lazar's claim to have worked at the Los Alamos National Laboratory was strenuously denied by officials. No records of his employment there could be found, they said. Confronted with Lazar's entry in the Lab's internal phone book, an exasperated official still insisted there were no records. More recently, officials have grudgingly admitted that Lazar worked briefly for 'a Lab sub-contractor in a non-sensitive position'. In spite of numerous inquiries over several months, neither the Lab nor the sub-contractor have provided copies of these records. Lazar's former co-workers have confirmed that he did indeed work on top secret projects, including SDI, and a 1982 front-page story about Lazar's jet car (the engine of which he designed and built) alludes to his employment at the Lab's Meson Physics Facility.[9] Finally, Lazar's W-2 tax forms provide proof of his employment there.

It has naturally been a formidable task to prove that Bob Lazar actually worked at S-4. US Naval Intelligence officials denied any knowledge of Lazar, yet incontrovertible proof of his employment by the US Department of Naval Intelligence, during the period he claims to have been there, is evident on his W-2 Wage and Tax Statement for 1989, which was located in August 1990. Equally significant is the reference to 'MAJ' – the 'Majestic' security clearance Lazar claims to have held at S-4 – which can be seen in the Office of Management & Budget number (Fig. 9.1).

Arrest

Bob Lazar is the first to admit that his colourful background has tended to augment his reputation as a maverick scientist. At Los Alamos, for example, police frowned on his noisy jet car, which had led to a number of complaints in the neighbourhood. Yet the car is a testimony to his ingenuity as a scientist and engineer. The engine (Lazar's second and installed in his Honda) was made of stainless steel and titanium and fuelled by liquid propane. In tests at a dry lake bed near Los Angeles, the car reached over 200 m.p.h., using its kerosene-powered afterburner. The conventional gasolene-powered engine was used to take the Honda up to a certain speed before the jet would be fired. Unlike most jet engines, Lazar's design did not incorporate bulky compressors, and used only 1.3 pounds of fuel for each pound of thrust. Prior to the car, Lazar had designed a jet-powered bike which reached up to 100 m.p.h. 'The cops saw that and put a stop to it for fear of safety,' he said.[10]

Lazar helped to produce record albums at one time, and also worked on a number of small engineering and photographic projects.

1 Control number		OMB No. 1545-0008	E-6722MAJ	
2 Employer's name, address, and ZIP code			3 Employer's identification number 46-1007639	4 Employer's state I.D. number N/A
United States Department of Naval Intelligence Washington, DC. 20038			5 Statutory Deceased Pension Legal employee plan rep. □ □ □ □	942 Subtotal Deferred Void emp. compensation □ □ □ □
			6 Allocated tips	7 Advance EIC payment
8 Employee's social security number 068-54-8190	9 Federal income tax withheld 168.24		10 Wages, tips, other compensation 958.11	11 Social security tax withheld 71.94
12 Employee's name, address, and ZIP code			13 Social security wages	14 Social security tips
Robert S. Lazar 1029 James Lovell Las Vegas, NV. 89128			16	16a Fringe benefits incl. in Box 10
			17 State income tax	18 State wages, tips, etc.	19 Name of state Nevada
			20 Local income tax	21 Local wages, tips, etc.	22 Name of locality

Form W-2 **Wage and Tax Statement 1989**
Employee's and employer's copy compared □ Copy 2 To be filed with employee's State, City, or Local Income tax return.

Fig. 9.1
Robert Lazar's W-2 Wage and Tax Statement for 1989 (after deductions), for a total of five non-consecutive days' work at the S-4 area. Proof of his employment by the US Department of Naval Intelligence is shown, as is his security clearance level – 'MAJ' for 'Majestic' (top right).

'There's a tremendous amount of things I've been involved with over the years,' Lazar said on a television interview in April 1990. 'Just because I have a wide variety of interests, a lot of it can be misconstrued and taken out of context. I'm sure it can be used to make me look pretty bad. There again, *maybe that's one of the reasons they looked at before hiring me.* I'm an easy person to hammer into the ground . . .'

It did not take long. During the same interview, Lazar responded to rumours that he had been involved in illegal drugs, that he had a meth lab in his home, that he was selling women to South America, and that he was involved with a prostitution ring. All the stories were demonstrably false, with one exception: his involvement in prostitution. Lazar openly admitted that he and his first wife Carol had owned a legal brothel, the 'Honeysuckle Ranch', in northern Nevada in the early 1980s, and that more recently he had installed some video equipment and helped with computer software and accounting for a friend who owned an illegal brothel in a residential area of Las Vegas, for which he had received money. His involvement had lasted only a matter of weeks, he said, and the business was operating before he came on the scene.

The police reacted swiftly to the televised admission, since it posed an embarrassment for the Las Vegas Metro Vice Squad and the Clark County District Attorney's office. The brothel owner, Toni Bulloch, had previously stated that the Vice Squad had come to an arrangement with her, whereby they would turn a blind eye to her operation if her girls did not make outside calls to hotels, and she had also agreed to act as an informant for the Squad, several of whose officers were alleged to have been clients. Within hours, officers raided the brothel, and Bulloch was arrested and charged with pandering, living off the earnings of a prostitute, conspiracy to commit prostitution, and keeping a disorderly house. Bulloch blamed Lazar for setting up the operation, and he was served with a search warrant at his home and charged with pandering ('pimping'), which in Nevada carries a sentence of from one to six years and a possible fine of $5,000.

On 18 June 1990, with some coaxing from his attorney, Lazar reluctantly pleaded guilty in the Las Vegas District Court, and on 20 August was sentenced to a three-year suspended sentence and 150 hours of community service. It was also recommended that Lazar, who is divorced from his second wife, should see a psychiatric counsellor, in view of his 'negligent circumstances'.

I have a video of the proceedings, and it is relevant to mention that nobody had a bad word to say for the defendant. Both the Las Vegas Vice Squad and the District Attorney had requested that Lazar should not be sent to jail, and even prosecutor John Lukens commented that Lazar did not fit the profile of a typical panderer. Judge Lehman expressed surprise that Lazar's partial involvement in the operation had not been plea-bargained down to a gross misdemeanour and that Toni Bulloch was not in court as a co-defendant (she had previously been charged only with keeping a disorderly house, a misdemeanour statute that goes back to 1911). He also took account of the fact that Lazar had lost his job with Naval Intelligence (the W-2 form cited as proof of his employment) and therefore needed to earn money.

Further Support

In spite of the suspended sentence, Lazar's credibility has suffered a severe blow, and one that he will not easily live down. Many will wonder why I have included his story here at all. The point is that we have firm evidence of his involvement in what could be the most secret project ever undertaken on this planet, and to dismiss Lazar's claims merely because of his involvement in prostitution is, in my opinion, premature. Perhaps, as he admits himself, he was recruited to work at S-4 precisely because of his colourful background.

Other experienced researchers who have met Lazar testify to his apparent honesty, including Dr Jacques Vallee, who is not predisposed to a belief in UFOs as solid, extraterrestrial spacecraft. 'He seems very credible,' he said on television in 1990. 'I think that he was in the places that he described. He also seemed to have concern with remembering some parts of the things that went on there. We asked him if he felt that his memory might have been tampered with. Now that is something . . . Could it be that he was exposed deliberately to certain things, perhaps to distract attention from other things? But I'm certainly of the opinion that he's not lying, and that he's talking the truth, and that he's genuinely concerned with finding out what happened to him.'[11]

Lazar has had difficulty in recollecting clearly all the events that took place at S-4. Although he recalls most of what happened, there were a couple of days when all he could remember was flying out to the test site and getting back on the plane to return to Las Vegas. Regression sessions with a clinical hypnotist, Layne Keck, tend to indicate that Lazar had been administered a drug (smelling like pine) and was subjected to periods of regimented hypnosis, including harassment, the purpose of which was to instigate a fear of breaking security. Further information may yet come to light, but it is significant that Keck has commented positively on Lazar's truthfulness. 'His subconscious mind believes, totally, all of these things,' he said in 1989.

In June 1990, former astronaut Dr Edgar Mitchell visited Lazar and spent three days talking with him. Afterwards, Dr Mitchell stated his conviction that Lazar had indeed been involved in a high-level 'black' project, because of his level of knowledge on these matters, and he has subsequently made his own investigations into the allegations about S-4.[12]

An Alien Presence?

It will be recalled that during Bob Lazar's initial interview in March 1989 he was asked if any aliens were present at S-4. 'Er, I really want to steer away from that right now,' he responded. I asked Bob the same question during one of our interviews.

'I don't know, I really don't,' he replied. 'You know, if you're walking by a door and glance in and think you see something, and when you walk by it again there's nothing there — the people, the configuration has changed in the room — how much credit can you put into that?'

Bob was more forthcoming in a private interview with George Knapp in 1989, although equally reluctant to confirm that what he saw could have been an alien, emphasizing how he disliked talking about aspects of his experiences at S-4 that he was unable to verify personally.

'OK. But what did you see?' insisted George.

'I walked down the hallway at one time I was working down there, and there were doors — the doors that go to the hangar are smaller doors than in the corridors and have a 9-inch or 12-inch square window with little wires running through it, just about head level. And as I was walking by, I just glanced in and I noticed — at a quick glance — there were two guys in white lab coats, facing me towards the door. And they were looking down and talking to something small, with long arms. I was just surprised as I walked by, and I only caught a glimpse. But I don't know what on earth that was.

'Now, UFO proponents right away say, "That was an alien — you saw an alien!" I don't know. I mean, there were so many weird things and they play so many mind games there. Maybe they stuck a doll in front of these guys and made me walk by it and look at it, just to see what my reaction would be. But, when we did turn around to do something, and walk back, it was gone, and the two guys were gone. So, I don't know what I saw.'

In the 1988 documentary, *UFO Cover-Up? Live*, Condor and Falcon claimed that the aliens not only operated from Area 51 but had complete control of the base. Could there be any truth to this scenario? Bob was sceptical when I put this to him, but did not totally discount the possibility of an alien presence, at least.

'The installation takes up a whole range of mountain, and I'm allowed into a little office area here, and all I know is the corridor that connects it,' he explained. 'The rest of it could be an alien haven for all I know. Maybe they never did open the door to let me into the whole bag. It could be tremendous. So who am I to say? I don't *think* that was the case. I don't know if there are any aliens running around. And then, what a waste of time this [research effort] would all be if there were!'

The Briefing Papers

Bob Lazar may not have seen aliens running around S-4, but he read a great deal about them in the 120 or so briefing papers that he was required to study.

Gene Huff told me that the papers dealt with a number of highly classified projects, including 'Galileo' (the disc-flying operation), 'Looking Glass' (research into the possibility of seeing back in time), and 'Sidekick' (dealing with powerful beam weapons), all under the umbrella of 'Project Overview'. Bob did not have time to read through everything, and concentrated mostly on those papers that dealt with his own area of expertise.

'Most of it did pertain to what I would be working with,' Bob told me, 'but there was a lot of it I didn't even understand.'

'Is it true that there was an interchange of information between the aliens and some scientists at the site at one time, and that there was an altercation resulting in many deaths, according to what you read in the briefing papers?'

'Right, that's *according* to what I read, that's what was going on. And I believe the altercation came about in 1979, or sometime like that. And I don't remember exactly how it was started, but it had something to do with the security personnel. The aliens were in a separate room. I think it had something to do with the bullets [the security guards] were carrying, and somehow they were trying to be told that they couldn't enter the area with the bullets, possibly because it was hazardous – the bullets could explode, through some field or whatever.

'I actually remember very little about the story, but either someone attempted to come into the room with the bullets, or had a gun in his hand or something, and the security people were killed – by head wounds. And it was very non-descriptive past that. And I think then that the scientists were all killed also.'

The incident is said to have led to the termination of an alien liaison at the Nevada Test Site.

I had heard an almost identical story from Paul Bennewitz in 1985. 'In 1979, something happened,' he wrote to me. 'The alien through the computer said [there had been] an argument over weapons . . . sixty-six were killed, forty-four got away.' The incident supposedly occurred at an alien base in Dulce, New Mexico – not at the Nevada Test Site.

Since Bennewitz had been fed liberal doses of disinformation, I put it to Bob that the briefing documents might have contained false information, too. He did not deny the possibility, but pointed out that everything he saw on paper pertaining to his own area of expertise turned out to be factual, so he assumes therefore that everything else he read could have been equally valid. Some of that information is controversial, to say the least, and is remarkably similar to the information (or disinformation) disseminated by Falcon and Condor.

There were references in the reports to 'The Kids' – presumably the little fellows who had manned at least one of the craft at S-4 – whose origin was said to be Reticulum 4, the fourth planet out from Zeta Reticuli 2. (Falcon mentioned the same point of origin during the 1988 documentary, but said that the home planet was the *third* out in the binary star system.)

The two stars that comprise the Zeta Reticuli system are similar to our sun (G2 type) and are approximately thirty-seven light years from our solar system, separated from each other by a distance of at least 350 billion miles, and requiring over 100,000 years to orbit their common centre of gravity. Both Zeta 1 and Zeta 2 are prime candidates for the search for life beyond Earth, and both could well have a system of planets similar to our own.[13]

It was stated in the briefing papers that humankind is the product of periodic genetic 'corrections' by the aliens. Bob has difficulty with this statement, as he emphasized in his private interview with George Knapp.

'It's easier to swallow things you can put your hands on and touch and then *work* with,' he said. 'That's no problem. But when you get a lot of spiritual stuff and religion – you know, that we were made by progressive corrections in evolution and that sort of thing . . . it's a tough thing to accept without hard-core proof. The only hard-core thing is that there is an *extremely* classified document dealing with religion, and it's extremely thick. But why should there be *any* classified documents dealing with religion?'

Knapp pressed Lazar for further information.

'Oh, come on, that's so weird . . .'

'I'm not asking you to say what you believe to be a fact; I'm asking you to say what you read in a report that is distributed at what may be the most top secret facility in the world.'

'It's just so far out . . .'

'All right. Your objection has been noted! What does it say?'

'That we're "containers". That's supposedly how the aliens look at us; that we are nothing but containers.'

'Containers of what?'

'Containers. Maybe containers of souls. You can come up with whatever theory you want. But we're containers, and that's how we're mentioned in the documents; that religion was specifically created so we have some rules and regulations for the sole purpose of not damaging the containers.'

Supposedly, Jesus and two other spiritual leaders were genetically engineered, in the sense that 'they were implanted in people on Earth and their births were closely monitored'. Again, a similar claim was made (specifically about Jesus) by Richard Doty, in conversation with Linda Howe in 1983.

The idea is hardly new, and has been put forward by a number of writers. For some reason, it outrages many devout Christians. Perhaps they should take note of the many passages in the Bible which, although open to alternative interpretations, nevertheless suggest the possibility of an out-of-this-world origin for Jesus, for example: the angel Gabriel's visit to Mary, informing her of an unusual conception; the star of Bethlehem which guided the Wise Men to the place of birth; the physical Ascension into 'heaven', with the two men standing by in 'white apparel'; and Saul's conversion on the road to Damascus, when Jesus apparently spoke to him from a 'great light' in the sky.

In addition, one could adduce the extraordinary abilities attributed to Jesus, and the occasional cryptic statements in reference to his origin, such as the following, recorded in John's Gospel: 'You belong to this world here below, but I come from above. You are from this world, but I am not from this world.'[14]

Is the idea really so far-fetched? Not according to Dr Barry Downing, for example, a theologian with a degree in physics, whose book, *The Bible and Flying Saucers*, traces the evidence for extraterrestrial liaison with mankind throughout biblical history.[15]

Bob Lazar's story should not be judged on what he read in the briefing papers, however, as he is the first to admit, but on the merits or otherwise of his alleged personal experiences at S-4. Based on my meetings with him, and on the considerable amount of related evidence that has come to light, I conclude that he is telling the truth, although I have reservations about some of the information that he has presented, and remain concerned about the lack of proof (so far) for his qualifications.

'Well, I am telling the truth – I've tried to prove that,' Bob Lazar insists. 'What's going on up there could be the most important event in history. You're talking about physical contact and proof from another system – another planet, another intelligence. That's got to be the biggest event in history – period. And it's real, and it's there.'[16]

Notes

1 Interview with the author, 30 March 1990.
2 Interview with the author, 5 September 1990.
3 Interview with the author, 30 March 1990.
4 KLAS-TV, Channel 8, P.O. Box 15047, Las Vegas, Nevada 89114, 1989.
5 *UFOs: The Best Evidence?*, KLAS-TV, 1990.
6 Interview with the author, 30 March 1990.

7 KLAS-TV, 1989.

8 *UFOs: The Best Evidence?*, KLAS-TV, 1990.

9 England, Terry: 'LA man joins the jet set – at 200 miles an hour', *Los Alamos Monitor*, 27 June 1982.

10 Ibid.

11 *UFOs: The Best Evidence?*, KLAS-TV, 1990.

12 Information supplied to the author by Gene Huff, who met Dr Mitchell during his meetings with Bob Lazar.

13 *Astronomy*, December 1974.

14 The Gospel According to John, 8:23, *Good News Bible*, The Bible Societies and Collins, American Bible Society, New York.

15 Downing, Dr Barry H.: *The Bible and Flying Saucers*, J. B. Lippincott Company, Philadelphia & New York, 1968.

16 Interviews with the author, March/April 1990; with George Knapp of KLAS-TV; and Billy Goodman, KVEG Radio, 1989. Bob Lazar has provided additional information on videotape. Write to: The Lazar Tape, 1324 S. Eastern, Las Vegas, Nevada 89104.

· 10 ·

Cosmic Journey

It was 13 May 1988. Admiral Bobby Ray Inman had just completed the keynote address at a ground-breaking ceremony for the National Security Agency's new top secret supercomputer facility for the Institute for Defense Analysis, of which Inman was a former director. Standing outside the speakers' tent at the University of Maryland's Science and Technology Center was former NASA mission specialist Bob Oechsler, waiting for an appropriate opportunity to approach the retired intelligence chief, who in his distinguished career had been a director of both the National Security Agency and Naval Intelligence.

The admiral bade his farewells and, fortuitously, headed in Oechsler's direction. 'Excuse me, Admiral,' said Oechsler, handing over his business card. 'I would be deeply appreciative if at some point you'd have someone contact me about how I can get closer to MJ-12.'

Inman studied the card, which briefly detailed Oechsler's expertise in robotics and mobilized security surveillance systems, then looked Bob straight in the eyes. With a knowing nod and half-smile, he placed the card neatly in the breast pocket of his jacket. 'OK,' he replied, in a Texas drawl.

The two men shook hands and Inman quickly departed, leaving Oechsler with the firm impression that Inman knew precisely about the nature of the inquiry.

Admiral Inman's impressive background in the Intelligence Community, his involvement with Government technology-related projects and organizations such as the Brookings Institution, the Council on Foreign Relations, the Defense Science Board as well as the Institute for Defense Analysis, had prompted Oechsler to make his request. 'I can think of no other individual in the entire United States of America who is more qualified to manage the most important covert operation in the history of mankind,' he believes.[1]

Born in 1931, Bobby Ray Inman graduated with a BA from the University of Texas in 1950 and entered the US Navy (Naval Reserve) in 1952, serving for two years on aircraft carriers, and occasionally working in London and Paris. From 1965 to 1967 he served as assistant to the Naval Attaché in Stockholm, and during this period became an analyst for the National Security Agency's Navy Field Operational Intelligence Office. In 1972 he was appointed assistant to the Chief of Staff of Intelligence, Office of the Commander of the Pacific Fleet. Two years later Inman became the Director of Naval Intelligence, a post he held until 1976, when he was made a vice admiral. Following a year as Vice Director of the Defense Intelligence Agency, he served as Director of the National Security Agency until 1981, when he advanced to the rank of admiral and was appointed Deputy Director of the CIA.[2]

Inman retired from Government service in 1982, and is currently chairman, president and chief executive officer of a Texas-based holding company specializing in micro-electronics. In July 1990 he was appointed to the President's Foreign Intelligence Advisory Board.

The son of an Air Force pilot, Bob Oechsler interrupted his education at the University of Maryland to join the Air Force in 1968, serving mostly with the American Forces Radio and Television Service in the continental United States. During the Vietnam War Bob also served in Cambodia, Thailand and Laos. Some of his work during this period required a Top Secret clearance, when each month he was flown into the demilitarized zone (DMZ) by helicopter to film classified prototype weapons systems. On returning to the US, he spent a year and a half at Wright-Patterson AFB. After leaving the Air Force in 1972, he returned to the University of Maryland, then joined NASA at the Goddard Space Flight Center in Greenbelt, Maryland, specializing in missions technical analysis as a prototype designer of sophisticated control systems and mobile surveillance systems. Among the projects he was involved in were the International Ultraviolet Explorer and the Apollo-Soyuz Test Project.

Now retired from NASA, Bob is currently chairman of Robots Internationale, Inc., where he has pioneered the field of mobilized security surveillance, drawing praise from the US Chamber of Commerce. He has lectured at the Franklin Institute in Philadelphia as a robotics expert in field application technologies. He is also Assistant State Director of the Mutual UFO Network (MUFON) in Maryland, as well as Director of the Annapolis Research and Study Group. Bob has been a broadcaster since 1968 and since 1987 has hosted a nationwide programme, *UFOs Today*, featuring interviews with witnesses and researchers, as part of the '21st-Century Radio' with Dr Robert Hieronimus and the American Radio Networks.

At my suggestion, Bob re-established contact with Admiral Inman by telephone in July 1989, and after reminding him of the meeting the previous year, requested guidance on the direction of our mutual research effort – the ultimate objective being to gain access to a craft for technical research and perhaps public display. I was also seeking guidance on behalf of Admiral of the Fleet, the Lord Hill-Norton, a former Chief of Defence Staff, who has been frustrated in his efforts at penetrating the shield of official secrecy surrounding UFOs.

'I've been spending a great deal of time researching the phenomenon,' Bob began, 'and technologically I think I might have some very interesting things to offer. I certainly would like to get some guidance in a number of different areas . . . on behalf of Admiral Lord Hill-Norton and Mr Good . . . They are more or less working together, Timothy Good as a consultant. Admiral Lord Hill-Norton is quite furious with his inability to gain knowledge on the issues . . . I had suggested to [Timothy] that the only individual I knew that possibly would be able to help him – if it was indeed possible to gain any information across country boundaries – would be you.'

'What is the general area of interest?' Inman asked.

'Two things,' replied Bob. 'One, it is my feeling from my research that there is a dichotomy of sorts, one in which there seems to be an indoctrination programme to educate the public to the realities that are involved here. The other must be a problem relating to security measures and the need-to-know level. I have the ability to [influence] a great mass of the public. I have a nationwide, regular broadcast [programme] on the subject matter . . . I am connected with all the major organizations. I've spent eighteen months investigating the Gulf Breeze situation . . . I have focused a great deal on the technological end, and I've studied a great deal of the things that have been going wrong along the Chesapeake Bay, in connection with the Electromagnetic Continuity Analysis Center and the EMP [Electromagnetic Pulse] projects.'

'All of those are areas in which I am vastly out of date,' Inman responded. 'When I made the decision to retire seven years ago, I made a conscious decision to sever ongoing ties with the US Intelligence Community. I have had some exposure on limited occasions, to some areas of activity over the succeeding seven years when I did the Embassy Security Survey as a consultant to the Defense Science Board. But overwhelmingly my efforts in these seven years have been focused on industrial competitiveness in the application of science and technology in the commercial world. So for many of the things – at least as I sort of infer from the conversation, of the interest of Mr Good and Peter Hill-Norton – they are areas where while I had some expertise, it's now, you know, seven years old. And the pace at which things move in that field, the odds of my being accurate are increasingly remote, in understanding those things.'

'Is it your understanding that there is a cultural dialogue going on . . . today?' Bob asked.

'Well, I guess I'd have to ask with whom? Between what parties?'

'Well, between any of the parties that presumably are behind the technology in the crafts?'

'I honestly don't know. I have no exposure at all. So I haven't a clue whether there are any ongoing dialogues or not. I'm trying to think who there is in the Washington area that is at least much closer to the issues, that might be able to at least give you some guidance . . . The Deputy Director for Science and Technology at the CIA is named Everett Hineman. He is in fact getting ready to retire in the very near future. That may make him somewhat more willing to have dialogues . . . When I knew him in the period seven to ten years ago, he was a person of very substantial integrity and just good common sense. So as a place to start he would clearly be high on the list, in the retired community of those who nonetheless were exposed to the intelligence business and stayed reasonably close to it. There is [also] a retired rear admiral, a former Director of Naval Intelligence named Sumner Shapiro . . . His level of competence again is very high, his integrity is very high. Whether he has any knowledge in the areas you are working on, I don't have a clue, because I don't have any ongoing dialogue with him. But those are at least two [people] for you that are there in the area where you are located, and who have a prospect of still having some currency. I don't know that they do. In my case, I don't have any.'

'Do you anticipate that any of the recovered vehicles would ever become available for technological research? Outside of the military circles?' Bob asked.

'Again, I honestly don't know,' replied Admiral Inman. '*Ten years ago the answer would have been no. Whether as time has evolved they are beginning to become more open on it, there's a possibility.* Again, Mr Hineman probably would be the best person to put that kind of question to . . .'[3]

CIA Headquarters

Bob Oechsler arranged to meet Everett Hineman at the CIA headquarters in Langley, Virginia, on 10 August 1989. During a stay at his Annapolis, Maryland, home in October 1989, Bob related the details of this meeting to me.

'I was escorted to a security room on the first floor when I first got inside the building,' he began. 'They summoned for an escort from the Office of Science and Technology, and she took me up to the sixth floor, and without much delay I found myself in the office of the Deputy Director for Science and Technology.'

The meeting with Hineman proved to be disappointing. Bob had brought with him a large portfolio of the extraordinary colour photographs taken by Ed and Frances Walters in Gulf Breeze, Florida,[4] and began by discussing the technology of one of the craft, gleaned from his extensive study of the pictures, keeping a close eye on Hineman to observe his reactions.

'Not only did he indicate he had no knowledge of the events in Gulf Breeze,' said Bob, 'he didn't even know where it was. Visibly, it did not appear as though he had ever seen the pictures before, although I'm not sure how that could have possibly been the case. He had to have known, in my opinion, that the Joint Chiefs of Staff met at Pensacola in August of 1988.'

Bob then raised the Lazar/S-4 story, discussing the alleged anti-matter reactor and gravity generators. But again, Hineman appeared to know nothing about S-4 or Area 51. 'It didn't even seem to strike a chord when I said Area 51 of the Nellis Test Range. But he seemed most interested in S-4, and intrigued by my suggestion that the Government had flying saucers – operational flying saucers at that. In fact, during that part of the conversation, he reached back over his desk and grabbed a phone and briefly chatted with his secretary; something about arranging for transport to Las Vegas. He even made the comment that he was going to check it out.'

Hineman seemed nervous throughout the meeting, Bob recalled. 'I got the feeling he was real uneasy about the subject.'

As well he might be. Assuming that he had knowledge of these matters, Hineman would have been unlikely to disclose any sensitive compartmented information to one who did not have the requisite clearance.

Bob had hoped to receive guidance on a number of related issues. One of his objectives, which had been proposed by the now late Dr Dan Overlade, was to try and establish a conduit for psychologists and scientists involved with abduction cases, so that they might gain some insight into the nature of the phenomenon. 'The problem is that they have no idea of what the source of the problem is,' Bob explained. 'Are we dealing with a purely psychological phenomenon, a physical phenomenon, or are we dealing with something totally outside the realm of psychiatric practice?'

Bob expressed the hope that either verbal or documentary information could be passed on to the investigators, or that a phone number could be given for them to contact those CIA personnel who were best informed on this aspect of the phenomenon. Hineman responded that he would make inquiries.

Another of Bob's proposals was to suggest the need for an independent historical account to be written about the Government's involvement in the UFO controversy, emphasizing that, in his opinion, the decisions that had been made and the actions that had been taken by the Government were all justified.

'I volunteered to conduct such an historical perspective,' Bob told me, 'pointing out that I would need clearance to have access to all UFO-related activities, and that I would work closely with them in order to maintain accuracy in my accounting of events.'

These may seem rather naïve proposals, but it must be borne in mind that the meeting with Hineman had been suggested by Admiral Inman, one of the most well-informed people in the Intelligence Community, specifically in order that guidance could be offered. In Hineman's case, it seemed fruitless.

'The bottom line, from the forty-five minutes I spent with him, was that he tried to conclusively give me the impression that he didn't know anything about flying saucers,' Bob said. 'But he indicated that either he or someone else would get back to me within the next week.'

After a reminder, Hineman called back on 1 September, the day he was due to retire from the CIA. 'I don't see any prospects for doing any business on the idea that you had when you were in here,' he began. 'I've done some checking with some folks, and there's no need for anything along these lines; at least at this time. I thank you for your interest and I appreciate your coming by.'

'Did you get out to the Las Vegas area?' asked Bob.

'I did not myself, no.'

'Well, then you were able to substantiate, I presume, the issues I was bringing up?'

'No. I come to different conclusions than you do.'

'Oh, really?'

'Yes. So I thank you for your interest.'

Bob was frustrated by the response to his proposals. 'It was surprising that he didn't reference the specific proposal about the psychologists,' he said, 'because in my opinion that was the most important issue that I had raised there that I thought needed some action on their part, and I was somewhat disappointed that there didn't seem to be anything forthcoming on that. I was also really surprised by his remark on S-4, since I didn't know that I'd offered any conclusions. All I did was offer data that was given to me, so I'm not sure what that was about . . .'

Naval Intelligence

Bob's two meetings with retired Rear Admiral Sumner Shapiro, the former Director of Naval Intelligence, proved to be considerably more productive.

Shapiro's career included two years as Assistant Naval Attaché at the US Embassy in Moscow (1963–5) and two years as Deputy Assistant Chief of Staff, Intelligence (Office of Naval Intelligence) in London (1967–9). After serving as Assistant Chief of Staff, Intelligence, for the US Atlantic Fleet, he was appointed Deputy Director of Naval Intelligence in 1976. From 1978 to 1982 Shapiro served as Director of Naval Intelligence, and on retirement from the Navy he worked as a business executive with the BDM Corporation.

Shapiro seemed to Bob not only to suggest that the United States was in possession of extraterrestrial space vehicles, but also to give every indication of having studied one at close quarters.

'He's an engineer by background,' Bob explained, 'and I could tell he had a fascination with certain aspects of the technology. He had "hands-on", there's no question about that. He told me how they would take them apart, pack them up and ship them around in trucks to different laboratories. He never told me specifically where things were taken: he was very careful about obvious breaches of security of classified information.'

I asked Bob if the retired intelligence chief had confirmed the existence of an antimatter reactor, as described by Lazar.

'Well, I guess you could say it was confirmed, because he had a real fascination with the antimatter reactor and described to me pretty much what it looked like, and its size and weight. He said it was real heavy for that size. There's nothing I've learned so far from the people in the Intelligence Community that would tend to corroborate anything that Lazar has said, other than the reference to an antimatter reactor.

'One of the things that was fascinating was the discovery of how they had the interlocking components of the craft. The whole thing comes apart in pieces, and apparently when it's locked together it's like one of those eastern puzzles: you can't get it apart unless you know the precise places to push . . . and everything has to be done in a specific sequence in order to get it to come apart. It's a real intricate process of putting things together, but it's relatively easy once you know how.'

In his 1950 book *Behind the Flying Saucers*, Frank Scully reported that a retrieved craft was eventually discovered to be assembled in segments, which fitted in grooves and were pinned together around the base. The craft was ingeniously put together, he wrote, and great care had to be exercised when dismantling it.[5] And in 1958, Dr Olavo Fontes was informed by Brazilian naval intelligence officials that at that time six flying discs had been recovered worldwide: three in the United States, the others in the Sahara Desert, the British Isles, and Scandinavia. 'All of them were made of a very light metal which was assembled in segments that fitted in deep grooves and were pinned together around the base,' he revealed in a private letter, a copy of which is in my possession. 'There was no sign of this on the outer surface of the ships . . .'[6]

I asked Bob if he had learned anything from Sumner Shapiro about the alleged test flights of these craft.

'Well, I don't think he ever made any reference to any kind of test flights, or anything relative to operations,' he replied. 'You know, I thought I was pushing it already as it was, and to start getting into questions about operational dynamics, navigational aspects and things like that would have been a little premature! There wasn't really anything discussed about the total craft or operational characteristics, other than the specific component operational characteristics.'

While the first meeting with Shapiro (at a Virginia restaurant in late 1989) had been cordial, it was less so at the second one, which took place in Shapiro's Virginia home on 21 June 1990, and concluded rather abruptly. 'It was as if the first time was much more "off-the-cuff", with no concern about impropriety on his part,' Bob explained. 'But he approached the second meeting from a much more official standpoint, which may be because he suspected that I was there under false pretences.'

The Cosmic Journey Project

In early September 1989 I received a letter from the director of a 'Special Development Group' associated with Ringling Brothers and Barnum and Bailey International, a huge entertainment corporation run by Kenneth Feld Productions which is particularly well known for its circuses. The director mentioned that one of his colleagues had been present at my lecture during the MUFON convention in Las Vegas in July that year. 'Our corporation is doing extensive research on the subject,' he wrote, 'as we are involved in preparing an International Touring Presentation which will include accurate information as well as be entertaining. We would appreciate if you could let us know, as soon as possible, if we could meet with you and have further discussions on the UFO Cover-Up.'[7]

In replying, I expressed my reservations regarding the association of the UFO subject with a circus company, but agreed to discuss the matter further. The reply came by return of post:

> Organizations, such as NASA, United States Government, Rockwell International, have agreed to work with our corporation to develop the main portion of this show, the future of space and the technical advances predicted over the next 100 years. Their reluctance at first was not the fact we owned circuses, but on how the UFO subject is going to be tastefully handled. We have now satisfied their concerns . . .[8]

Following further discussion by telephone, I was invited to become the 'Official Consultant on UFO research' to the Special Development Group. A personal meeting in Orlando, Florida, was a prerequisite, the director said, and since I would be visiting Gulf Breeze during October, I made arrangements to fly to Orlando. Unfortunately, difficulties with airline scheduling arose, allowing inadequate time for the trip, and I was obliged to postpone the meeting.

Back in England, the director made it clear to me over the telephone that the exhibition programme had reached a critical stage. 'We are looking for a manner and a form to develop our UFO portion of this particular exhibition,' he explained, 'and we are in a position now where we are trying to decide what is the best method to go forward with a post-show exhibit of 5 or 6,000 square feet on UFOs, and we need to make sure that if our discussions were fruitful, you can be of assistance to us on this or give us a name or supply somebody that could help us to develop this properly.'[9]

I mentioned that my friend Bob Oechsler was uniquely qualified to assist the group, not only because of his competence as a UFO researcher but also owing to his background as a NASA mission specialist and project engineer. (I learned later that Jun-Ichi Yaoi, the well-known television director and UFO researcher, who had been asked to assist with the exhibition in Japan, had also recommended Bob.) The director thanked me for the recommendation, and Bob contacted him later. I never heard from the Special Development Group again.

As it transpired, Bob was more suitably qualified for the position than I, partly because of his NASA background, which had immediately endeared him to the NASA team involved with the project. Perhaps his military background in the Air Force was another contributory factor in the decision to employ him, as well as his contacts with the Intelligence Community.

Bob and I had often discussed the various official attempts at indoctrinating the public about the UFO phenomenon which invariably have been aborted for one reason or another, such as the approaches to Bob Emenegger, Linda Howe, and Bill Moore. Perhaps the exhibition project was another such attempt, we reasoned. As it turned out, we were right.

Bob met the Special Development Group in Orlando on 1/2 November 1989, and after signing a non-disclosure agreement was given a briefing on the project, known as 'Cosmic Journey'. The theme of the exhibition was to be an international historical outlook on the space programmes of the US and the Soviet Union, and participants included the former astronauts Alan Bean, Charles 'Pete' Conrad, Gene Cernan, and Alexei Leonov. The project had the approval of President George Bush, Vice-President Dan Quayle and the National Space Council (an organization based in the White House and protected under Executive Order).

With the co-operation of NASA and Rockwell International, the exhibition was to feature a full-scale mock-up of the shuttle, called the

Ambassador, and encompassed 134,000 square feet of exhibits, including a 15,000-square-foot 'space camp'. Fully one third of the exhibition was to feature UFOs and extraterrestrials, including a 600-seat auditorium that became a Bio-Tech spaceship and a UFO pre-show area with interactive case history kiosks. Additionally, the project was to involve a tri-level educational curriculum for 25,000 schools in the US, due to commence on 1 January 1990. The travelling exhibition was originally scheduled to be completed by 1 September 1990.

'Their interest in me was multifaceted,' Bob told me, 'with focuses on my contacts in the Intelligence Community regarding UFOs, my NASA background, with particular interest in my limited involvement with the mechanical-arm assembly created for the shuttle project by a Canadian firm, and a keen interest in my robotics expertise regarding sophisticated remote-control devices for character robots, of which they planned extensive use as guides for the travelling exhibition.'

The Pentagon Meeting

On 13 November 1989 Bob reported to the Pentagon in Washington, DC for a meeting with a general who was the Intelligence Community contact for the Cosmic Journey project. The security check included walking through an unusual type of electronic screen, Bob told me.

'It resembled an airport security metal detector, but left me with a series of strange sensations such as the feeling that I had just passed through a physical mesh of some sort, similar to the perceived feeling of walking through a screened door or window, if one could do such a thing. There was a residual tingling sensation experienced in the cortex area of the cerebellum, and apparently affecting the pons area of the brain stem: both cerebella hemispheres were equally affected.

'In somewhat of a groggy state, but with equilibrium pretty much intact, I approached the general's office with the security guard. The office was not far down the corridor from the security station, and on the same level. The security guard knocked once and without waiting for a reply opened the door and motioned me inside. He quickly saluted the general and closed the door behind me. The general, apparently just finishing a telephone conversation, greeted me with a genuine smile and offered me a chair next to his expansive cherry-wood desk. I recognized him immediately from the photographs of the project team that were shown to me at the Cosmic Journey meeting in Orlando.

'My first remarks related to the concern I had about going through that machine at security. "What was that?" I asked. He laughed, dismissing my inquiry by saying, "That damn thing gave me headaches the first two weeks I was here!"

'He immediately got into a discussion about the exhibits for the Cosmic Journey project. He wanted to know where I was planning to get material for the kiosks to show photographs and case histories of UFO events and encounters, what military archives, and so on. I indicated that we hadn't come that far in the planning and that I was hoping to get his guidance on that and other issues. He indicated that NASA and NPIC (the National Photographic Interpretation Center) would be good places to start.'

(The NPIC, established by the CIA in 1961 and staffed by CIA and DIA analysts, is located in the six-storey Federal Building 213, at the corner of M and First Streets, eight blocks down Jersey Avenue from the Capitol in Washington, DC, and looks like a bricked-in warehouse. Much of the work there involves the evaluation of photographs taken by spy planes and satellites.[10])

'One of the more intriguing elements of the discussion involved an exhibit showing an alien/ET corpse in a cryogenic tank,' Bob continued. 'The general described the tank as a space-age-looking coffin with blue tube lighting inside the clear lexan cover, propped up at an angle so it wouldn't look so much like a casket. It seems he was concerned about using the real thing versus a mock-up, and he queried me at length about my thoughts on public perception and whether or not the public would believe such an exhibit was real, or how could it be authenticated with official plaques of some sort. I suggested that a companion autopsy report with colour photographs might help the credibility aspect.'

Bob insists that it was his impression that the idea of exhibiting an actual alien corpse was proposed in all seriousness. 'As a matter of fact, I got the impression they had a lot of bodies to choose from!' he told me.

'The general also had the same concerns about showing a real versus a mock-up craft, and tended to doubt the feasibility of altering a real vehicle to show a cutaway view. I suggested that the real thing would be preferable if on-board access for the public could be achieved. The objective of the project was to provide hands-on experience and to be interactive.

'The other primary areas of discussion involved my robotics expertise and the minor role that I played in the development of the shuttle arm, which was initially designed to provide life support to astronauts and a diagnostic instrument for repairing satellites in orbit. My expertise with character robots convinced him of my innovative capabilities with regard to control systems – especially prototype reconfigured design. This was the genesis of a subsequent training trip to Houston and my involvement with reconfiguring the shuttle arm from a zero-gravity environment to a gravity environment on the shuttle mock-up – the centre-piece of the Cosmic Journey project.

'We also discussed the UFO pre-show and theatre concept. I expressed my objections to the Bio-Tech spaceship idea and the total concept of military-type aggression. It was my opinion that the concept was out of line with the reality-based objectives of the overall project. Maybe my view is the unrealistic one?

'I have no doubts that he knew far more about the subject matter than I. It was clear that he was trying to get my reaction to things and I freely gave it. The single surprise was my awakening to the level of intelligence that I was dealing with. It had not occurred to me that the general was perhaps tied in with the establishment that could monitor my every move and conversation. I was very taken aback when he casually blurted out that since I was going to Dallas that weekend, he'd have someone from Carswell AFB meet with me. I don't know if it was clear that I would be met at the airport or later during my stay, but I was absolutely certain that I had not made mention to anyone of my travel plans.

'The meeting ended and seemed productive for both of us. I was escorted out through a different route than I had taken coming in.

'Although I had expected further contact from the general, there have been no further meetings or calls to date. Having a local area consultant practice, the general no doubt aborted further work on the project when the funds were halted. In fact the only time I've heard his name mentioned was when I arrived at NASA's Ellington air base and my orders were reviewed by the duty officer. I have not seen him since that meeting at the Pentagon.'

There is no doubt, in my opinion, that Bob's contacts with the Intelligence Community and his involvement in the Cosmic Journey project had made him a target for surveillance. And although the general's comment had alerted him to the possibility, he was totally unprepared for the next development. No one from Carswell AFB showed up in Dallas, but what occurred on the first evening there was so bizarre that Bob began to question his sanity.

Alien Intrusion?

On 17 November 1989, while relaxing in a Dallas cocktail lounge with a friend, Melanie King, Bob suddenly experienced an almost indescribable sensation, similar to that reported by a witness in the Colorado ranch case (see Chapter 3). Lasting no more than about thirty seconds, the sensation began with a series of 'waves' of energy at the back of his head, simultaneously inducing a sense of acute panic. 'It was as if a whole range of memories, information and emotions was being retrieved or generated at tremendous speed,' Bob tried to explain.

Melanie, sitting beside him, felt nothing, but realized something was wrong by the look of panic on Bob's face. He became aware of a man, standing some distance away, whom he somehow felt convinced was responsible for the mental 'intrusion'. The man appeared to be in his late twenties, was around 6 feet tall, with fair hair and 'real clean, reddish tanned skin,' Bob said.

'I jumped up and pointed right at him and said, "That's him!" And Melanie took off towards the entrance where the guy turned to walk out, ran out and caught up with him. I was really scared, just looking for security, like a mouse in a corner, looking for a way out. A little while later she came back, and I could tell from the look in her eyes that she was real stunned. She said she caught up with the man, went past him, stopped and looked him right in the eyes. But he didn't look at her; it was like she was not even there – he walked right past her. In fact, she was doubting herself when she came back. "That can't be," she said. "His pupils were diamond-shaped – laterally" – you know, like a cat's would be vertical, these were horizontal.'

The sensation in the back of Bob's head reminded him of the security machine at the Pentagon, which had induced a 'tingling' sensation at the back of his head. Was there some connection, perhaps? The immediate consequence of Bob's encounter, however, was an incessant itching on his forehead, which lasted about thirty minutes; a sensation which had not occurred at the Pentagon. The impression left with Bob was that the man was 'searching' for a certain piece of information – and that he had retrieved it.

On his return to Maryland, Bob began to experience severe difficulties with his short-term memory. 'I would have a telephone conversation with somebody in the morning, for example, and they'd call me back an hour later and would be referring to something that we had talked about an hour earlier and I had no recollection of even talking to this person. It got so bad that I had to record every single phone call. It was a frightening experience. It slowly started to get better after a week or so, and after ten days I was fully back to normal.'

In addition, however, Bob experienced temporary enhancement of perception, enabling him to anticipate events and read others' thoughts.

The Microgravity Chamber

Bob's work with the Cosmic Journey project entailed a period during the second week of January 1990 when he was billeted at NASA's Ellington air base, near the Johnson Space Flight Center in Houston. The problem he was asked to assist in solving was how to reconfigure the mechanical arm in the shuttle, which is configured to operate in a zero-gravity environment. The mechanics associated with the manipulation of the arm are significantly different in a gravity environment, he explained to me.

'The whole thing had to be reconfigured in order to make it capable of public interaction. Essentially, what needed to be done was that they had to have limit stops put in. When you start the motor, it keeps going unless you stop it. In a gravity environment, you have other forces that are acting on that manipulation that you don't have out in space. So the point was, they wanted first to get me accustomed to how it works in a microgravity environment.'

In order to become accustomed to microgravity, Bob, together with some astronauts and engineers, was flown by helicopter to a NASA facility about 20 miles south-west of Ellington. No roads led to the building. On arrival, he went in to what he assumed was a 'clean room', where dust and dirt particles were removed automatically from his clothes, and changed into special clothing in preparation for entry into another room. He had no idea what to expect.

'I stepped through this hatch into this other room – and I was air-borne! I mean, I took a step and – wow! – it was weird, because it's like the loss of balance and equilibrium and everything. I was totally unprepared for this. Obviously, the astronauts had done a lot of train-ing: they were so accustomed to it, and they were laughing at me.

'The first step you take, you're airborne, and there's a tendency to fall forward. The boots you have on have a natural attraction for the material on the floor, but you could never use your whole foot for trac-tion. You learn to skip around. It takes about fifteen minutes to become accustomed to the biomechanics: the muscle forces change. It feels almost similar to getting into a pool of water – the arms tend to swing out.

'I was working on a model – a series of mechanical arms – and there were several different devices that measured the energy calories re-quired to do each motion, which were all registered on computer. Then you had to compute what it took to turn so many screws, and so on. It was essentially a workshop facility in a weightless environment.'

No more than about eight astronauts or engineers worked on a variety of projects in the chamber at any one time, and sometimes only four, Bob told me. A biophysicist, for example, was engaged in working with protein crystals, possibly for developing materials used in superconductivity experiments. 'Everyone was wearing the same clothing. Several of the others I knew, but they really wouldn't let us talk among ourselves. It was pretty much forbidden to talk about any-thing that had to do with what we were doing.'

The chamber was rectangular in shape, measuring about 30 feet long, 20 feet wide, and 9 feet high. Recessed in the ceiling was a strange, plasma-like light, which Bob felt was responsible for generating microgravity. He had never heard of such a device before and none of his NASA contacts had ever mentioned it to him. Although unable to divulge certain information, Bob nevertheless assures me that the device employs advanced technology acquired as a result of studying recovered alien vehicles. 'No question about it,' he said, 'because I knew where it was being generated from, right there in the ceiling. You could hardly look at it for long; your eyes would start burning like you were in chlorine.'

Another visit was to a bunker-like building north of Houston, where Bob learned how to operate a peculiar panel that he believes must have come from an alien craft. 'It had a series of vertical cylinders made of multicoloured lights that terminated in a hood about 4 feet above the panel. When one inserts a hand to break the beam, and then raises or lowers the hand, a comparable action takes place with what appears to be some kind of clear-looking cylinder that resides in the base of the console corresponding to each beam. It was some kind of control panel – that was all I learned. I think it was being considered for use in the UFO exhibit area of Cosmic Journey.'

The NORAD Platform

One evening in January 1990, following his trip to the bunker-like building, Bob was invited to visit an interesting North American Aerospace Defense Command (NORAD) installation in the Gulf of Mexico. Three helicopters of a highly advanced type made the trip.

'They were black and extremely sleek,' Bob said, 'with black windows, and showed no seams. You couldn't see where the door was until it popped open.' Additionally, it was relatively quiet in flight. 'There was noise, but it was more like a humming noise, and certainly a lot quieter than you would get inside a commercial jet.'

Bob believes that a highly advanced and secret type of propulsion system was being utilized in the helicopter, and further speculates that some other aircraft – such as the B-2 and F-117a stealth planes – might likewise incorporate an auxiliary device of unconventional type.

'I was just along for the ride on this trip,' Bob explained to me, during a visit to London with his wife and daughter in September

1990 which had been arranged specifically in order to clarify and elaborate on the details of his remarkable experiences. 'The trip was for the benefit of two other guys, who seemed to be state-of-the-art radar technicians. The technology they were discussing was way over my head, other than that it had something to do with computer software configurations. The computer system they were working on dealt exclusively with optical fibre communications.

'Our pilot was wearing a black jump suit with a white helmet, and on the left pocket of his jump suit was a black patch with a white circle around it, and inside it had "NORAD" embroidered in white. The "N" was exactly like the NASA "N". We left at twilight from Ellington, flew out across Galveston Bay and out into the Gulf.'

The flight lasted no more than thirty-five to forty-five minutes, Bob estimated, which astonished him since a distance of over 500 miles had been covered. The helicopter began its descent shortly after passing Mobile, Alabama, and landed on what looked like an oil-rig platform, possibly 20 miles south of Pensacola, Florida (where an intensive wave of UFO sightings has been reported since 1986).

'Our group was the first to land. The two fellows who had come with us were immediately whisked off down a corridor and we didn't see them again. We went through a hatchway with "NORAD" written in black, on white. Inside, we went down a corridor, passed to the left, went down a ladderway and on to a mezzanine level where you could look out over what looked like a very typical control room, not unlike the facilities at Johnson, really – a series of consoles. Everyone was dressed in black pants, white shirts and black ties, and some even had black jackets.

'There was an enormous screen that was many times the size of a normal cinema screen, and curved. It had a three-dimensional quality to it with a great deal of depth, so that in effect you could see up-range. They had it on what I estimate would be a 35-degree angle. We were looking at a quadrant of the United States, which included the lower Gulf, Florida, Alabama, Mississippi, and on up to about halfway up the States. I would say it covered roughly a third or fourth of the south-eastern quadrant of the United States.

'It had altitude to it as well, and the entire area was covered with a grid that was moving: it appeared to "float". On the grid was a "vortex" area, with a sort of "weakening" area to it, in the general area of Keesler AFB, Mississippi. And it was in that area that I noticed a series of blips on the top of the screen that moved laterally to the left. There were five, as I recall, and all of them slipped down through this vortex, and they were labelled, like a typical radar screen where blips usually designate aircraft. In fact, there was ground movement as well, that was also coded and numbered. But these particular ones that were up top were all labelled "ASC". They didn't have any specific numbers – just ASC.

'I overheard someone say "Alternative Spacecraft". And they came down and spread out – all five of them. Two immediately went off the screen to the north-west and one came around the Gulf "horn", meaning to the east, and then down to the south, almost as if they were following the shoreline. There was one – possibly two, I forget – that stopped what looked like just across the border of Florida into Georgia – somewhere in that area. And as soon as it stopped, it glowed: there was like a red glow that came off of it. I don't know what that meant. There was another one that moved to the left . . . I guess over Texas – the area we had come from in the choppers.

'Everyone was quite busy. I was essentially there along for the ride. I guess we were there probably about forty-five minutes. Shortly after that we went into a holding room for about twenty minutes, waiting for the pilots to come back. And then we left and headed back . . .'

'NORAD SECRET'

The implications of the scenario described by Bob Oechsler are that NORAD keeps regular track of extraterrestrial, intelligently controlled vehicles, designated as 'Alternative Spacecraft', and that these are clearly differentiated from more prosaic unidentified flying objects.

NORAD has never denied that it tracks thousands of objects each day with the Space Detection and Tracking System (SPADATS) and the Naval Space Surveillance System (NAVSPASUR) and acknowledges that a certain percentage relates to 'uncorrelated observations'. A number of documents relating to the intrusions of UFOs over Strategic Air Command (SAC) bases, including nuclear missile bases in the USA and Canada in 1975, have been released under provisions of the Freedom of Information Act, but many more are being withheld. When Citizens Against UFO Secrecy (CAUS) filed a request for this data in NORAD files, they were quoted a search fee of over $155,000![11]

More recently, CAUS has obtained further information regarding NORAD's Unknown Track Reporting System (NUTR). An extract from the *Directory of Databases* (Appendix, Fig. 10.1) defines the scope of the NUTR as follows:

> The NORAD Unknown Track Reporting System records details of all air traffic declared unknown in North America and the Greenland–Iceland–United Kingdom Gap. Data are used by a wide variety of users in NORAD, USAF, Joint Chiefs of Staff, Canadian NDHQ, and region commanders in a continuing assessment of airspace sovereignty.

The NUTR document states that 7,000 trackings of unknown objects had been recorded since 1971 (a nineteen-year period) but details are classified Secret.[12] As a result of further Freedom of Information requests for data by Robert Todd, CAUS was informed by the Air Force Space Command (AFSPACECOM) in February 1990 that no such records existed. Then in May 1990 the Air Force's FOIA Manager, Barbara Carmichael, confirmed that the records did indeed exist but were exempt from disclosure in the interests of national security.

In June 1990, W. M. McDonald, Director of Freedom of Information and Security Review for the Office of the Assistant Secretary of Defense, explained that a decision to release NUTR tracking records had been made, and Robert Todd was supplied with five examples. The released documents – classified 'NORAD SECRET' (Appendix, Fig. 10.2) – are almost completely censored, however, providing further proof of the extreme secrecy attached to the subject.[13]

Local Intrusions

More surprises were in store for Bob Oechsler. On the early morning of 25 January 1990, he observed an unusual aerial object from his Maryland home. 'I first saw it at a distance, then it moved out straight towards me over the field behind my house. After about thirty seconds, it took off – straight up.'

The object looked rather like a 'golf ball sitting in a dish' when at a distance, Bob related, and at its closest approach a kind of Celtic cross was clearly visible underneath, as depicted in his sketch (Fig. 10.3).

On 18 March 1990, alerted by the sound of low-flying helicopters while working in his study, Bob went outside to take a look. One of the dark green helicopters circled about 100 yards from the house and appeared to be scanning the street. 'It stopped, nose pointed down between my house and the house next door,' Bob told me. 'They were probably waiting for clearance to land at the nearby Lee Airport.' He went back inside and returned to work.

'About fifteen minutes later, I heard the doorbell ring. My wife and daughter had gone to the shopping mall, so I ran upstairs and pulled open the door. There was this big burly colonel with a big bushy moustache, with no hat on and real thick hair. I got the impression he was a little older than I am – probably fifty or late forties. He was wearing a dark green fatigue-type uniform, but the material was a summer-type similar to what I had worn in South-East Asia, but with long sleeves, which I hadn't seen before. It had "US Army" embroidered on it. There were two other guys in the driveway, but I never got a good look. I saw no vehicle.

'This guy got my attention immediately. He said, "We'd like you to stand by on the report for a few days." I couldn't figure what he was talking about, so he said, "We'd like you to stand by on that Walters report for a few days." So I said, "I wasn't planning on delivering a report yet: I was planning on giving an overview this afternoon at a reception." "That's OK. We'd appreciate it if you would stand by on that report for a few days." And it was still unclear as to whether it was OK to give the condensed synopsis or not.

'This guy really scared me. Only Ed Walters knew what was in that report. So either my phone or Ed's is tapped. Anyway, I did not release the report . . .'

Bob waited a while after the colonel had left, then grabbed his video camera and three fully charged batteries, jumped in his car, and headed for Lee Airport, hoping to get some film of the helicopters leaving. As he drove up to the airfield, the video camera went dead.

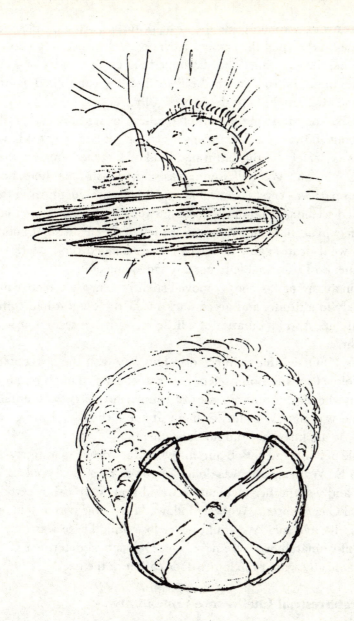

Fig. 10.3
The unusual aerial object seen by Bob Oechsler near his Maryland home in
January 1990. The sketches show the object as it first appeared (above), looking like
'a golf ball sitting in a dish', and the underside (below). A similar object was seen in
March 1990 and January 1991. *(Robert Oechsler)*

'I went down the road beside the airfield, turned around, reloaded the batteries and turned the camera back on. As I turned to go down the flightline, the car stalled and I stopped my camera to try and get the car running. Halfway down the flightline, the car stalled again. And then I saw a bright light down in a gully.

'It was like the sun rising up out of a valley down at the end of the airfield about 100 yards away, except it was bright white, not yellowish. It was extremely bright, but it had kind of darkened areas, rather like the dimples on a golf ball, and it was set in a dish-type thing, and the bottom part was crystal clear, like a Celtic cross – identical to the object I had seen on 25 January. It came swooping up, not more than about 30 feet in altitude and 20 feet to the left of the car. At that point, the video went dead again, although I had changed the batteries a second time. So I was unable to get any videotape of it.

'It left in an arcing fashion. It moved slightly to my left, increasing very quickly in altitude, and arced back in the direction it had come from – only up. And in a matter of a little more than a second, it was out of sight.'

Was the UFO sighting connected in any way with the helicopters and the colonel's visit? Bob prefers not to speculate, though remains puzzled by the extraordinary series of coincidences. As for the helicopters, he was unable to locate them at the airfield or hear them taking off, so assumes they did not land there.

A couple of hours later, Bob and his wife Mary drove to Virginia to meet with Ed Walters, who was doing a book-signing in Crystal City, Virginia, and yet another incident occurred that is typical in certain cases of UFO encounters. 'We were followed the whole trip by a black Mercedes,' he told me. 'We could never lose him. There was only a driver. Unfortunately we were never close enough to determine if he was the same guy who came to my door earlier in the day.'

The Extraterrestrial Intelligence Community

At the Ozark UFO Conference held in Eureka Springs, Arkansas, in April 1990, Bob told me that he had invited Admiral Inman to give the keynote address, either in person or on video. Inman declined the invitation, and during the ensuing correspondence and phone calls made it clear (through his executive assistant) that any public discussion of the information which Bob had acquired from the former Intelligence Community directors would be in violation of national secrecy laws.

Bob Oechsler's contacts with the Intelligence Community have led to a continuing exchange of information. On 2 October 1990, for example, he gave, together with Dr Bruce Maccabee, an illustrated lecture on the mysterious cropfield circles at the CIA headquarters, which was arranged by the Office of Scientific & Weapons Research and attended by about fifty Agency personnel.

As for the Cosmic Journey project, plans for the exhibition were temporarily shelved in early 1990, ostensibly for budgetary reasons. Indeed, a number of NASA projects were also cancelled or cut back later in the year, including the SETI (Search for Extraterrestrial Intelligence) programme, for which NASA had requested $12.1 million in its fiscal 1991 appropriations bill.

Although there will always remain a need to search for signs of life and communications from the extraterrestrial intelligence community that in my view is undoubtedly widespread throughout the cosmos, the SETI programme seems to me to be something of an anachronism, in the sense that NASA and other agencies already have proof – though highly classified – of the existence of at least one extraterrestrial intelligence agency right here on Earth.

In the last few years alone, the massive scale of bewildering sightings, landings, contacts and abductions might convey the impression that Earth has become a kind of cosmic Clapham Junction. Some idea of the variety of occupants reported may be gleaned from the following brief selection:

The small bug-eyed being wearing a type of helmet and shield, who harassed Ed and Frances Walters at their home in Gulf Breeze, Florida, in December 1987;[14] silver-suited humanoids seen by three witnesses in Kiev, USSR, in July 1989, described as having long, golden hair and large, radiant eyes (and who said they took one person from Earth each day!); silver-suited spacemen, about 3 metres tall, accompanied by a robot, going for a walkabout in Voronezh, USSR, observed by a considerable number of witnesses in September/October 1989 (the reports endorsed by TASS and local officials); the

4-foot-tall fluorescent-green figure inspecting a parked aircraft, seen by soldiers in Kecskemét, Hungary, in October 1989; 10-foot-tall figures 'moving as if they were chess pieces', observed by a soldier at the Tarnaszentmaria barracks, Hungary, in November 1989; and the 7-foot-tall guy with a bald head and cat-like eyes seen wandering around a parking lot by a security guard in Miami, Florida, in December 1989.[15]

One of the more recent reports to come to my attention concerns an encounter with aliens during the small hours of 31 August 1990, in the Laguna Cartagena, Cabo Rojo area of south-west Puerto Rico, where many unusual incidents have taken place. Ten carloads of witnesses reportedly observed five humanoids walking down a dirt road, heading in the direction of the Laguna Cartagena. One of the witnesses, Miguel Figueroa, pursued the beings in his car, but as he approached them, they 'lit up', and he was somehow prevented from getting any closer. When the light dissipated, Figueroa again gave chase and managed to get a better look. He described the figures as grey, varying between 3 and 4 feet in height, with almond-shaped eyes and long pointed ears! The following day, there were reports of discs flying out over the Laguna Cartagena.[16]

What makes these reports particularly frustrating for an investigator such as myself is that I was actually in that very area on the afternoon of 31 August, together with Jorge Martín and other investigators. We saw nothing, of course, and the reports did not come to our attention until later.

It is rumoured that an alien base is located in this vicinity and that liaison has been established with US military personnel. Such rumours are bound to circulate, given the large number of sightings, combined with the presence of US (NSA?) monitoring and communications stations in the area, as well as the fact that much of the land there – including the Laguna Cartagena – has been appropriated by the federal government. And according to Jorge Martín, Puerto Rico's top researcher, George Bush made a clandestine visit to the Cabo Rojo area prior to becoming President.

Although the disappearance of US Navy jets during close approaches to UFOs seen over this area in 1988 (as related in Chapter 1) could have sinister implications, we should consider the possibility

– however bizarre – that some kind of a liaison with aliens has been established, and that the pilots survived the experience. 'We know where they are', Jorge was told by a Navy source.

In my last book I related the case of 'Mel Noel' (Guy Kirkwood), a US Air Force lieutenant who together with other pilots succeeded in obtaining 16 mm gun-camera film of UFOs on several occasions in 1953/4. Kirkwood told me that radio contact with the UFOs was established during the third encounter, and a considerable amount of information was given. Colonel Peterson, the flight leader, claimed later to have had direct physical contact with human-appearing extra-terrestrials. In 1959 he disappeared over the Atlantic without any trace of his aircraft being found, having previously informed Kirkwood that he had made arrangements to join the extraterrestrials.[17]

I am *not* suggesting that a similar 'arrangement' was made with the US Navy pilots; just that we should not assume that hostile aliens are snatching our pilots out of the skies for some nefarious purpose. As to the actual agenda of the extraterrestrial community, I can only speculate.

Culture Shock

Our own galaxy – one of countless billions – is comprised of over 100 billion stars, and statistically it is probable that life has evolved on some planetary systems to the extent that space travel and colonization are commonplace.

In assuming that the lifetime of advanced civilizations is ten million years, science writer Ian Ridpath speculates that there could be as many as one million advanced civilizations 'like ourselves or more advanced' in our galaxy, and surmises that the main interest of an old and advanced civilization may be in 'developing creatures of the galaxy, as the anthropologists of the western world are increasingly fascinated by the stone-age societies that remain on Earth'.[18] Dr Bernard Oliver, of NASA's SETI project, believes in the possibility that an 'interconnecting galactic community of advanced cultures already exists.'[19]

But many astronomers and exobiologists concur that although we might have been visited in the past, and are certain to be visited in the future, present-day visits are out of the question. The logic of such reasoning escapes me.

That contact has so far been restricted to relatively few people, rather than on a massive scale, may be for a number of sound reasons. Some visitors, for example, may not want us to know what they are doing here, and in any event can probably go about their business without needing to contact anyone at all; when they do, they ensure that the contactee is left in a state of confusion. Disinformation could well be an inevitable consequence of contact.

Others may be so far advanced, technologically, culturally and spiritually, that contact with our relatively retarded species might be seen as disadvantageous for both parties. In this regard, the comments allegedly made by Daniel Fry's extraterrestrial friend in 1949 are worth noting. 'We will never attempt to thrust either our knowledge or our culture upon your people,' he said, 'and will never offer it unless there is substantial evidence that they desire it, and that it would be advantageous to them. There is certainly no such evidence at the present time.

'It is also true that the purpose of this visit is not entirely philanthropic, since there are some materials upon your planet which we could use to the advantage of both our peoples; materials which you have in great abundance but which are rather scarce elsewhere in this solar system. While the use of some of these materials would be of assistance to us, our services to your people will not be made contingent upon such use. Any knowledge or aid which we can give will be freely offered . . .

'If we took steps to force the acceptance of our reality upon their consciousness,' Fry was told, 'about 30 per cent of the people would consider us as gods, and could attempt to place upon us all responsibility for their welfare. This is a responsibility we could not be permitted to assume, even if we were able to discharge it, which of course, we are not. Most of the remaining 70 per cent would adopt the belief that we were potential tyrants or dictators, who were planning to enslave their world, and many would begin to seek means to destroy us.'[20]

Regardless of whether or not we believe Daniel Fry's contact story to be pure fiction (I, for one, do not), the sentiments expressed by the alleged extraterrestrial accord well with some modern-day thinking.

The perceptive writer Michael Michaud, Director of the Office of Advanced Technology at the US Department of State, for example, points out that we are likely to project our hopes, fears and prejudices on to a hypothetical alien culture. 'At one extreme,' he writes, 'we think of aliens as altruistic teachers, who will show us the road to survival, wisdom and prosperity, or God-like figures who will raise humanity from its fallen condition. At the other, we see the aliens as implacable, grotesque conquerors whose miraculous but malevolently applied technology can only be overcome by simple virtues . . .'

Michaud goes on to speculate that contact would probably cause many people to attribute events to alien intervention, citing the present cultural response to the UFO phenomenon as an example.[21] And in discussing other problems of contact, Michaud also comes remarkably close to the truth, as I see it. He reasons that individual nations or special interest groups might try and conduct exclusive dialogues with the aliens in order to exploit the contact, and continues:

> Political and governmental leaders would be concerned about the impact that contact could have on their populations, and might try to let through only those ideas they considered safe. National security policy-makers might argue for classification of the contact and the information received. Some scholars, particularly those personally involved in the first contact, might be equally possessive about the information and the channel, especially if they distrusted governments and held a low opinion of the general population.[22]

As Bob Lazar stresses, although advanced alien technology could be put to use for the benefit of all, the same technology could equally well be used for destructive purposes, such as the construction of a super-bomb.

Michael Michaud foresees another problem relating to the acquisition of alien technology: that it could undermine our 'spirit of invention and independent initiative, forcing massive readjustment and unemployment, and threatening existing economic institutions.'[23]

I take the view that those few within governments who are aware of the situation are acting in our best interests by gradually presenting the information in such a way that it will lessen the political, economic, religious and psychological shock to our culture. But eventually, the ultimate secret will be revealed.

'The truth about UFOs may be painful for us to face, and this might provide a continuing rationale for the Government to maintain secrecy,' says the astronomer and former astronaut, Dr Brian O'Leary. 'But the truth will and must be known eventually. Continuing our denials and fears, in my opinion, [is] only adding to the problem. We are all in this together.'[24]

The evidence available to me suggests that – regardless of any move by governments – we are being visited by a number of extraterrestrial groups. Some could be visiting for less than benign purposes, others perhaps as anthropologists or tourists, but it seems logical that some groups have established a liaison with a relatively small number of our people, partly perhaps to lend us a helping hand as we reach, falteringly, towards the stars.

If any of the contactees have been told the truth, we may owe our very survival to some of these beings from elsewhere, since it is claimed that on several occasions they have intervened to prevent nuclear catastrophe. In addition to being motivated by compassion, they may also have a vested interest in the survival of our planet and its species.

Is it really so absurd to suggest that contact has already taken place? Most of our notions about alien contact are predicated on what we have absorbed from science fiction. The facts are infinitely more complex than we have been led to believe, as I have tried to show.

Let us hope that the advantages of contact will ultimately outweigh the disadvantages, leading to a more complete and profound understanding of our place in the universal scheme.

Notes

1 Oechsler, Bob, with Regimenti, Debby: *The Chesapeake Connection: An Implication of Corporate Involvement in the Cover-Up*, The Annapolis Research & Study Group, 136 Oakwood Road, Edgewater, Maryland 21037 (1989).

2 Various sources, including *Directors and Deputy Directors of Central Intelligence: Dates and Data 1946–1983*, by the History Staff, Central Intelligence Agency, Washington, DC 20505, November 1983

3 Phone conversation, 20 July 1989.

4 Walters, Ed and Walters, Frances: *UFOs: The Gulf Breeze Sightings*, Bantam Press, London, 1990.

5 Scully, Frank: *Behind the Flying Saucers*, Henry Holt & Co., New York, 1950, pp. 132–3.

6 Letter to Coral Lorenzen from Dr Olavo Fontes, 27 February 1958.

7 Letter to the author from Robert W. Kirchgessner, Director, Special Development Group, Ringling Bros. and Barnum & Bailey International, Inc., 31 August 1989.

8 Letter to the author from Robert Kirchgessner, 21 September 1989.

9 Communication with the author, 17 October 1989.

10 Burrows, William E.: *Deep Black: The Secrets of Space Espionage*, Bantam, London, 1988, pp. 216–18.

11 Fawcett, Lawrence and Greenwood, Barry J.: *Clear Intent: The Government Cover-up of the UFO Experience*, Prentice-Hall, Englewood Cliffs, New Jersey, 1984, pp. 9–11.

12 *Just Cause*, Citizens Against UFO Secrecy, P.O. Box 218, Coventry, Connecticut 06238, December 1989.

13 Ibid., June 1990.

14 Walters, Ed and Walters, Frances: op.cit.

15 Good, Timothy: 'World Round-Up of Selected Reports', *The UFO Report 1991*, edited by Timothy Good, Sidgwick & Jackson, London, 1990, pp.214–39.

16 Information supplied to the author by Bob Oechsler, Bob Pratt, and Wilson Sosa.

17 Good, Timothy: *Above Top Secret: The Worldwide UFO Cover-Up*, Sidgwick & Jackson, London, 1987, pp. 266–9, 567–8.

18 Ridpath, Ian: *Messages from the Stars*, Fontana, London, 1978, pp. 17, 24.

19 Ibid., p. 24.

20 Fry, Daniel W.: *To Men of Earth* (including the White Sands Incident), Merlin Publishing Co., Merlin, Oregon, 1973, pp. 98–9.

21 Michaud, Michael: 'A Unique Moment in Human History', *First Contact: The Search for Extraterrestrial Intelligence*, edited by Ben Bova and Byron Preiss, Headline, London, 1990, pp. 243–4.

22 Ibid., p. 248.

23 Ibid., p. 249.

24 Press release by Dr Brian O'Leary, New York, 6 October 1989.

Appendix

**Some Major UFO Organizations
(Australia, Canada, UK and USA)**

Australia
Australian Centre for UFO Studies, P.O. Box 728, Lane Grove, NSW 2066.
UFO Research Australia, P.O. Box 229, Prospect, South Australia 5082.
UFO Research Queensland, P.O. Box 111, North Quay, Queensland 4002.
Victorian UFO Research Society, P.O. Box 43, Moorabbin, Victoria 3189.

Canada
Canadian UFO Research Network, P.O. Box 15, Station 'A', Willowdale, Ontario, M2N 5S7.
Centrale de Compilation Ufologique de Quebec, CP 103, Drummondville, Quebec, J2B 2V6.
UFO Research Institute of Canada, Dept. 25, 1665 Robson Street, Vancouver, British Columbia, V6G 3C2.
Ufology Research of Manitoba, P.O. Box 1918, Winnipeg, Manitoba, R3C 3R2.

United Kingdom

British UFO Research Association, 10 Southway, Burgess Hill, Sussex RH15 9ST.

Contact International (UK), 11 Ouseley Close, New Marston, Oxford OX3 OJS.

Essex UFO Research Group, 95 Chilburn Road, Great Clacton, Essex CO15 4PE.

Quest International, 18 Hardy Meadows, Grassington, Skipton, North Yorkshire BD23 5DL.

United States of America

Citizens Against UFO Secrecy, 3518 Martha Custis Avenue, Alexandria, Virginia 22302.

J. Allen Hynek Center for UFO Studies, 2547 W. Peterson Avenue, Chicago, Illinois 60659.

Fund for UFO Research, P.O. Box 277, Mount Rainier, Maryland 20712.

Mutual UFO Network, 103 Oldtowne Road, Seguin, Texas 78155-4099.

UFO Reporting & Information Service, P.O. Box 832, Mercer Island, Washington 98040.

Pennsylvania Association for the Study of the Unexplained, 6 Oak Hill Avenue, Greensburg, Pennsylvania 15601.

Some UFO Journals

Flying Saucer Review, P.O. Box 162, High Wycombe, Buckinghamshire HP13 5DZ, UK.

Focus, 4219 W. Olive, Suite 247, Burbank, California 91505, USA.

International UFO Reporter, 2547 W. Peterson Avenue, Chicago, Illinois 60659, USA.

Just Cause, P.O. Box 218, Coventry, Connecticut 06238, USA.

MUFON UFO Journal, 103 Oldtowne Road, Seguin, Texas 78155-4099, USA.

UFO, 1536 S. Robertson Boulevard, Los Angeles, California 90035, USA.

Quest International, 15 Pickard Court, Temple Newsam, Leeds, Yorkshire LS15 9AY, UK.

Services

Books on UFOs
Those requiring books on UFOs which are not available in the bookshops should write, enclosing a stamped addressed envelope, to: Susanne Stebbing, 41 Terminus Drive, Herne Bay, Kent CT6 6PR, UK, or to Arcturus Book Service, P.O. Box 831383, Stone Mountain, Georgia 30083-0023, USA.

UFO Newsclippings
Those interested in obtaining news clippings on UFOs should send a stamped addressed envelope to CETI Publications, 247 High Street, Beckenham, Kent BR3 1AB, UK, or to the UFO Newsclipping Service, Route 1, Box 220, Plumerville, Arkansas 72127, USA.

UFO Call
The British UFO Research Association and British Telecom run a 24-hour UFO news update service on (0898) 121886.

UFO Hotline
Quest International has a 24-hour UFO hotline for reporting sightings in the UK on (0756) 752216.

Computer UFO Network/UFO Reporting & Information Service
Connect at 300 or 1200 bauds, eight data bits, no parity, one stop bit: USA (206) 721 5035, from 20.00 – 08.00 hrs. WST. The UFO Reporting & Information Service functions from 08.00 – 20.00 hrs.

MUFON Amateur Radio Net
80 metres –   3.990 MHz, Saturdays, 22.00 hrs.
40 metres –   7.237 MHz, Saturdays, 08.00 hrs.
10 metres – 28.460 MHz, Thursdays, 20.00 hrs.
10 metres – 28.470 MHz, Sundays, 15.00 hrs.

DATE: October 11, 1975
OWNER: Sam Britt - 33 miles West of Clayton, New Mexico
ANIMAL DESCRIPTION: Hereford bull, 3 years, 1400-1500 lbs.
DATE DIED: 36-48 hours before October 11
POSITION FOUND IN: Right side
ORGANS TAKEN: Scrotum, penis, rectum
TRACK EVIDENCE: None stated
INSPECTOR: Frank Best

DATE: October 13, 1975
OWNER: Alvin Stocton - Raton, New Mexico
ANIMAL DESCRIPTION: Bull
DATE DIED: October 11, 1975
POSITION FOUND IN: Right side
ORGANS TAKEN: Scrotum, testicles, penis and end of sheath
TRACK EVIDENCE: Only those made by Mr. Stocton, Sheriff Grubilnik,
                and Ben Wooten
INSPECTOR: Ben Wooten

DATE: October 15, 1975
OWNER: W. F. Martin - Springer, New Mexico
ANIMAL DESCRIPTION: Black bull
DATE DIED: October 15, 1975
POSITION FOUND IN:
ORGANS TAKEN: Rectum, penis, testicles
TRACK EVIDENCE: None stated
INSPECTOR: Harold Gilbert

DATE: October 18, 1975
OWNER: Rock Ranch - Nara Visa, New Mexico
ANIMAL DESCRIPTION: Black angus cow
DATE DIED: Found October 16 - had been dead seven to eight days prio
POSITION FOUND IN: Laying on back
ORGANS TAKEN: Rectum and vagina
TRACK EVIDENCE: None noted
INSPECTOR: Dwayne Massey

Fig. 2.1
A small selection of official reports on the cattle mutilations by the New Mexico
State Police. *(FBI)*

DATE: May 19, 1976
OWNER: Sharp Ranch - Corona, New Mexico
ANIMAL DESCRIPTION: Black angus bull
DATE DIED: May 15, 1976
POSITION FOUND IN: Left side on back
ORGANS TAKEN: Testicles removed
TRACK EVIDENCE: None
INSPECTOR: Claude Foster

DATE: June 29, 1976
OWNER: Tony Lamb -
ANIMAL DESCRIPTION: Yearling steer
DATE DIED: 48 hours prior to date
POSITION FOUND IN: Left side
ORGANS TAKEN: Right ear and right eye, the tongue, circle cut
              out at his navel, penis was gone, and he had also
              been cut around his rectum.
TRACK EVIDENCE: None stated
INSPECTOR: Harold Gilbert

DATE: July 10, 1976
OWNER:
ANIMAL DESCRIPTION: Buffalo calf
DATE DIED: July 10, 1976
POSITION FOUND IN:
ORGANS TAKEN: Tongue, testicles and penis. Cut at the rectum,
              also gone was large intestine.
TRACK EVIDENCE: A white helocopter was seen the morning of July 8

DATE: July 1, 1976
OWNER: Stanley Cisneros- Questa, New Mexico
ANIMAL DESCRIPTION: Solid red cow - pregnant
DATE DIED: June 29 or June 30, 1976
POSITION FOUND IN: Laying on right side
ORGANS TAKEN: Left eye, udder was cut off
TRACK EVIDENCE: None
INSPECTOR: Milton Culbertson

COMMITTEE ON COMMERCE,
SCIENCE, AND TRANSPORTATION

COMMITTEE ON BANKING,
HOUSING, AND URBAN AFFAIRS

SELECT COMMITTEE ON ETHICS

United States Senate
WASHINGTON, D.C. 20510

December 21, 1978

The Honorable Griffin B. Bell   RECEIVED
Attorney General
Department of Justice   2
10th and Constitution Avenue, N.W.
Washington, D.C.   20530

Dear Mr. Attorney General: O.L.A.

During the past several years, ranchers throughout the West,
including my home state of New Mexico, have been victimized
by a series of cattle mutilations. As a result, these ranchers
have as a group and individually suffered serious economic
losses.

These mysterious killings have been the subject of at least
two articles in national publications, copies of which are
enclosed. Mr. Cockburn's article in the December 1975 issue
of Esquire states that there had been a federal investigation
into this matter, but it was dropped. Mr. Cockburn implies
the investigation may have been terminated because cattle
mutilation per se is not a federal offense.

While an individual cattle mutilation may not be a federal
offense, I am very concerned at what appears to be a continued
pattern of an organized interstate criminal activity. Therefore,
I am requesting that the Justice Department re-examine its
jurisdiction in this area with respect to the possible reopening
of this investigation.

Enclosed are copies of my files on this subject. While awaiting
what will hopefully be a favorable reply, I shall continue to
gather materials that could be of help in such an investigation.
If you need further information in studying this matter, please
do not hesitate to contact me.

Sincerely,

Harrison Schmitt

HS:jri
Enclosures

DEPARTMENT
23   DEC 23 1978
R.R.O.
CRIMINAL-GEN.

Fig. 2.2
Letter regarding the cattle mutilations from Senator Harrison Schmitt to the US
Attorney General, 21 December 1978. *(FBI)*

January 10, 1979

Honorable Harrison H. Schmitt
United States Senate
1251 DSOB
Washington, D.C.   25010

Dear Senator Schmitt:

As I told you over the telephone yesterday, I
have asked Philip Heymann, head of the Criminal Division,
to look into our jurisdiction over the cattle mutilation
problem with which you are concerned. We will be in
touch with you at an early date.

I must say that the materials sent me indicate the
existence of one of the strangest phenomenons in my
memory.

Warm regards.

Sincerely,

Griffin B. Bell

CBS kmm

bcc: w/materials to Terry Adamson
              Ray Calamaro
          ✓ Phil Heymann - Please have someone look into
                            this matter at an early date.
                            Sen. Schmitt is our freind and
                            there have been about 60
                            mutilations in New Mexico in
                            recent months. GRBBB

Fig. 2.3
Letter from the US Attorney General to Senator Harrison Schmitt. *(FBI)*

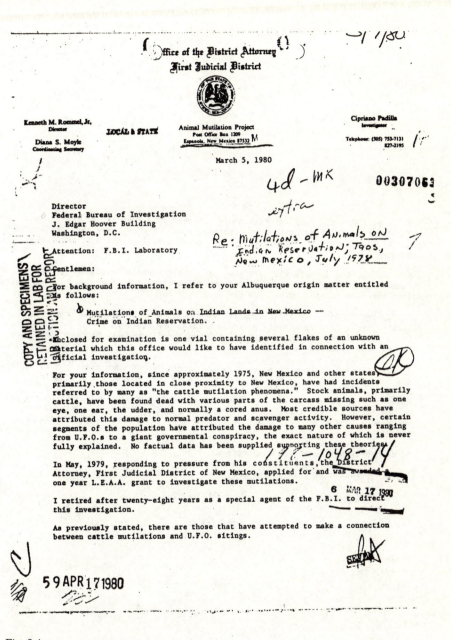

Fig. 2.4
Letter regarding the cattle mutilations from Kenneth Rommel Jr. to the Director of the FBI, 5 March 1980. *(FBI)*

Director
Federal Bureau of Investigation

In July, 1978, a U.F.O. was reportedly observed by a resident of Taos, New Mexico, reportedly hovering over a pickup truck. The next morning, the enclosed powder flakes were reportedly recovered from the roof of the aforementioned pickup.

Some of the individuals that are most vocal to the media have inferred that these flakes are identical with a substance that was taken from cowhides in a controlled test conducted in the Dulce, New Mexico area.

Dulce, New Mexico, which has been the site of several reported mutilations, is located approximately seventy miles from Taos, New Mexico. I have not been able to locate a sample of the substance reportedly collected in the Dulce test, but it has been described as a florescent material.

I have, to-date, been able to confirm any connection between these two substances, and have been told by those that have seen both that they are not identical.

However, I would appreciate it if through the use of a G.S. Mas spectroscopy test or any other logical test, that these flakes can be identified. This in itself would go a long way to assisting me to discredit the U.F.O. -- Cow Mutilation association theory.

If need be, the flakes can be destroyed during your examination.

Your cooperation in this investigation is appreciated.

Sincerely,

KENNETH M. ROMMEL, JR.

KMR/dsm
enclosure

ENLISTED RECORD AND REPORT OF SEPARATION
HONORABLE DISCHARGE

1. LAST NAME - FIRST NAME - MIDDLE INITIAL	2. ARMY SERIAL NO.	3. GRADE	4. ARM OR SERVICE	5. COMPONENT
BROWN MELVIN E	6 578 751	TEC 5	CAC	RA

6. ORGANIZATION	7. DATE OF SEPARATION	8. PLACE OF SEPARATION
743RD AAA GUN BN	2 DEC 45	SEP CEN FT MACARTHUR CALIF

9. PERMANENT ADDRESS FOR MAILING PURPOSES	10. DATE OF BIRTH	11. PLACE OF BIRTH
RFD 1 BOX 319 CHICO CALIF	14 OCT 16	DEL RAY CALIF

12. ADDRESS FROM WHICH EMPLOYMENT WILL BE SOUGHT	13. COLOR EYES	14. COLOR HAIR	15. HEIGHT	16. WEIGHT	17. NO. DEPEND.
NONE	BLUE	BROWN	5' 6"	130 LBS.	0

18. RACE	19. MARITAL STATUS	20. U.S. CITIZEN	21. CIVILIAN OCCUPATION AND NO.
WHITE X NEGRO OTHER(specify)	SINGLE X MARRIED OTHER (specify)	YES X NO	COOK

MILITARY HISTORY

22. DATE OF INDUCTION	23. DATE OF ENLISTMENT	24. DATE OF ENTRY INTO ACTIVE SERVICE	25. PLACE OF ENTRY INTO SERVICE
	11 DEC 39	11 DEC 39	FT MC DOWELL CALIF

SELECTIVE SERVICE DATA	26. REGISTERED YES X NO	27. LOCAL S.S. BOARD NO.	28. COUNTY AND STATE	29. HOME ADDRESS AT TIME OF ENTRY INTO SERVICE
				GRIDLEY CALIF

30. MILITARY OCCUPATIONAL SPECIALTY AND NO.	31. MILITARY QUALIFICATION AND DATE (i.e., infantry, aviation and marksmanship badges, etc.)
COOK 060	EXPERT M1 CARBINE

32. BATTLES AND CAMPAIGNS
NORTHERN SOLOMONS

33. DECORATIONS AND CITATIONS AMERICAN DEFENSE SERVICE MEDAL   AMERICAN CAMPAIGN MEDAL
ASIATIC PACIFIC CAMPAIGN MEDAL   PHILIPPINE LIBERATION RIBBON WITH 1
BRONZE STAR   GOOD CONDUCT MEDAL   VICTORY MEDAL

34. WOUNDS RECEIVED IN ACTION
NONE

35. LATEST IMMUNIZATION DATES				36. SERVICE OUTSIDE CONTINENTAL U.S. AND RETURN			
SMALLPOX	TYPHOID	TETANUS	OTHER (specify) PLAGUE	DATE OF DEPARTURE	DESTINATION		DATE OF ARRIVAL
DEC 42	MAR 43	MAY 43	SEP 45	23 JUN 43	ASIATIC PACIFIC THEATER		18 JUL 45

37. TOTAL LENGTH OF SERVICE					38. HIGHEST GRADE HELD			
CONTINENTAL SERVICE			FOREIGN SERVICE				UNITED STATES	22 NOV 45
YEARS	MONTHS	DAYS	YEARS	MONTHS	DAYS		9 NOV 45	
3	6	23	2	4	29	S SGT		

39. PRIOR SERVICE
NONE

40. REASON AND AUTHORITY FOR SEPARATION
CONVENIENCE OF THE GOVERNMENT   AR 615-365 15 DEC 44 AND CIR 310 WD 45

41. SERVICE SCHOOLS ATTENDED	42. EDUCATION (Years)		
COOKS & BAKERS SCHOOL 3 MONTHS COOK & BAKER	Grammar 8	High School 0	College 0

PAY DATA

YOU 00120

43. LONGEVITY FOR PAY PURPOSES		44. MUSTERING OUT PAY		45. SOLDIER DEPOSITS	46. TRAVEL PAY	47. TOTAL AMOUNT, NAME OF DISBURSING OFFICER
YEARS 5	MONTHS 22	TOTAL $300	THIS PAYMENT $300	NONE	NONE	$ 406 15 F FRIEDMAN CAPT FD

INSURANCE NOTICE

IMPORTANT IF PREMIUM IS NOT PAID WHEN DUE OR WITHIN THIRTY-ONE DAYS THEREAFTER, INSURANCE WILL LAPSE. MAKE CHECKS OR MONEY ORDERS PAYABLE TO THE TREASURER OF THE U. S. AND FORWARD TO COLLECTIONS SUBDIVISION, VETERANS ADMINISTRATION, WASHINGTON 25, D. C.

48. KIND OF INSURANCE			49. HOW PAID		50. Effective Date of Allotment Discontinuance	51. Date of Next Premium Due (One month after 50)	52. PREMIUM DUE EACH MONTH	53. INTENTION OF VETERAN TO		
Nat. Serv.	U.S. Govt.	None	Allotment	Direct to V. A.				Continue	Continue Only	Discontinue

54. | **55. REMARKS** (This space for completion of above items or entry of other items specified in W. D. Directives)

RIGHT THUMB PRINT

ASR SCORE (2 SEP 44)-91   HONORABLY DISCHARGED FOR THE
CONVENIENCE OF THE GOVERNMENT TO ENLIST IN THE REGULAR
ARMY WD CIR 310 1945.   DISCHARGED AS TEMPORARY TECHNICIAN
FIFTH GRADE AUS, PERMANENT PRIVATE REGULAR ARMY.

56. SIGNATURE OF PERSON BEING SEPARATED	57. PERSONNEL OFFICER (Type name, grade and organization - signature)
Melvin E Brown	M E HOFT 1ST LT AC M. E. Hoft

WD AGO FORM 53 - 55
1 November 1944

This form supersedes all previous editions of
WD AGO Forms 53 and 55 for enlisted persons
entitled to an Honorable Discharge, which
will not be used after receipt of this revision.

Fig. 5.1
1945 military record of Melvin Brown, who claimed to have stood guard over the wreckage of a flying disc at Roswell Army Air Field and to have been involved in the recovery of alien bodies from the New Mexico desert in July 1947. *(US Army)*

HEADQUARTERS
TASK UNIT 7.4.1
AIR TASK GROUP 7.4 (PROV) FWD
APO 187-1, c/o Postmaster
San Francisco, California

7 May 1948

SUBJECT: Recommendation for Promotion of Enlisted Man

TO: Commanding Officer
           Squadron "D"
           509th Airdrome Group
           Walker Air Force Base
           Roswell, New Mexico

1. Pursuant to AR 615-5, as amended, and Department of the Army Circular 51, dated 26 February 1948, I recommend that Sergeant Melvin E. Brown, AF 6578751, be promoted to the grade of Staff Sergeant.

2. Sergeant Brown has diligently and industriously performed all duties assigned to him while on duty with Task Unit 7.4.1. During the peculiar and tedious circumstances resulting from this project, he clearly demonstrated the qualities and abilities desired of a Staff Sergeant.

3. Sergeant Brown's Service Record indicates no record of previous conviction by Courts-Martial. His WD AGO Form 20 indicates that he has a primary SSN of Mess Steward (824) and a Duty SSN of Cook (060). His Form 20 further verifies the facts that he enlisted 3 December 1945 for a period of three (3) years and received the MOS of 824 on 10 April 1943. He was appointed to the grade of Sergeant 4 February 1947. His AGCT is 97 and he is skilled in his MOS. Sergeant Brown has met a Board of Officers at this headquarters and is recommended for this promotion.

JACK J. CATTON
Lt Col, USAF
Commanding

Fig. 5.3
Letter recommending promotion of Sergeant Brown, May 1948. *(US Air Force)*

GERALD LIGHT
10545, SCENARIO LANE
LOS ANGELES 24, CALIFORNIA

[Letter Received:
4-16-54]   4/16/54

Mr. Meade Layne
San Diego, California

My dear Friend: I have just returned from Muroc. The report is true---
devastatingly true!

I made the journey in company with Franklin Allen of the Hearst papers and
Edwin Nourse of Brookings Institute (Truman's erstwhile financial adviser)
and Bishop MacIntyre of L.A. (confidential names, for the present, please.)

When we were allowed to enter the restricted section, (after about six hours
in which we were checked on every possible item, event, incident and aspect
of our personal and public lives) I had the distinct feeling that the world
had come to an end with fantastic realism. For I have never seen so many
human beings in a state of complete collapse and confusion as they realized
that their own world had indeed ended with such finality as to beggar description. The reality of "otherplane" aeroforms is now and forever removed from
the realms of speculation and made a rather painful part of the consciousness
of every responsible scientific and political group.

During my two days visit I saw five separate and distinct types of aircraft
being studied and handled by our airforce officials---with the assistance and
permission of The Etherians! I have no words to express my reactions.

It has finally happened. It is now a matter of history.

President Eisenhower, as you may already know, was spirited over to Muroc one
night during his visit to Palm Springs recently. And it is my conviction that
he will ignore the terrific conflict between the various "authorities" and go
directly to the people via radio and television---if the impasse continues
much longer. From what I could gather, an official statement to the country
is being prepared for delivery about the middle of May.

I will leave it to your own excellent powers of deduction to construct a fitting
picture of the mental and emotional pandemonium that is now shattering the consciousness of hundreds of our scientific "authorities" and all the pundits of
the various specialized knowledges that make up our current physics. In some
instances I could not stifle a wave of pity that arose in my own being as I
wtached the pathetic bewilderment of rather brilliant brains struggling to make
some sort of rational explanation which would enable them to retain their familiar theories and concepts. And I thanked my own destiny for having long ago
pushed me into the metaphysical woods and compelled me to find my way out. To
wtach strong minds cringe before totally irreconcilable aspects of "science" is
not a pleasant thing. I had forgotten how commonplace such things as the dematerialization of "solid" objects had become to my own mind. The coming and going
of an etheric, or spirit, body has been so familiar to me these many years I had
just forgotten that such a manifestation could snap the mental balance of a man
not so conditioned. I shall never forget those forty-eight hours at Muroc!

Fig. 4.1
Part of the letter from Gerald Light to his friend and associate Meade Layne,
describing his experiences at Edwards AFB, California, 16 April 1954. *(Borderland
Sciences Research Foundation)*

· 229 ·

OFFICE OF THE PRESIDENT-ELECT

RICHARD M. NIXON

WASHINGTON, D.C.

December 2, 1968

Mr. D. Fry
Merlin, Oregon 97532

Dear Mr. Fry:

As you may know, I have pledged to bring into this
Administration men and women who by their qualities of
youthfulness, judgment, intelligence and creativity,
can make significant contributions to our country. I
seek the best minds in America to meet the challenges
of this rapidly changing world. To find them, I ask for
your active participation and assistance.

You, as a leader, are in a position to know and
recommend exceptional individuals. The persons you select should complete the enclosed form and return it to
you. I ask that you then attach your comments. My staff
will carefully review all recommendations for inclusion
in our reservoir of talent from which appointments will
be made.

I will appreciate greatly, Mr. Fry, your taking
time from your busy schedule to participate in this
all-important program.

Sincerely,

Richard M. Nixon

Fig. 4.2
Letter from President-elect Richard Nixon to UFO contactee Daniel Fry, 2
December 1968.

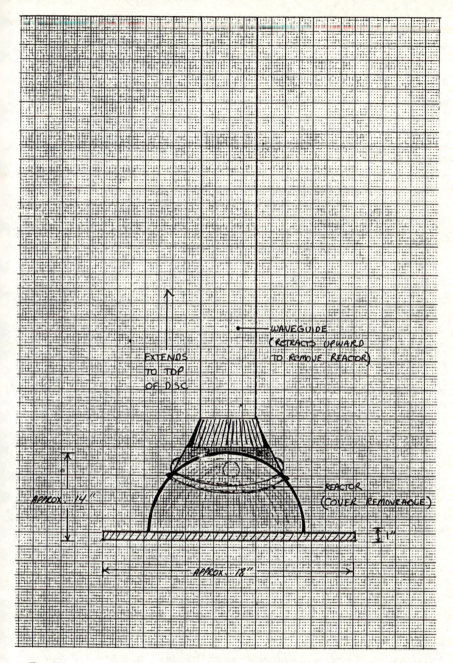

Fig. 8.2
Diagram by Robert Lazar showing part of the extraterrestrial propulsion unit he claims to have worked on. (© *Robert Lazar*)

ACCESSION NUMBER: 339

Database Name	NORAD Unknown Track Reporting System
Acronym	NUTR
Update Frequency	Monthly
Beginning Date	1971
Size	7,000

Producer

		COMMERCIAL	AUTOVON
Name	North American Aerospace Defense Command		
Address	HQ NORAD/NPY, Peterson AFB, CO 80914-5001		
Contact	Wingeard, R. O.	(303) 554-3758	692-3758

Distributor

		COMMERCIAL	AUTOVON
Name	North American Aerospace Defense Command		
Address	HQ NORAD/NPY, Peterson AFB, CO 80914-5001		
Contact	Wingeard, R. O.	(303) 554-3758	692-3758

Generator

		COMMERCIAL	AUTOVON
Name	North American Aerospace Defense Command		
Address	HQ NORAD/NPY, Peterson AFB, CO 80914-5001		
Contact	Wingeard, R. O.	(303) 554-3758	692-3758

Availability	Limited
Database Type	Alphanumeric
Program Language	Pascal
Computer	Zenith-150
Documentation	Available
Classification	Secret
Online Access	No
Cost	———————
Military Sponsor	Air Force
Descriptors	Air Force; Aircraft; Greenland; Iceland; Identification; Latitude; Longitude; North America; Number of Unknowns; Region; Scramble Actions; Scramble Bases; Soviet Traffic; Tracking; United Kingdom
Abstract	The NORAD Unknown Track Reporting System records details of all air traffic declared unknown in North America and the Greenland- Iceland-United Kingdom Gap. Data are used by a wide variety of users in NORAD, USAF, Joint Chiefs of Staff, Canadian NDHQ, and region commanders in a continuing assessment of airspace sovereignty.

Fig. 10.1
An extract from the North American Aerospace Defense Command's Directory of Databases, relating to the NORAD Unknown Track Reporting System. 7,000 unknown objects were tracked from 1971–1990, but details are classified Secret (see Fig. 10.2). *(NORAD/Citizens Against UFO Secrecy)*

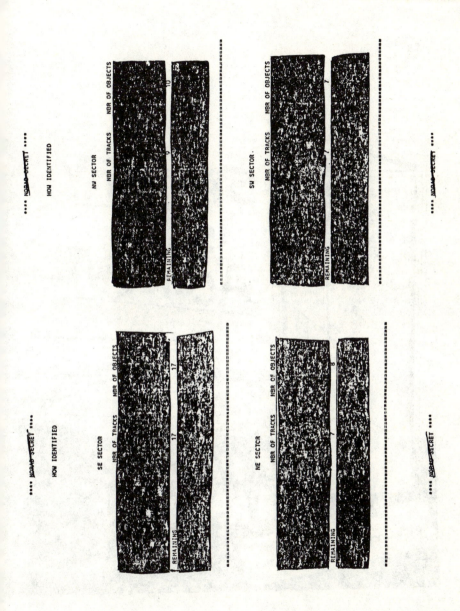

Fig. 10.2
Censored information from the records of NORAD's Unknown Track Reporting
System. *(NORAD/Citizens Against UFO Secrecy)*

A hitherto classified Defense Intelligence Agency security poster, 1984. *(Robert Shuping/DIA)*

Index